THE SIMPLE FEELING OF BEING

Best wishes,
Ken Wilber

THE SIMPLE FEELING OF BEING

*Embracing Your
True Nature*

Ken Wilber

Compiled and edited by
Mark Palmer, Sean Hargens,
Vipassana Esbjörn, and Adam Leonard

SHAMBHALA
Boston & London
2004

SHAMBHALA PUBLICATIONS
Horticultural Hall
300 Massachusetts Avenue
Boston, Massachusetts 02115
www.shambhala.com

9 8 7 6 5 4 3 2 1

FIRST EDITION
Printed in the United States of America
⊗ This edition is printed on acid-free paper that meets the
American National Standards Institute z39.48 Standard.
Distributed in the United States by Random House, Inc.,
and in Canada by Random House of Canada Ltd

Library of Congress Cataloging-in-Publication Data
Wilber, Ken. The simple feeling of being: embracing your true nature /
Ken Wilber; Compiled and edited by Mark Palmer . . . [et al.]
p.   cm.
Includes bibliographical references and index.
ISBN 1-59030-151-X (pbk.: alk. paper)
1. Spiritual life. I. Palmer, Mark. II. Title.
BL624 .W535 2004
204'.4—dc22
2003026741

We are part and parcel of a single and all-encompassing evolutionary current that is itself Spirit-in-action, the mode and manner of Spirit's creation, and thus is always going beyond what went before—that leaps, not crawls, to new plateaus of truth, only to leap again, dying and being reborn with each new quantum lurch, often stumbling and bruising its metaphysical knees, yet always getting right back up and jumping yet again.

And do you remember the Author of this Play? As you look deeply into your own awareness, and relax the self-contraction, and dissolve into the empty ground of your own primordial experience, the simple feeling of Being—right now, right here—is it not obvious all at once? Were you not present from the start? Did you not have a hand to play in all that was to follow? Did not the dream itself begin when you got bored with being God? Was it not fun to get lost in the productions of your own wondrous imagination, and pretend it all was other? Did you not write this book, and countless others like it, simply to remind you who you are?

cw 2: *Up from Eden,* 304

Contents

The Invitation of Spirit   ix

1. The Witness   1

2. Memoirs   32

3. Spirit-in-Action   66

4. Immediate Awareness   111

5. Passionate Philosophy   139

6. Always Already   175

7. Being-in-the-World   197

8. One without a Second   224

9. The Brilliant Clarity of Ever-Present Awareness   239

Sources   259

Index   265

The Invitation of Spirit

WHILE KEN WILBER is known prominently for his development of the Integral Approach—which some critics regard as the most comprehensive and inclusive philosophy available—Wilber's writings are ultimately grounded in his commitment to spiritual practice and the truths that are revealed through the wondrous opening of body in mind, mind in soul, soul in Spirit.

As the world's foremost integral philosopher, Wilber has achieved rare distinction through his unique, all-inclusive framework. This theoretical framework not only explores the vast range of potential in self, culture, and nature, but is also deeply committed to honoring Spirit in its myriad forms. Wilber's efforts are nothing short of a profound manifestation of the bodhisattva vow to liberate all sentient beings, through the honoring and integration of all perspectives.

Ken Wilber continually invites his readers to recognize the value of words and concepts as a means for going beyond words and concepts entirely to a direct realization of Emptiness or Reality itself. This is also the path of jnana yoga, where one studies the world and accumulates knowledge, until they are cracked open to the Mystery by the very profundity of the manifest realm.

In many mystical traditions, there are often two components to any visualization or meditative practice: the creation stage and the completion stage. In the first, one creates through ritual visualization a complex image or mandala, which represents the sacred dwelling of a particular divine energy. In the latter, one transforms oneself into a divine energy (such as compassion or wisdom) and then dissolves the entire visualization into emptiness, leaving only the Clear Light of primordial awareness.

Likewise, throughout his many books and articles, Wilber invites his readers to visualize the Kosmos as a four-quadrant mandala with multiple layers (such as levels, lines, types, bodies). In effect, Wilber, through his theoretical musings, is providing his readers with meditation instructions by which they can transform the world into a divine integral palace. At the end of sections, chapters, or books, Wilber reminds readers that they are this mandala, they are the awareness that brings forth and discloses this world matrix. As a result, the entire intellectual edifice dissolves into Suchness, and the integral map becomes a springboard into the waters of the Eternal Now. In this way Wilber's work, even at its most intellectual, has always been in the service of remembering Spirit. He offers a clarion call to all sentient beings to awaken as the Source that is always already the point and play of life.

The Simple Feeling of Being is a collection of the specifically spiritual aspects of his work—a treatise of his soul, expressing the mystical core that permeates both his life and work. This anthology gives a glimpse into the spiritual essence and experience of Ken Wilber as pandit and scholar, student and practitioner, visionary and sage. Many of the sections in this volume are those used by him to spring from intellectual knowledge to direct, experiential knowledge of our Original Face, reminding readers of their own eternal nature. The passages in this volume are arranged according to themes, though many selections could have easily been included in multiple chapters. "The Witness" presents instructions on how to become disidentified from our discursive thinking and feeling through contacting the Witness in our own lived awareness. "Memoirs" provides significant moments from Ken Wilber's own life. "Spirit-in-Action" explores the currents of evolution and involution and Spirit's manifestation in the world. "Immediate Awareness" highlights the various modes of being that are always available to us in our moment-to-moment experience. "Passionate Philosophy" is a journey through the beauty of thought. "Always Already" exposes the Suchness of our true nature. "Being-in-the-World" sings the splendor of the manifest realm and its community of beings interacting. "One without a Second" presents the undivided One Taste of each moment. "The Brilliant Clarity of Ever-Present Awareness" is a reminder of the tremendous display of Spirit through Form and Openness.

Each passage in this volume invites you to enter the experience behind the words, to engage the perennial path beyond all description, to release into the Divine space that transcends all language. Prepare to surrender your mind and allow the poetic waves to wash you into your own contemplative heart. Flow with the illuminated awareness of a contemporary master to where you already are in this moment.

For years, many individuals have accepted Wilber's invitation to Spirit. Travelers, seekers, students, and teachers have been marking passages, dog-earing pages, and transcribing sections into journals:

> Clamoring along well-torn train tracks, on the road from New Delhi to Rishikesh, the sweet stench of India is both welcoming and repugnant. Scrunched between the sticky metal cabin wall and the sweaty limbs of my travel companion, I gaze out at the ancient and beautiful landscape that is India. My travel partner is a dear and longtime friend in the dharma. We are both exhausted from long hours on airplanes, filthy, and filled with the wonder and awe that many who have made a spiritual pilgrimage to India will recognize. Too excited to sleep, I pull from my bag the one book I have brought with me on this sacred journey, *One Taste: The Journals of Ken Wilber.*
>
> I have already read the book once, highlighting particular passages that provide "pointing-out instructions." These are writings in which Wilber "points out" for the reader an aspect of his or her awareness or consciousness; the Witness; or the true nature of one's Mind. In these passages, it is as if Wilber gently takes our hand and walks us into the vastness that is our own true Self, and then nudges us to dwell there, just a little longer, in this luminous expanse of infinite Spaciousness.
>
> And so, while rolling through the lush December countryside of India, I prepare to read Wilber's pointing-out instructions aloud to my fellow traveler. Sitting in half-lotus on my bunk, my body bouncing up and down with the rhythm of the train, I begin to read from *One Taste*, the November 19th entry. In this passage, Wilber leads us into the heart of our awareness. His words beckon us beyond the hum of fellow passengers and below the clattering of our busy minds, to that still point that is vast Emptiness and simply Spirit:
>
>> Is this not obvious? Aren't you *already* aware of existing? Don't you *already* feel the simple Feeling of Being? Don't

you already possess this immediate gateway to ultimate Spirit, which is nothing other than the simple Feeling of Being? You have this simple Feeling now, don't you? And you have it now, don't you? And now, yes?

And don't you already realize that this Feeling is Spirit itself? Godhead itself? Emptiness itself? Spirit does not pop into existence: it is the *only* thing that is constant in your experience—and that is the simple Feeling of Being itself, a subtle, constant, background awareness that, if you look very closely, very carefully, you will realize you have had ever since the Big Bang and before—not because *you* existed way back when, but because you truly exist *prior* to time, in this timeless moment, whose feeling is the simple Feeling of Being: now, and now, and always and forever now.

You feel the simple Feeling of Being? Who is not *already* enlightened?

Now these chai-stained pages and underlined words are gathered together in one place. May this volume of passages from the heart-mind of Ken Wilber stir your simple Feeling of Being, and awaken you to your Original Face.

Mark Palmer
Sean Hargens
Vipassana Esbjörn
Adam Leonard

THE SIMPLE FEELING OF BEING

1

The Witness

Within the deep silence of the great unborn, Spirit whispers a sub-
lime secret, an otherwise hidden truth of one's very essence: You, in
this and every moment, abide as Spirit itself, an immutable radiance
beyond the mortal suffering of time and experience. Spirit itself is the
very heart of one's own awareness, and it has always been so.

In this first chapter, Wilber urges us to stand as this native Self, and
to realize the source of our being that impartially witnesses the world
and life, illuminating all things sacred and profane. In these passion-
filled expressions, he guides us toward this most profound awaken-
ing, a depth in the well where even the soul cannot drink. Do you not
remember this Self of yours, this great Witness? Is it not always your
constant realization?

DIVINITY HAS one ultimate secret, which it will also whisper in
your ear if your mind becomes quieter than the fog at sunset: the
God of this world is found within, and you know it is found within: in
those hushed silent times when the mind becomes still, the body relaxes into infinity, the senses expand to become one with the world—
in those glistening times, a subtle luminosity, a serene radiance, a
brilliantly transparent clarity shimmers as the true nature of all manifestation, erupting every now and then in a compassionate Radiance
before whom all idols retreat, a Love so fierce it adoringly embraces
both light and dark, both good and evil, both pleasure and pain
equally; for "I make the Light to fall on the good and bad alike; I the
Lord do all these things"; a passionately embroiling Heat so painful it
will melt your bones while you hurl yourself to the ground with awe
and supplication and reverence and surrender.

And just when you are bowing to that Radiance, thrown to the ground by a Force that crushes mind and body and ego into microscopically insignificant dust, just at that point exactly: that is when it whispers, in barely audible words, a whisper like a beautiful woman calling your name on a shining, silvery, moonlit night: You are bowing to yourself. Don't you remember who and what you really are? Did not even Saint Clement say, He who knows himself knows God?

Deeper than nature, deeper than the body, deeper than the mind, deeper than thoughts altogether: a luminous shimmering radiance pours out of the Heart, reflects through the crown, and lights up the entire universe. The real secret of the subtle Divine: the light of the sun and the stars and all of nature comes directly from your very own Heart. Wordsworth saw that Light: "An auxiliar light, Came from my mind, which on the setting sun, Bestowed new splendour." And you can see it, too, in those quiet times when you forget the Shadows in the Cave and start to turn toward the blazing radiant Light of it all.

The directions to finding God, which are printed on the box in which your Heart came, are simple: relax the mind and body; with reverence and devotion, gaze into the Heart; feel the Love-Light radiance that permeates your entire body, and your entire mind, and all of nature, and all nations everywhere. A Current of Luminous Compassion creates and sustains the entire gross and manifest realm, a Current known by many, many names—the Holy Ghost, the Sambhogakaya, saguna Brahman, Arwah or divine luminosity, Keter, the subtle body— but a Current that, in all events, is simply the sound of the beating of your Heart keeping rhythm to the pulsing of the world.

Don't play favorites, don't pick and choose, don't deny that you fathered and mothered every single thing and event in this Kosmos that is yours.

Still, still, and at the same time, the radiant Current of the Kosmos is itself an Eros, pushing and crashing and pulling and yearning to find a greater Light-Life and Love that is beyond good and evil—but not beneath it. Subtle Divinity—kundalini itself—the Serpent Power of the Kosmos—senses obstructions, contractions, snarls and snags, and moves spontaneously to uncoil them. The Prime Directive of the gross realm issues from the subtle Divine itself: These are my children; what can I do to help each and every one of them grow through the great Spiral that has formless Spirit as its ultimate destination?

And if you rise to that level in your very own Heart—the level where you and I are one—then this very world itself will start to take on the nature of a dream, a shimmering shining gossamer film, less and less to be taken seriously than to be rejoiced in as it passes. Leave seriousness at the door, and please take off your shoes, for this is hallowed ground, and bow to the Lightness and Humor that begins to replace solemnity. The entire world begins to take on a glimmering transparency as material atoms are replaced by light, and the days and nights pass before you like so many wandering dreams, while attention increasingly turns to the divine Dreamer itself, your very own Self, radiant in the midst of the madness.

Go deeper yet, dear souls. As nature retreats before God, so God retreats before the Abyss. The entire manifest realm, gross and subtle, even God and the Goddess herself, issue forth from a vast Emptiness, an infinite Formlessness, a radiant Ursprung that is the Ground and Goal of manifestation itself. As the great sages East and West have long proclaimed, in many different voices: beyond God is the unqualifiable Godhead. This vast Emptiness cannot be characterized in any fashion whatsoever (including that one)—it is neither absolute nor relative, neither one nor many, neither universal nor plural, neither good nor bad—because every word has meaning only in terms of its opposite, and This has no opposite. It can be felt, but not known; it is an atmosphere, not an object; it is infinite Release, the great Liberation, a radical Fullness on the other side of fear. Timeless and therefore eternal, it gives rise to all time; spaceless and therefore infinite, it gives rise to all space; formless and therefore ever present, it gives rise to all the worlds, even here and now. Look! Look! Can you find it? It is closer to you right now than you are to yourself! I promise you, it is closer than your heartbeat, nearer than your breath. It is staring you in the face, right here, right now! Can you find it?

If we must think of it, many poetic metaphors have been used: it is Consciousness without an object; the pure Self that sees but can never be seen; the selfless Witness that is the mirror-mind of all space; a radiant Emptiness that is the transparency of the entire Kosmos. But in all ways, and from the start, it is the great I AMness, the One without a second, the Nature of all natures and the Condition of all conditions, the discovery of which is the Great Liberation that leads to a realm beyond death and mortality, finitude and pain, suffering and separation, tears and terror.

But those are mere words—bloodless, heartless words, as all words are. Listen to me, dear souls, and go beyond the words:

How is the radiant Abyss of the Great Liberation found? It is never found, because it has never been lost. This pure formless Witness is the only thing you have never been without. It is the only constant in the entire Kosmos. You have known this utterly obvious secret for 15 billion years, and before that, you knew it eternally. It is nothing other than your own Original Face, the face you had before the Big Bang. Would you like to see it? Really, truly see it? Right here, right now? A dear friend of mine gave its pointing-out instructions as follows:

Let your mind relax. Let your mind relax and expand, mixing with the sky in front of it. Then notice: the clouds float by in the sky, and you are effortlessly aware of them. Feelings float by in the body, and you are effortlessly aware of them, too. Thoughts float by in the mind, and you are aware of them as well. Nature floats by, feelings float by, thoughts float by . . . and you are aware of all of them.

So tell me: Who are you?

You are not your thoughts, for you are aware of them. You are not your feelings, for you are aware of them. You are not any objects that you can see, for you are aware of them too.

Something in you is aware of all these things. So tell me: What is it in you that is conscious of everything?

What is it in you that is always awake? Always fully present? Something in you right now is effortlessly noticing everything that arises. What is that?

That vast infinite witnessing awareness, don't you recognize it? What is that Witness?

You are that Witness, aren't you? You are the pure Seer, pure awareness, the pure Spirit that impartially witnesses everything that arises, moment to moment. Your awareness is spacious, wide open, empty and clear, and yet it registers everything that arises.

That very Witness is Spirit within, looking out on a world that it created. It sees but cannot be seen; it hears but cannot be heard; it knows but cannot be known. It is Spirit itself that sees with your eyes, speaks with your lips, hears with your ears, reaches out with your arms. When will you confess this simple secret and awaken from the gruesome nightmare?

Can you see the words on this page? Then 100% of Spirit is present, looking out through your eyes.

Can you feel the book in your hands? Then 100% of Spirit is present, taking the world in its hands.

Can you hear the sound of that bird singing? Then 100% of Spirit is present, listening to that song.

You cannot look for this Spirit, for it is doing the looking. You cannot see this Spirit, for it is doing the seeing. You cannot find this Spirit, for it does all the finding. If you understand this, then Spirit is doing the understanding; if you don't understand this, Spirit is doing that. Understand it or not, just that is Spirit.

Hence the amazing, secret, ultimate truth that slowly starts to dawn: the enlightened mind—pure Spirit itself—is not hard to attain but impossible to avoid. How could you ever be without that Spirit which is reading this sentence right now?

Show me the Self you had before the Big Bang, and I will show you the Spirit of the entire Kosmos. And as for that pure, timeless, formless Spirit: *You . . . Are . . . That.*

And then the strangest thing happens. Resting in the pure Self, abiding as the timeless Witness, noticing that the clouds float by in the vast expanse of Emptiness that is my own ever-present awareness, the Witness itself suddenly cannot be found. The Seer vanishes into everything that is seen and never again returns to haunt the universe as a separate and separating force. Subject and object vanish into One Taste, the Nondual announces itself as a Presence that has no within or without, the ultimate Mystery permeates the Kosmos with an Obviousness that is too simple to believe, too close to see, too present to be reached, too This to be noticed.

The Seer vanishes into everything seen, which sees itself eternally. I no longer witness the clouds, I am the clouds; I do not hear the rain, I am the rain; I can no longer touch the earth, for I am the earth; I cannot hear the robin singing, because I am the robin singing, here in the painful brilliant clarity of ever-present One Taste. If nature arises, I am that. If nature vanishes, I am that. If God arises, I am that. If God dies, I am that. I am the terrorists with unforgivable murder in their hearts; I am the victims in the Towers who crashed to a fiery death; I am the love in the hearts of those who care, I am the hatred in the heartless souls of those who massacre without remorse.

Precisely because I am not this, not that, I am fully this, fully that. Beyond nature, I am nature; beyond God, I am God; beyond the Kosmos altogether, I am the Kosmos in its every gesture. Where there is

call me by my true names

pain, I am there; where there is love, I am present; where there is death, I breathe easily; where there is suffering, I move unconstrained. On September 11, 2001, I attacked me in a distant part of the galaxy on an unremarkable planet in a speck of dust in the corner of manifestation, all of which are wrinkles in the fold of what I am. And none of which affects me in the slightest, and therefore I am totally undone, I cry endlessly, the sadness is infinite, the despair dwarfs galaxies, my heart weeps monsoons, I can't breathe in this torture.

Totally insignificant, infinitely significant—no difference, truly. Atoms and Gods are all the same, here in the world of One Taste; the smallest insult is equal to the greatest; I am happy beyond description with every act of torture, I am sad beyond compare with every act of goodness. I delight in seeing pain, I despise seeing love. Do those words confuse you? *Are you still caught in those opposites?* Must I believe the dualistic nonsense that the world takes as real? Victims and murderers, good and evil, innocence and guilt, love and hatred? What dream walkers we all are!

Love in your heart? You are caught in illusions. Compassion in your soul? People, wake up! You are a million miles off the mark, wondering what to do, what it means, how to respond, where to find love, how to show compassion—all totally off the mark, careening between the opposites, caught in endless roving dreams that have no reality at all! Let the Spiral do what it must to handle these affairs, and then tell me: Can you show me your Original Face, exactly here and now? *Who* is aware of wanting to love? *Who* is aware of the pain of the attacks? *Who* is aware of wanting to practice compassion?

Who is aware of all those objects? *Forget those objects and show me this Self,* and I will show you the Kosmos.

"The Deconstruction of the World Trade Center"

There are many things that I can doubt, but I cannot believably doubt my own consciousness in this moment. My consciousness IS, and even if I tried to doubt it, it would be my consciousness doing the doubting. I can imagine that my senses are being presented with a fake reality—say, a completely virtual reality or digital reality, which looks real but is merely a series of extremely realistic images. But even then, I cannot doubt the consciousness that is doing the watching. . . .

The very undeniability of my present awareness, the undeniability of my consciousness, immediately delivers to me a certainty of existence in this moment, a certainty of Being in the now-ness of this moment. I cannot doubt consciousness and Being in this moment, for it is the ground of all knowing, all seeing, all existing. . . .

Who am I? Ask that question over and over again, deeply. Who am I? What is it in me that is conscious of everything?

If you think that you know Spirit, or if you think you don't, Spirit is actually that which is thinking both of those thoughts. So you can doubt the objects of consciousness, but you can never believably doubt the doubter, never really doubt the Witness of the entire display. Therefore, rest in the Witness, whether it is thinking that it knows God or not, and that witnessing, that undeniable immediacy of now-consciousness, is itself God, Spirit, Buddha-mind. The certainty lies in the pure self-felt Consciousness to which objects appear, not in the objects themselves. You will never, never, never see God, because God is the Seer, not any finite, mortal, bounded object that can be seen. . . .

This pure I AM state is not hard to achieve but impossible to escape, because it is ever present and can never really be doubted. You can never run from Spirit, because Spirit is the Runner. To put it very bluntly, Spirit is not hard to find but impossible to avoid: it is that which is looking at this page right now. Can't you feel That One? Why on earth do you keep looking for God when God is actually the Looker?

Simply ask, Who am I? Who am I? Who am I?

I am aware of my feelings, so I am not my feelings—Who am I? I am aware of my thoughts, so I am not my thoughts—Who am I? Clouds float by in the sky, thoughts float by in the mind, feelings float by in the body—and I am none of those because I can Witness them all.

Moreover, I can doubt that clouds exist, I can doubt that feelings exist, I can doubt that objects of thought exist—but I cannot doubt that the Witness exists in this moment, because the Witness would still be there to witness the doubt.

I am not objects in nature, not feelings in the body, not thoughts in the mind, for I can Witness them all. I am that Witness—a vast, spacious, empty, clear, pure, transparent Openness that impartially notices all that arises, as a mirror spontaneously reflects all its objects. . . .

You can already feel some of this Great Liberation in that, as you rest in the ease of witnessing this moment, you already feel that you are free from the suffocating constriction of mere objects, mere feelings, mere thoughts—they all come and go, but you are the vast, free, empty, open Witness of them all, untouched by their torments and tortures.

This is actually the profound discovery of . . . the pure divine Self, the formless Witness, causal nothingness, the vast Emptiness in which the entire world arises, stays a bit, and passes. And you are That. You are not the body, not the ego, not nature, not thoughts, not this, not that—you are a vast Emptiness, Freedom, Release, and Liberation.

With this discovery . . . you are halfway home. You have dis-identified from any and all finite objects; you rest as infinite Consciousness. You are free, open, empty, clear, radiant, released, liberated, exalted, drenched in a blissful emptiness that exists prior to space, prior to time, prior to tears and terror, prior to pain and mortality and suffering and death. You have found the great Unborn, the vast Abyss, the unqualifiable Ground of all that is, and all that was, and all that ever shall be.

But why is that only halfway home? Because as you rest in the infinite ease of consciousness, spontaneously aware of all that is arising, there will soon enough come the great catastrophe of final Freedom and Fullness: the Witness itself will disappear entirely, and instead of witnessing the sky, you are the sky; instead of touching the earth, you are the earth; instead of hearing the thunder, you are the thunder. You and the entire Kosmos become One Taste—you can drink the Pacific Ocean in a single gulp, hold Mt. Everest in the palm of your hand; supernovas swirl in your heart and the solar system replaces your head. . . .

You are One Taste, the empty mirror that is one with any and all objects that arise in its embrace, a mindlessly vast translucent expanse: infinite, eternal, radiant beyond release. And you . . . are . . . That. . . .

So the primary Cartesian dualism—which is simply the dualism between . . . in here and out there, subject and object, the empty Witness and all things witnessed—is finally undone and overcome in nondual One Taste. Once you actually and fully contact the Witness, then—and only then—can it be transcended into radical Nonduality, and halfway home becomes fully home, here in the ever-present wonder of what is. . . .

And so how do you know that you have finally and really over-come the Cartesian dualism? Very simple: if you have really over-come the Cartesian dualism, then you no longer feel that you are on this side of your face looking at the world out there. There is only the world, and you are all of that; you actually feel that you are one with everything that is arising moment to moment. You are not merely on this side of your face looking out there. "In here" and "out there" have become One Taste with a shuddering obviousness and certainty so profound it feels like a five-ton rock just dropped on your head. It is, shall we say, a feeling hard to miss.

At that point, which is actually your ever-present condition, there is no exclusive identity with this particular organism, no constriction of consciousness to the head, a constriction that makes it seem that "you" are in the head looking at the rest of the world out there; there is no binding of attention to the personal bodymind: instead, consciousness is one with all that is arising—a vast, open, transparent, radiant, infinitely Free and infinitely Full expanse that embraces the entire Kosmos, so that every single subject and every single object are erotically united in the Great Embrace of One Taste. You disappear from merely being behind your eyes, and you become the All, you directly and actually feel that your basic identity is everything that is arising moment to moment (just as previously you felt that your identity was with this finite, partial, separate, mortal coil of flesh you call a body). Inside and outside have become One Taste. I tell you, it can happen just like that!

From *Boomeritis*, Sidebar E: "The Genius Descartes Gets a Postmodern Drubbing: Integral Historiography in a Postmodern Age"

Notice first of all the broad, distinguishing marks of the transcendent self: it is a center and expanse of awareness which is creatively detached from one's personal mind, body, emotions, thoughts, and feelings. So if you would like to begin to work at intuiting this transcendent self within you that goes beyond you, the you that is not you, then proceed as follows:

Slowly begin to silently recite the following to yourself, trying to realize as vividly as possible the import of each statement:

I *have* a body, but I am *not* my body. I can see and feel my body, and what can be seen and felt is not the true Seer. My body may be tired or excited, sick or healthy, heavy or light, but that has nothing to do with my inward I. I *have* a body, but I am *not* my body.

I *have* desires, but I am *not* my desires. I can know my desires, and what can be known is not the true Knower. Desires come and go, floating through my awareness, but they do not affect my inward I. I *have* desires but I am *not* desires.

I *have* emotions, but I am *not* my emotions. I can feel and sense my emotions, and what can be felt and sensed is not the true Feeler. Emotions pass through me, but they do not affect my inward I. I *have* emotions but I am *not* emotions.

I *have* thoughts, but I am *not* my thoughts. I can know and intuit my thoughts, and what can be known is not the true Knower. Thoughts come to me and thoughts leave me, but they do not affect my inward I. I *have* thoughts but I am *not* my thoughts.

This done—perhaps several times—one then affirms as concretely as possible: I am what remains, a pure center of awareness, an unmoved witness of all these thoughts, emotions, feelings, and desires.

If you persist at such an exercise, the understanding contained in it will quicken and you might begin to notice fundamental changes in your sense of "self." For example, you might begin intuiting a deep inward sense of freedom, lightness, release, stability. This source, this "center of the cyclone," will retain its lucid stillness even amid the raging winds of anxiety and suffering that might swirl around its center. The discovery of this witnessing center is very much like diving from the calamitous waves on the surface of a stormy ocean to the quiet and secure depths of the bottom. At first you might not get more than a few feet beneath the agitated waves of emotion, but with persistence you may gain the ability to dive fathoms into the quiet depths of your soul, and lying outstretched at the bottom, gaze up in alert but detached fashion at the turmoil that once held you transfixed.

Here we are talking of the transpersonal self or witness—we are not yet discussing pure unity consciousness. In unity consciousness, the transpersonal witness itself collapses into everything witnessed. Before that can occur, however, one must first discover that transpersonal witness, which then acts as an easier "jumping-off point" for unity consciousness. And we find this transpersonal witness by disidentifying with all particular objects, mental, emotional, or physical, thereby transcending them.

cw 1: *No Boundary*, 546–547

"Who am I?" The query has probably tormented humankind since the dawn of civilization, and remains today one of the most vexing of all human questions. Answers have been offered which range from the sacred to the profane, the complex to the simple, the scientific to the romantic, the political to the individual. But instead of examining the multitude of answers to this question, let's look instead at a very specific and basic process which occurs when a person asks, and then answers, the question "Who am I? What is my real self? What is my fundamental identity?"

When someone asks, "Who are you?" and you proceed to give a reasonable, honest, and more or less detailed answer, what in fact, are you doing? What goes on in your head as you do this? In one sense you are describing your self as you have come to know it, including in your description most of the pertinent facts, both good and bad, worthy and worthless, scientific and poetic, philosophic and religious, that you understand as fundamental to your identity. You might, for example, think that "I am a unique person, a being endowed with certain potentials; I am kind but sometimes cruel, loving but sometimes hostile; I am a father and lawyer, I enjoy fishing and basketball. . . ." And so your list of feelings and thoughts might proceed.

Yet there is an even more basic process underlying the whole procedure of establishing an identity. Something very simple happens when you answer the question, "Who are you?" When you are describing or explaining or even just inwardly feeling your "self," what you are actually doing, whether you know it or not, is drawing a mental line or boundary across the whole field of your experience, and everything on the inside of that boundary you are feeling or calling your "self," while everything outside that boundary you feel to be "not-self." Your self-identity, in other words, depends entirely upon where you draw that boundary line.

You are a human and not a chair, and you know that because you consciously or unconsciously draw a boundary line between humans and chairs, and are able to recognize your identity with the former. You may be a very tall human instead of a short one; and so you draw a mental line between tallness and shortness, and thus identify yourself as "tall." You come to feel that "I am this and not that" by drawing a boundary line between "this" and "that" and then recognizing your identity with "this" and your nonidentity with "that."

So when you say "my self," you draw a boundary line between what is you and what is not you. When you answer the question, "Who are you?," you simply describe what's on the inside of that line. The so-called identity crisis occurs when you can't decide how or where to draw the line. In short, "Who are you?" means "Where do you draw the boundary?"

All answers to that question, "Who am I?," stem precisely from this basic procedure of drawing a boundary line between self and not-self. Once the general boundary lines have been drawn up, the answers to that question may become very complex—scientific, theological, economic—or they may remain most simple and unarticulated. But any possible answer depends on first drawing the boundary line.

The most interesting thing about this boundary line is that it can and frequently does shift. It can be redrawn. In a sense the person can remap her soul and find in it territories she never thought possible, attainable, or even desirable. As we have seen, the most radical re-mapping or shifting of the boundary line occurs in experiences of the supreme identity, for here the person expands her self-identity boundary to include the entire universe. We might even say that she loses the boundary line altogether, for when she is identified with the "one harmonious whole" there is no longer any outside or inside, and so nowhere to draw the line.

CW 1: *No Boundary*, 435–437

The Witness simply observes the stream of events both inside and outside the mind-body in a creatively detached fashion, since, in fact, the Witness is not exclusively identified with either. In other words, the individual realizes that his mind and his body can be perceived objectively, he spontaneously realizes that they cannot constitute a real subjective self.

CW 1: "Psychologia Perennis," 19

The Witness is a huge step forward, and it is a necessary and important step in meditation, but it is not ultimate. When the Witness or the soul is finally undone, then the Witness dissolves into everything that is witnessed. The subject/object duality collapses and there is only pure nondual awareness, which is very simple, very obvious.

Like a famous Zen Master said when he got his enlightenment, "When I heard the bell ring, suddenly there was no 'I' and no 'bell,' just the ringing."

CW 5: *Grace and Grit*, 121

When, as a specific type of meditation, you pursue the observing Self, the Witness, to its very *source* in pure Emptiness, then no objects arise in consciousness at all. This is a discrete, identifiable state of awareness—namely, *unmanifest absorption* or *cessation*, variously known as nirvikalpa samadhi, jnana samadhi, ayin, vergezzen, nirodh, classical nirvana, the cloud of unknowing.

This is the causal state, a discrete state, which is often likened to the state of deep dreamless sleep, except that this state is not a mere blank but rather an utter fullness, and it is experienced as such—as infinitely drenched in the fullness of Being, so full that no manifestation can even begin to contain it. Because it can never be seen as an object, this pure Self is pure Emptiness.

cw 7: *A Brief History of Everything*, 251

The contemplative traditions are based on a series of experiments in awareness: what if you pursue this Witness to its source? What if you inquire within, pushing deeper and deeper into the source of awareness itself? What if you push beyond or behind the mind, into a depth of consciousness that is not confined to the ego or the individual self? What do you find? As a repeatable, reproducible experiment in awareness, what do you find?

"There is a subtle essence that pervades all reality," begins one of the most famous answers to that question. "It is the reality of all that is, and the foundation of all that is. That essence is all. That essence is the real. And thou, thou art that."

In other words, this observing Self eventually discloses its own source, which is Spirit itself, Emptiness itself. And that is why the mystics maintain that this observing Self is a ray of the Sun that is the radiant Abyss and ultimate Ground upon which the entire manifest Kosmos depends. Your very Self intersects the Self of the Kosmos at large—a supreme identity that outshines the entire manifest world, a supreme identity that undoes the knot of the separate self and buries it in splendor.

So from matter to body to mind to Spirit. In each case consciousness or the observing Self sheds an exclusive identity with a lesser and shallower dimension, and opens up to deeper and higher and wider occasions, until it opens up to its own ultimate ground in Spirit itself.

And the stages of transpersonal growth and development are basically the stages of following this observing Self to its ultimate abode, which is pure Spirit or pure Emptiness, the ground, path, and fruition of the entire display.

CW 7: *A Brief History of Everything*, 232–233

So who is this real Seer? Who or what is this observing Self?

Ramana Maharshi called this Witness the I-I, because it is aware of the individual I or self, but cannot itself be seen. So what is this I-I, this causal Witness, this pure observing Self?

This deeply inward Self is witnessing the world out there, and it is witnessing all your interior thoughts as well. This Seer sees the ego, and sees the body, and sees the natural world. All of those parade by "in front" of this Seer. But the Seer itself cannot be seen. If you see anything, those are just more objects. Those objects are precisely what the Seer is not, what the Witness is not.

So you pursue this inquiry, Who am I? Who or what is this Seer that cannot itself be seen? You simply "push back" into your awareness, and you *dis-identify* with any and every object you see or can see.

The Self or the Seer or the Witness is not any particular thought—I can see that thought as an object. The Seer is not any particular sensation—I am aware of that as an object. The observing Self is not the body, it is not the mind, it is not the ego—I can see all of those as objects. What is looking at all those objects? What in you right now is looking at all these objects—looking at nature and its sights, looking at the body and its sensations, looking at the mind and its thoughts? What is looking at all that?

Try to feel yourself right now—get a good sense of being yourself—and notice, that self is just another object in awareness. It isn't even a real subject, a real self, it's just another object in awareness. This little self and its thoughts parade by in front of you just like the clouds float by through the sky. And what is the real you that is witnessing all of that? Witnessing your little objective self? Who or what is that?

As you push back into this pure Subjectivity, this pure Seer, you won't see it as an object—you can't see it as an object, because it's not an object! It is nothing you can see. Rather, as you calmly rest in this observing awareness—watching mind and body and nature float by—you might begin to notice that what you are actually feeling is simply a sense of freedom, a sense of release, a sense of not being bound to any of the objects you are calmly witnessing. You don't see anything in particular, you simply rest in this vast freedom.

In front of you the clouds parade by, your thoughts parade by, bodily sensations parade by, and you are none of them. You are the vast expanse of freedom through which all these objects come and go. You are an opening, a clearing, an Emptiness, a vast spaciousness, in which all these objects come and go. Clouds come and go, sensations come and go, thoughts come and go—and you are none of them; you are that vast sense of freedom, that vast Emptiness, that vast opening, through which manifestation arises, stays a bit, and goes.

So you simply start to notice that the "Seer" in you that is witnessing all these objects is itself just a vast Emptiness. It is not a thing, not an object, not anything you can see or grab hold of. It is rather a sense of vast Freedom, because it is not itself anything that enters the objective world of time and objects and stress and strain. This pure Witness is a pure Emptiness in which all these individual subjects and objects arise, stay a bit, and pass.

So this pure Witness is not anything that can be seen! The attempt to see the Witness or know it as an object—that's just more grasping and seeking and clinging in time. The Witness isn't out there in the stream; it is the vast expanse of Freedom in which the stream arises. So you can't get hold of it and say, Aha, I see it! Rather, it is the Seer, not *anything* that can be seen. As you rest in this Witnessing, all that you sense is just a vast Emptiness, a vast Freedom, a vast Expanse— a transparent opening or clearing in which all these little subjects and objects arise. Those subjects and objects can definitely be seen, but the Witness of them cannot be seen. The Witness of them is an utter *release* from them, an utter Freedom not caught in their turmoils, their desires, their fears, their hopes.

Of course, we tend to *identify* ourselves with these little individual subjects and objects—and that is exactly the problem! We identify the Seer with puny little things that can be seen. And that is the beginning of bondage and unfreedom. We are actually this vast expanse of Freedom, but we identify with unfree and limited objects and subjects, all of which can be seen, all of which suffer, and none of which is what we are.

Patanjali gave the classic description of bondage as "the identification of the Seer with the instruments of seeing"—with the little subjects and objects, instead of the opening or clearing or Emptiness in which they all arise.

So when we rest in this pure Witness, we don't see this Witness as an object. Anything you can see is *not* it. Rather, it is the absence of any subjects or objects altogether, it is the *release* from all of that. Resting in the pure Witness, there is this background absence or Emptiness, and this is "experienced," *not* as an object, but as a vast expanse of Freedom and Liberation from the constrictions of identifying with these little subjects and objects that enter the stream of time and are ground up in that agonizing torrent.

So when you rest in the pure Seer, in the pure Witness, you are invisible. You cannot be seen. No part of you can be seen, because you are not an object. Your body can be seen, your mind can be seen, nature can be seen, but you are not any of those objects. You are the pure source of awareness, and not anything that arises in that awareness. So you abide as awareness.

Things arise in awareness, they stay a bit and depart, they come and they go. They arise in *space*, they move in *time*. But the pure Witness does not come and go. It does not arise in space, it does not move in time. It is as it is; it is ever-present and unvarying. It is not an object out there, so it never enters the stream of time, of space, of birth, of death. Those are all experiences, all objects—they all come, they all go. But you do not come and go; you do not enter that stream; you are aware of all that, so you are not caught in all that. The Witness is aware of space, aware of time—and is therefore itself free of space, free of time. It is timeless and spaceless—the purest Emptiness through which time and space parade.

So this pure Seer is prior to life and death, prior to time and turmoil, prior to space and movement, prior to manifestation—prior even to the Big Bang itself. This doesn't mean that the pure Self existed in a time before the Big Bang, but that it exists prior to time, period. It just never enters that stream. It is aware of time, and is thus free of time— it is utterly timeless. And because it is timeless, it is eternal—which doesn't mean everlasting time, but free of time altogether.

It was never born, it will never die. It never enters that temporal stream. This vast Freedom is the great Unborn, of which the Buddha said: "There is an unborn, an unmade, an uncreate. Were it not for this unborn, unmade, uncreate, there would be no release from the born, the made, the created." Resting in this vast expanse of Freedom is resting in this great Unborn, this vast Emptiness.

And because it is Unborn, it is Undying. It was not created with your body, it will not perish when your body perishes. It's not that it lives on beyond your body's death, but rather that it never enters the stream of time in the first place. It doesn't live on after your body, it lives prior to your body, always. It doesn't go on in time forever, it is simply prior to the stream of time itself.

Space, time, objects—all of those merely parade by. But you are the Witness, the pure Seer that is itself pure Emptiness, pure Freedom, pure Openness, the great Emptiness through which the entire parade passes, never touching you, never tempting you, never hurting you, never consoling you.

And because there is this vast Emptiness, this great Unborn, you can indeed gain liberation from the born and the created, from the suffering of space and time and objects, from the mechanism of terror inherent in those fragments, from the vale of tears called samsara.

CW 7: *A Brief History of Everything*, 252–255

I know I've talked about witnessing awareness persisting through waking, dreaming, and deep sleep. But the Witness is *fully* available in *any* state, including your own *present* state of awareness *right now*. So I'm going to talk you into this state, or try to, using what are known as "pointing-out instructions." I am *not* going to try to get you into a *different* state of consciousness, or an altered state of consciousness, or a nonordinary state. I am going to simply point out something that is *already* occurring in your own present, ordinary, natural state.

So let's start by just being aware of the world around us. Look out there at the sky, and just relax your mind, let your mind and the sky mingle. Notice the clouds floating by in the sky. Notice that this takes no effort on your part. Your present awareness, in which these clouds are floating, is very simple, very easy, effortless, spontaneous. You simply notice that there is an *effortless awareness* of the clouds. The same is true of those trees, and those birds, and those rocks. You simply and effortlessly witness them.

Look now at the sensations in your own body. You can be aware of whatever bodily feelings are present—perhaps pressure where you are sitting, perhaps warmth in your tummy, maybe tightness in your neck. But even if these feelings are tight and tense, you can easily be aware of them. These feelings arise in your present awareness, and that awareness is very simple, easy, effortless, spontaneous. You simply and effortlessly witness them.

Look at the thoughts arising in your mind. You might notice various images, symbols, concepts, desires, hopes, and fears, all *spontaneously* arising in your awareness. They arise, stay a bit, and pass. These thoughts and feelings arise in your present awareness, and that awareness is very simple, effortless, spontaneous. You simply and effortlessly witness them.

So notice: you can see the clouds float by, because you are *not* those clouds—you are the witness of those clouds. You can feel bodily feelings, because you are *not* those feelings—you are the witness of those feelings. You can see thoughts float by, because you are *not* those thoughts, you are the witness of those thoughts. Spontaneously and naturally, these things all arise, on their own, in your present *effortless* awareness.

So who are you? You are not objects out there, you are not feelings, you are not thoughts—you are effortlessly aware of all those, so you are not those. Who or what are you?

Say it this way to yourself: I *have* feelings, but I am not those feelings. Who am I? I *have* thoughts, but I am not those thoughts. Who am I? I *have* desires, but I am not those desires. Who am I?

So you push back into the source of your own awareness. You push back into the Witness, and you rest in the Witness. I am not objects, not feelings, not desires, not thoughts.

But then people usually make a big mistake. They think that if they rest in the Witness, they are going to see something, or feel something, something really neat and special. But you won't see anything. If you see something, that is just another object—another feeling, another thought, another sensation, another image. But those are all objects; those are what you are *not*.

No, as you rest in the Witness—realizing, I am not objects, I am not feelings, I am not thoughts—all you will notice is a sense of Freedom, a sense of Liberation, a sense of Release—release from the terrible constriction of identifying with these puny little finite objects, your little body and little mind and little ego, all of which are objects that can be seen, and thus are not the true Seer, the real Self, the pure Witness, which is what you really are.

So you won't see anything in particular. Whatever is arising is fine. Clouds float by in the sky, feelings float by in the body, thoughts float by in the mind—and you can effortlessly witness all of them. They *all* spontaneously arise in your own present, easy, effortless awareness. And this witnessing awareness is not itself anything specific you can see. It is just a vast, background sense of Freedom—or *pure Emptiness*—and in that pure Emptiness, which you are, the entire manifest world arises. You *are* that Freedom, Openness, Emptiness—and not any itty bitty thing that arises in it.

Resting in that empty, free, easy, effortless witnessing, notice that the clouds are arising in the vast space of your awareness. The clouds are arising within you—so much so, you can taste the clouds, you are one with the clouds, it is as if they are on this side of your skin, they are so close. The sky and your awareness have become one, and all things in the sky are floating effortlessly through your own aware-ness. You can kiss the sun, swallow the mountain, they are that close. Zen says "Swallow the Pacific Ocean in a single gulp," and that's the easiest thing in the world, when inside and outside are no longer two, when subject and object are nondual, when the looker and looked at are One Taste. You see?

CW 8: *One Taste*, 358–360

Ramana [Maharshi], echoing Shankara, used to say:

> The world is illusory;
> Brahman alone is real;
> Brahman is the world.

The world is illusory, which means you are not any object at all—nothing that can be seen is ultimately real. You are *neti, neti*, not this, not that. And under no circumstances should you base your salva-tion on that which is finite, temporal, passing, illusory, suffering-enhancing and agony-inducing.

Brahman alone is real, the Self (unqualifiable Brahman-Atman) alone is real—the pure Witness, the timeless Unborn, the formless Seer, the radical I-I, radiant Emptiness—is what is real and all that is real. It is your condition, your nature, your essence, your present and your future, your desire and your destiny, and yet it is always ever-present as pure Presence, the alone that is Alone.

Brahman is the world, Emptiness and Form are not-two. *After* you realize that the manifest world is illusory, and *after* you realize that Brahman alone is real, *then* you can see that the absolute and the relative are not-two or nondual, then you can see that nirvana and samsara are not-two, then you can realize that the Seer and everything seen are not-two, Brahman and the world are not-two—

all of which really means, the sound of those birds singing! The entire world of Form exists no-where but in your own present Formless Awareness: you can drink the Pacific in a single gulp, because the entire world literally exists in your pure Self, the ever-present great I-I.

Finally, and most important, Ramana would remind us that the pure Self—and therefore the great Liberation—*cannot be attained*, any more than you can attain your feet or acquire your lungs. You are *already* aware of the sky, you *already* hear the sounds around you, you *already* witness this world. One hundred percent of the enlightened mind or pure Self is present right now—not ninety-nine percent, but one hundred percent. As Ramana constantly pointed out, if the Self (or knowledge of the Self) is something that comes into existence—if your realization has a beginning in time—then that is merely another object, another passing, finite, temporal state. There is no reaching the Self—the Self is reading this page. There is no looking for the Self—it is looking out of your eyes right now. There is no attaining the Self—it is reading these words. You simply, absolutely, cannot attain that which you have never lost. And if you do attain something, Ramana would say, that's very nice, but that's not the Self.

So, if I may suggest, as you read the following words from the world's greatest sage: if you think you don't understand Self or Spirit, then rest in that which doesn't understand, and just that is Spirit. If you think you don't quite "get" the Self or Spirit, then rest in that which doesn't quite get it, and just that is Spirit.

Thus, if you think you understand Spirit, that is Spirit. If you think you don't, that is Spirit. And so we can leave with Ramana's greatest and most secret message: the enlightened mind is not hard to attain but impossible to avoid. In the dear Master's words:

> There is neither creation nor destruction,
> Neither destiny nor free-will;
> Neither path nor achievement;
> This is the final truth.

cw 8: *One Taste*, 465–468

Truly, adopting a new holistic philosophy, believing in Gaia, or even thinking in integral terms—however important those might be, they are the least important when it comes to spiritual transformation. Finding out who believes in all those things: There is the doorway to God.

A Theory of Everything, 137

People make two common mistakes on the way to One Taste. The first occurs in contacting the Witness, the second occurs in moving from the Witness to One Taste itself.

The first mistake: In trying to contact the Witness (or I-I), people imagine that they will *see something*. But you don't see anything, you simply rest as the Witness of all that arises—you are the pure and empty Seer, *not anything that can be seen*. Attempting to see the Seer as a special light, a great bliss, a sudden vision—those are all *objects*, they are not the Witness that you are. Eventually, of course, with One Taste, you will be *everything* that you see, but you cannot *start* trying to do that—trying to see the Truth—because that is what blocks it. You have to start with "neti, neti": I am not this, I am not that.

So the first mistake is that people sabotage the Witness by trying to make it an object that can be grasped, whereas it is simply the Seer of all objects that arise, and it is "felt" only as a great background sense of Freedom and Release *from* all objects.

Resting in that Freedom and Emptiness—and impartially witnessing all that arises—you will notice that the *separate-self* (or ego) simply arises in consciousness *like everything else.* You can actually *feel* the self-contraction, just like you can feel your legs, or feel a table, or feel a rock, or feel your feet. The self-contraction is a feeling of interior tension, often localized behind the eyes, and anchored in a slight muscle tension throughout the bodymind. It is an effort and a sensation of contracting in the face of the world. It is a subtle whole-body tension. Simply notice this tension.

Once people have become comfortable resting as the empty Witness, and once they notice the tension that is the self-contraction, they imagine that to finally move from the Witness to One Taste, they have to get rid of the self-contraction (or get rid of the ego). Just that is the second mistake, because it actually locks the self-contraction firmly into place.

We assume that the self-contraction hides or obstructs Spirit, whereas in fact it is simply a radiant manifestation of Spirit itself, like absolutely every other Form in the universe. All Forms are not other than Emptiness, including the form of the ego. Moreover, the only thing that *wants* to get rid of the ego is the ego. Spirit loves everything that arises, just as it is. The Witness loves everything that arises, just as it is. The Witness loves the ego, because the Witness is the impartial *mirror-mind* that equally reflects and perfectly embraces *everything* that arises.

But the ego, convinced that it can become even more entrenched, decides to play the game of getting rid of itself—simply because, *as long as it is playing that game*, it obviously continues to exist (who else is playing the game?). As Chuang Tzu pointed out long ago, "Is not the desire to get rid of the ego itself a manifestation of ego?"

The ego is not a thing but a subtle *effort*, and you cannot use effort to get rid of effort—you end up with two efforts instead of one. The ego itself is a perfect manifestation of the Divine, and it is best handled by resting in Freedom, not by trying to get rid of ego, which simply increases the effort of ego itself.

And so, the practice? When you rest in the Witness, or rest in I-I, or rest in Emptiness, simply notice the self-contraction. Rest in the Witness, and *feel* the self-contraction. When you feel the self-contraction, you are *already* free of it—you are already *looking at it*, instead of identifying with it. You are looking at it from the position of the Witness, which is always already free of all objects in any case.

So rest as the Witness, and feel the self-contraction—just as you can feel the chair under you, and feel the earth, and feel the clouds floating by in the sky. Thoughts float by in the mind, sensations float by in the body, the self-contraction hovers in awareness—and you effortlessly and spontaneously witness them all, equally and impartially.

In that simple, easy, effortless state—while you are *not* trying to get rid of the self-contraction but simply feeling it—and while you are therefore resting as the great Witness or Emptiness that you are— One Taste might more easily flash forth. There is nothing that you can do to bring about (or cause) One Taste—it is always already fully present, it is not the result of temporal actions, and you have never lost it anyway.

The most you can do, by way of temporal effort, is to avoid these two major mistakes (don't try to see the Witness as an object, just rest in the Witness as Seer; don't try to get rid of the ego, just feel it), and that will bring you to the edge, to the very precipice, of your own Original Face. At that point it is, in every way, out of your hands.

Rest as the Witness, feel the self-contraction: that is exactly the space in which One Taste can most easily flash forth. Don't do this as a strategic effort, but randomly and spontaneously throughout the day and into the night, standing thus always on the edge of your own shocking recognition.

So here are the steps:

Rest as the Witness, feel the self-contraction. As you do so, notice that the Witness is *not* the self-contraction—it is aware of it. The Witness is *free* of the self-contraction—and *you are the Witness*.

As the Witness, you are free of the self-contraction. *Rest in that Freedom*, Openness, Emptiness, Release. Feel the self-contraction, *and let it be*, just as you let all other sensations be. You don't try to get rid of the clouds, the trees, or the ego—just let them all be, and relax in the space of Freedom that you are.

From that space of Freedom—and at some unbidden point—you may notice that the *feeling* of Freedom has no inside and no outside, no center and no surround. Thoughts are floating in this Freedom, the sky is floating in this Freedom, the world is arising in this Freedom, and you are That. The sky is your head, the air is your breath, the earth is your body—it is all that close, and closer. You are the world, as long as you rest in this Freedom, which is infinite Fullness.

This is the world of One Taste, with no inside and no outside, no subject and no object, no in here versus out there—without beginning and without end, without ways and without means, without path and without goal. And this, as Ramana said, is the final truth.

That is what might be called a "capping exercise." Do it, not instead of, *but in addition to*, whatever other practice you are doing—centering prayer, vipassana, prayer of the heart, zikr, zazen, yoga, etc. All of these other practices train you to enter a specific state of consciousness, *but One Taste is not a specific state*—it is compatible with any and all states, just as wetness is fully present in each and every wave of the ocean. One wave may be bigger than another wave, but it is not wetter. One Taste is the wetness of the water, not any particular wave, and therefore specific practices, such as prayer or vipassana or yoga, are *powerless* to introduce you to One Taste. All specific practices are designed to get you to a particular wave—usually a Really Big Wave—and that is fine. But One Taste is the wetness of even the smallest wave, so any wave of awareness you have right now is fine. Rest with that wave, feel the self-contraction, and stand Free.

But continue your other practices, first, because they will introduce you to specific and important waves of your own awareness (psychic, subtle, and causal), which are all important vehicles of your full manifestation as Spirit. Second, precisely because One Taste is too simple to believe and too easy to reach by effort, most people will never notice that the wave they are now on is wet. They will never notice the Suchness of their own present state. They will instead dedicate their lives to wave hopping, always looking for a Bigger and Better wave to ride—and frankly, that is fine.

Those typical spiritual practices, precisely by introducing you to subtler and subtler *experiences*, will inadvertently help you *tire of experience altogether*. When you tire of wave jumping, you will stand open to the wetness or Suchness of whatever wave you are on. The pure Witness itself is *not an experience*, but the opening or clearing in which all experiences come and go, and as long as you are chasing experiences, including spiritual experiences, you will never rest as the Witness, let alone fall into the ever-present ocean of One Taste. But tiring of experiences, you will rest as the Witness, and it is as the Witness that you can notice Wetness (One Taste).

And then the wind will be your breath, the stars the neurons in your brain, the sun the taste of the morning, the earth the way your body feels. The Heart will open to the All, the Kosmos will rush into your soul, you will arise as countless galaxies and swirl for all eternity. There is only self-existing Fullness left in all the world, there is only self-seen Radiance here in Emptiness—etched on the wall of infinity, preserved for all eternity, the one and only truth: there is *just this*, snap your fingers, nothing more.

CW 8: *One Taste*, 533–536

The Witness is not identified with the ego or with any other mental object, it just impartially witnesses all objects. But that's just it: the Witness is still separate from all the objects that it witnesses. In other words, there is still a very subtle form of the subject/object dualism. The Witness is a huge step forward, and it is a necessary and important step in meditation, but it is not ultimate. When the Witness or the soul is finally undone, then the Witness dissolves into everything that is witnessed. The subject/object duality collapses and there is only pure nondual awareness, which is very simple, very obvious. . . . Everything continues to arise, moment to moment, but there's nobody divorced or alienated from it. What you are looking out of is what you are looking at. There's no separation or fragmentation between subject and object, there is just the ongoing stream of experience, perfectly clear and luminous and open. What I am is now everything that is arising.

CW 5: *Grace and Grit*, 121–122

The soul, as I am using the term, is a sort of halfway house, halfway between the personal ego-mind and the impersonal or transpersonal Spirit. The soul is the Witness as it shines forth in you and nobody else. The soul is the home of the Witness in that sense. Once you are established on the soul level, then you are established as the Witness, as the real Self. Once you push through the soul level, then the Witness itself collapses into everything witnessed, or you become one with everything you are aware of. You don't witness the clouds, you are the clouds. That's Spirit. . . .

In a sense the soul or the Witness in you is the highest pointer toward Spirit and the last barrier to Spirit. It's only from the position of the Witness that you can jump into Spirit, so to speak. But the Witness itself eventually has to dissolve or die. Even your own soul has to be sacrificed and released and let go of, or died to, in order for your ultimate identity with Spirit to radiate forth. Because ultimately the soul is just the final contraction in awareness, the subtlest knot restricting universal Spirit, the last and subtlest form of the separate-self sense, and that final knot has to be undone. That's the last death, as it were. First we die to the material self—that is, disidentify with it—then we die to an exclusive identity with the bodily self, then to the mental self, and then finally to the soul. The last one is what Zen calls the Great Death.

CW 5: *Grace and Grit*, 120–121

[Sri Ramana] Maharshi's unique contribution to the ways of liberation is his insistence that the "I-thought" is the source of all other thoughts. That is, every time you think of your "self," that is the I-thought, and Ramana declares it to lie behind every other thought:

> The first and foremost of all the thoughts that arise in the mind is the primal "I"-thought. It is only after the rise or origin of the "I"-thought that innumerable other thoughts arise.

Thus the suspension of the I-thought marks the suspension of all other thoughts and mental objects. Now Sri Ramana Maharshi realizes that the I-thought cannot be suppressed—for who would suppress "I" except another "I"? Spiritual altruism is spiritual hypocrisy. The I-thought, like any other thought, is to be suspended, not suppressed, and for this suspension, Ramana recommends what he calls "Self-Inquiry (*nan yar*)," which is the intensively active inquiry "Who am I?" . . .

How does this self-inquiry work? Let us suppose, for example, that I ask you, "Who are you?" and you reply, "Well, I am so-and-so, I work at this particular job, I'm married, and I am of such-and-such religion. Is that what you mean?" "No," I would answer, "those are all objects of perception, they are mere ideas. Who are you that sees these objects, these ideas?" "Well, I am a human being, an individual organism endowed with certain biological faculties. Is that closer?" "Not really," I would have to counter, "for those are still ideas and thoughts. Now deeply, *who are you*?" As your mind keeps turning back in on itself in search of the answer, it gets quieter and quieter. If I kept asking "Who are you? Who are you?" you would quickly enter a mental silence, and that mental silence would be identical to the one produced by Benoit's question, "How do you feel from all possible views at once?" That *object-less silence* produced by active attention, by vigilant watchfulness, by intense inquiry, is a Bodhimandala, for right at the point where no mental answer, image, or object is forthcoming, you are open to seeing the Real in a flash.

CW 1: *The Spectrum of Consciousness*, 351–353

People typically feel trapped by life, trapped by the universe, because they imagine that they are actually *in* the universe, and therefore the universe can squish them like a bug. This is not true. You are not in the universe; the universe is in you.

The typical orientation is this: my consciousness is in my body (mostly in my head); my body is in this room; this room is in the surrounding space, the universe itself. That is true from the viewpoint of the ego, but utterly false from the viewpoint of the Self.

If I rest as the Witness, the formless I-I, it becomes obvious that, right now, I am not in my body, my body is IN my awareness. I am aware of my body, therefore I am not my body. I am the pure Witness in which my body is now arising. I am not in my body, my body is in my consciousness. Therefore, *be* consciousness.

If I rest as the Witness, the formless I-I, it becomes obvious that, right now, I am not in this house, this house is IN my awareness. I am the pure Witness in which this house is now arising. I am not in this house, this house is in my consciousness. Therefore, *be* consciousness.

If I look outside this house, to the surrounding area—perhaps a large stretch of earth, a big patch of sky, other houses, roads and cars—if I look, in short, at the universe in front of me—and if I rest as the Witness, the formless I-I, it becomes obvious that, right now, I am not in the universe, the universe is IN my awareness. I am the pure Witness in which this universe is now arising. I am not in the universe, the universe is in my consciousness. Therefore, *be* consciousness.

It is true that the physical matter of your body is inside the matter of the house, and the matter of the house is inside the matter of the universe. But you are not merely matter or physicality. You are also Consciousness as Such, of which matter is merely the outer skin. The ego adopts the viewpoint of matter, and therefore is constantly trapped by matter—trapped and tortured by the physics of pain. But pain, too, arises in your consciousness, and you can either be in pain, or find pain in you, so that you surround pain, are bigger than pain, transcend pain, as you rest in the vast expanse of pure Emptiness that you deeply and truly are.

So what do I see? If I contract as ego, it appears that I am confined in the body, which is confined in the house, which is confined in the large universe around it. But if I rest as the Witness—the vast, open, empty consciousness—it becomes obvious that I am not in the body, the body is in me; I am not in this house, the house is in me; I am not in the universe, the universe is in me. All of them are arising in the vast, open, empty, pure, luminous Space of primordial Consciousness, right now and right now and forever right now.

Therefore, *be* Consciousness.

CW 8: One Taste, 448–449

Death: the mystics are unanimous that death contains the secret to life—to eternal life, in fact. As Eckhart put it, echoing the mystics everywhere: "No one gets as much of God as those who are thoroughly dead." Or Ramana Maharshi: "You will know in due course that your glory lies where you cease to exist." Or the *Zenrin*: "While alive, live as a dead person, thoroughly dead."

They don't mean physically dead; they mean dead to the separate-self sense. And you can "test" your own spiritual awareness in relation to death by trying to imagine the following items:

1. A famous Zen koan says, "Show me your Original Face, the Face you had before your parents were born." This is not a trick question or a symbolic question; it is very straightforward, with a clear and simple answer. Your Original Face is simply the pure formless Witness, prior to the manifest world. The pure Witness, itself being timeless or prior to time, is equally present at all points of time. So of course this is the Self you had before your parents were born; it is the Self you had before the Big Bang, too. And it is the Self you will have after your body—and the entire universe—dissolves.

This Self existed prior to your parents, and prior to the Big Bang, because it exists prior to time, period. And you can directly contact the Self you had before your parents were born by simply resting in the pure Witness right now. They are one and the same formless Self, right now, and right now, and right now.

By "imagining" what you were like before your parents were born, you are forced to drop all identity with your present body and ego. You are forced to find that in you which actually goes beyond you—namely, the pure, empty, formless, timeless Witness or primordial Self. To the extent you can actually rest as the timeless Witness ("I am not this, not that"), then you have died to the separate self—and discovered your Original Face, the face you had before your parents were born, before the Big Bang was born, before time was born. You have found, in fact, the great Unborn, which is just this.

2. Similarly, imagine what the world will be like a hundred years after you die. You don't have to imagine specific details, just realize that the world will be going on a century after you are gone. Imagine that world without you. So many things will have changed—different people, different technologies, different cars and planes. . . . But one thing will not have changed; one thing will be the same: Emptiness, One Taste, Spirit. Well, you can taste that right now. One and the same formless Witness will look out from all eyes, hear with all ears, touch with all hands . . . the same formless

Witness that is your own primordial Self right now, the same One Taste that is yours, right now, the same radiant Spirit that is yours, right now.

Were you somebody different a thousand years ago? Will you be somebody different a thousand years from now? What is this One Self that is forever your own deepest being? Must you believe the lies of time? Must you swallow the insanity that One Spirit does not exist? Can you right now show me your Original Face, of which there is One and Only One in all the entire World?

Listen to Erwin Schroedinger, the Nobel Prize–winning cofounder of quantum mechanics, and how can I convince you that he means this literally?

> Consciousness is a singular of which the plural is unknown. It is not possible that this unity of knowledge, feeling, and choice which you call your own should have sprung into being from nothingness at a given moment not so long ago; rather, this knowledge, feeling, and choice are essentially eternal and unchangeable and numerically one in all people, nay in all sensitive beings.
>
> The conditions for your existence are almost as old as the rocks. For thousands of years men have striven and suffered and begotten and women have brought forth in pain. A hundred years ago [there's the test], another man sat on this spot; like you he gazed with awe and yearning in his heart at the dying light on the glaciers. Like you he was begotten of man and born of woman. He felt pain and brief joy as you do. Was he someone else? Was it not you yourself?

WAS IT NOT YOU, YOUR PRIMORDIAL SELF? Are you not humanity itself? Do you not touch all things human, because you are its only Witness? Do you not therefore love the world, and love all people, and love the Kosmos, because you are its only Self? Do you not weep when one person is hurt, do you not cry when one child goes hungry, do you not scream when one soul is tortured? You *know* you suffer when others suffer. You already know this! "*Was* it someone else? Was it not you yourself?"

3. By thinking of what you were like a thousand years ago or a thousand years hence, you drop your identity with the present body

and ego, and find that in you which goes beyond you—namely, the pure, formless, timeless Self or Witness of the entire World. And once every twenty-four hours you completely drop your egoic identity, not as a mere imaginative exercise but as a fact. Every night, in deep dreamless sleep, you are plunged back into the formless realm, into the realm of pure consciousness without an object, into the realm of the formless, timeless Self.

This is why Ramana Maharshi said, "That which is not present in deep dreamless sleep is not real." The Real must be present in all three states, including deep dreamless sleep, and the only thing that is present in all three states is the formless Self or pure Consciousness. And each night you die to the separate-self sense, die to the ego, and are plunged back into the ocean of infinity that is your Original Face.

All three of those cases—the Self you had before your parents were born, the Self you will have a hundred years from now, and the Self you have in deep dreamless sleep—point to one and the same thing: the timeless Witness in you which goes beyond you, the pure Emptiness that is one with all Form, the primordial Self that embraces the All in radical One Taste. And *That*, which is *just this*, has not changed, will not change, will never change, because it never enters the corrupting stream of time with all its tears and terror.

The ultimate "spiritual test," then, is simply your relation to death (for all three of those cases are examples of death). If you want to know the "ultimate truth" of what you are doing right now, simply submit it to any of those tests. Practicing astrology? If it is not present in deep dreamless sleep, it is not real. Running with wolves? If it is not present a hundred years from now, it is not real. Care of the Soul? If it is not present in deep dreamless sleep, it is not real. Healing your inner child? If it was not present prior to your parents' birth, it is not real. You remember your reincarnated past lives? If it is not present in deep dreamless sleep, it is not real. Using diet for spiritual cleansing? If it is not present a hundred years from now, it is not real. Worshipping Gaia? If it is not present in deep dreamless sleep, it is not real.

All of those relative practices and translative beliefs are fine, and can be very useful—I truly don't wish to belittle any of them—but never forget they are secondary to the great Unborn, your Original Face, the Face of Spirit in all its radiant forms, the forms of your very own being and becoming, now and again, now and forever, always and already.

"*Was* it someone else? Was it not you yourself?"

cw 8: *One Taste*, 619–622

"Let your mind relax. Let your mind relax and expand, mixing with the sky in front of it. Then notice: the clouds float by in the sky, and you are effortlessly aware of them. Feelings float by in the body, and you are effortlessly aware of them, too. Thoughts float by in the mind, and you are aware of them as well. Nature floats by, feelings float by, thoughts float by . . . and you are aware of all of them.

"So tell me: Who are you?

"You are not your thoughts, for you are aware of them. You are not your feelings, for you are aware of them. You are not any objects that you can see, for you are aware of them.

"Something in you is aware of all these things. So tell me: What is it in you that is conscious of everything?"

Boomeritis, 336

2

Memoirs

Many readers discovered Wilber's work through Grace and Grit,
*a heart-opening book that chronicles both the terminal cancer and
the spiritual journey of his late wife, Treya Killam Wilber. After
the book's publication, an outpouring of appreciation was sent to
Wilber through letters expressing such sentiments as this:*

> *With fullest of hearts, I write to you thanks for living your
> story of* Grace and Grit *with such candor, love, honesty, and
> acceptance. I have set your book down a few days ago, and
> the story runs through my being, so powerful, even many
> years after her passing. The experience for me has been one of
> those lovely mystical events that opens me in new and better
> ways (not without a few floods!), changing me once again.*

*Because he brings such a personal voice to his writings, Wilber's
memoirs especially touch people in a distinct way—with candor and
emotional immediacy. This intimate expression complements his
more academic prose, making his writings personal as well as metaphysical. A Zen teacher was once asked, "What happens to the individual style and unique expression of one who attains liberation?"
The teacher responded, "While the separate self may eventually dissolve, each person still maintains their own unique* scent.*" In this
chapter, extensive excerpts from* Grace and Grit, *as well as memoirs
drawn from other books, introduce us to Ken Wilber the man, to
the joy, humor, heartache, passion, sensuality, and spiritual realization that make up his particular* scent.

K EN WILBER is just a scab on my Original Face, and this morning I flick it off like a tiny insect, and disappear back into the infinite space that is my true abode.

But that infinite space is impulsive. It sings its songs of manifestation, it dances the dance of creation. Out of sheerest purest gossamer nothingness, now and now and forever now, this majestic world arises, a wink and a nod from the radiant Abyss. So I finish unpacking the books, and go on about the morning business.

CW 8: *One Taste*, 421

In my first year of college (Duke), I chanced to pick up a very small book, whose opening lines were:

> The Way that can be told of is not the eternal Way.
> The name that can be named is not the eternal name.
> The Nameless is the origin of Heaven and Earth.
> The Named is but the mother of ten thousand things.
> Truly, only he that rids himself forever of desire can
>   see the Secret Essences;
> He that has never rid himself of desire can see only
>   the Outcomes.
> These two things issue from the same Source, but
>   nevertheless are different in form.
> This Source we can but call the Mystery,
> The Doorway whence issue all secret essences.
>
> —Lao Tzu, *Tao-te Ching*

I had never been exposed to such ideas before. Or perhaps I should say, if I had on occasion seen such words they had made no impression on me whatsoever. My life up to that point had been largely involved with science (physics, chemistry, biology, and mathematics). During my early youth I was rebellious and trouble-making enough to be normal and healthy; nonetheless my earliest memory of intellectual satisfaction was buying a chemistry text at age ten, and my happiest moments were spent in various home laboratories I would rig up. While in late high school and early college, I drank enough beer and became obsessed with enough women also to be normal and healthy. Nonetheless my true passion, my inner daemon, was for science. I fashioned a self that was built on logic, structured by physics, and moved by chemistry. I was precociously successful in that world, obtaining numerous awards and honors, and I was at college to corner that success and extrapolate it into a life's destiny. My mental youth was an idyll of precision and accuracy, a fortress of the clear and evident.

And so, as I stood reading the first chapter of the *Tao-te Ching*, it was as if I were being exposed, for the first time, to an entirely new and drastically different world—a world beyond the sensical, a world outside of science, and therefore a world quite beyond myself. The result was that those ancient words of Lao Tzu took me quite by surprise; worse, the surprise refused to wear off, and my entire world outlook began a subtle but drastic shift. Within a period of a few months— months spent in introductory readings of Taoism and Buddhism—the meaning of my life, as I had known it, simply began to disappear. Oh, it was nothing dramatic; more like waking up one morning, after twenty years of marriage, with the "sudden" realization that you no longer loved (or even recognized) your spouse. There is really no upset, no bitterness, no tears—just the tacit realization that it is time to sepa- rate. Just so, the old sage had touched a chord so deep in me (and so much stronger due to its twenty-year repression) that I suddenly awoke to the silent but certain realization that my old life, my old self, my old beliefs could no longer be energized. It was time for a separation.

CW 2: "Odyssey," 15–16

A small stream, softly murmuring, runs down behind my house; you can hear it actually singing, if you listen with ears of light. The sun plays on the green leaves, sparkling emeralds each and all, and Spirit speaks in times like these just a little louder. "I become a transparent eyeball; I am nothing, I see all." There is nothing solid here, all that is hard melts into air, all that is rigid softens to transparency, the world is diaphanous, not in appearance but essence. I disappear into the transparent show, and we are all light in light, images in images, floating effortlessly on a sea of the serene.

Nature is the outer form of Buddha, nature is the corporeal body of Christ. Take, eat, for this is my flesh; take, drink, for this is my blood. Poor dear nature, expression of the Real, impulse of the Infinite, transparent to Eternity, is merely a shining surface on an ocean of unending Spirit, dancing in the daylight of the Divine, hiding in the night of ignorance. For those who do not know the Timeless, nature is all they have; for those who do not taste Infinity, nature serves its last supper. For those in need of redemption, nature tricks you into thinking it alone is real. But for those who have found release, nature is the radiant shell in which a deeper truth resides. So it is—nature, mind, and spirit—Nirmanakaya, Sambhogakaya, and Dharmakaya—gross, subtle, and causal—are an eternal trinity in the folds of the Kosmos, never lost, never found.

Except today, where we are all light in light, and images in images, floating effortlessly on a sea of the serene.

CW 8: *One Taste*, 346

By the time I had finished writing *No Boundary* (1979), my meditation practice, while not exactly advanced, was no longer in the beginner's phase. The leg pain (from the lotus posture) was manageable, and my awareness was growing in its capacity to maintain an alert yet relaxed, active yet detached stance. But my mind was, as the Buddhists say, that of a monkey: compulsively active, obsessively motive. And there I came face to face with my own Apollo complex, the difficulty in transforming from the mental sphere to the subtle sphere. The subtle sphere (or the "soul," as Christians mystics use that term) is the beginning of the transpersonal realms; as such, it is supramental, transegoic, and trans-verbal. But in order to reach that sphere, one must (as in all transforma-tions) "die" to the lower sphere (in this case, the mental-egoic). The failure to do so or the incapacity to do so is the Apollo complex. As the person with an Oedipus complex remains unconsciously attached to the body and its pleasure principle, so the person with an Apollo complex remains unconsciously attached to the mind and its reality principle. ("Reality" here means "institutional, rational, verbal reality," which, although conventionally real enough, is nevertheless only an intermedi-ate stage on the path to Atman; that is, it is merely a description of ac-tual Reality itself, and thus, if clung to, eventually and ultimately prevents the discovery of that actual Reality.)

The struggle with my own obsessive/compulsive thinking—not *particular* obsessive thoughts, as per specific neurosis (which is often indicative of an Oedipus-complex holdover), but the very stream of thought itself—was an arduous task. As it was, I was fortunate to make some progress, to be able eventually to rise above the fluctua-tions of mental contractions and discover, however initially, a realm incomparably more profound, more real, more saturated with being, more open to clarity. This realm was simply that of the subtle, which is disclosed, so to speak, after weathering the Apollo complex. In this realm, it is not that thinking *necessarily* ceases (although it often does, especially at the beginning); it is that, even when thinking arises, it does not detract from this broader background of clarity and awareness. From the subtle, one no longer "gets lost in thoughts"; rather, thoughts enter consciousness and depart much as clouds traverse the sky: with smoothness, grace, and clarity. Nothing sticks, nothing rubs, nothing grates. Chuang Tzu: "The perfect man employs his mind as a mirror. It grasps nothing; it refuses nothing; it receives, but does not keep."

While in actual meditation, however, the experiences of the subtle realm can be (and usually are) quite extraordinary, awesome, profound. For this is the realm of the archetypes and of archetypal deity—confrontation with which is always numinous, as Jung pointed out. This was a very real and very intense period for me; it was my first direct and unequivocal experience of the actual sacredness of the world, this world which, as Plotinus said, emanates from the One and plays as an expression of It. Oh, I had earlier had brief and initial glimpses into the subtle realm—and even the causal beyond it—but I had not yet really been introduced to, or initiated in, that realm. A Zen Master once said that the proper response to the first strong kensho (small satori) is not to laugh but to cry, and that is exactly what I did, for hours, it seemed. Tears of gratitude, of compassion, of unworthiness, and finally, of infinite wonder. (That is not false humility; I have never met anyone who did not feel unworthy of this realm.) Laughter—great laughter—came later; at this early point, it would have been sacrilegious.

There followed, in my meditation practice, a "tour" of the subtle realm. My favorite description of this realm is from Dante, and I assure you he means this literally:

> Fixing my gaze upon the Eternal Light
> I saw within its depths,
>   Bound up with love together in one volume,
> The scattered leaves of all the universe. . . .
> Within the luminous profound subsistence
>   Of that Exalted Light saw I three circles
>   Of three colors yet of one dimension

And by the second seemed the first reflected
As rainbow is by rainbow, and the third
Seemed fire that equally from both is breathed.

It was at that time that I discovered the works of Kirpal Singh, who did much to clarify my own experiences in this realm. Singh is, to my mind, the unsurpassed master of the subtle realms, and without his guidance (even if only by book) I doubt seriously I would have passed as easily and quickly through some of these realms as I apparently did. Singh's whole point is that there is, within the subtle realm, a hierarchy of successively subtler audible illuminations, or shabd "chakras," at and beyond the chakras (such as the ajna and the sahasrara), considered to be ultimate by older and less sophisticated yogic schools. His whole approach was hierarchical, developmental, and dynamic, which meshed perfectly with my own philosophy so that I didn't have to waste time either learning or arguing with his position. I could simply use it.

I was getting, then, a taste of the subtle realms, an introduction to archetype, to deity, to yidam (the Buddhist term) and ishtadeva (the Hindu term). These were, without doubt, the most profound experiences I had ever encountered. More important, because I was already quite familiar (in theory, and in fact) with the experiences that can be produced by *subconscious* impulses, all the "magical" and "hallucinatory" images described by Freud et al., I was not led into the fallacy of confusing superconscious experiences with subconscious revivals. In my opinion, anyone who has carefully and personally studied these various realms will recognize at once the profound differences between prepersonal, subconscious, and instinctual displays as opposed to those that are transpersonal, superconscious, and archetypal. The Eastern schools themselves are very explicit on the differences between pranamayakosha (or emotional-sexual displays) and anandamayakosha (or archetypal intuitions).

THE LIMITS OF EXPERIENCE

But the more these superconscious experiences progressed, the more it began to dawn on me that all of it was just that—mere experience. For experience by definition is that which has a beginning and that which has an end (strictly temporal, strictly relative). The more deeply I began to see into the nature of experience, the more profoundly I became disillusioned with it. Granted, these realms were, in a special sense, more real than the material or bodily or mental planes, at least as I knew them, but the point was that this experiential display could go on forever. I could be introduced into subtler and subtler *experiences* ad infinitum.

There is a saying, by Hanns Sachs, I think, that psychoanalysis ends when the patient realizes it can go on forever. The same type of realization, as it were, began to cure me of the subtle-level fixation, the Vishnu complex. For the Vishnu complex is precisely the difficulty in moving from subtle soul to causal spirit. The subtle experiences are so blissful, so awesome, so profound, so salutary, that one wants never to leave them, never to let go, but rather to bathe forever in their archetypal glory and immortal release—and *there* is the Vishnu complex. If the Apollo complex is the bane of beginning meditators, the Vishnu complex is the great seducer of intermediate practitioners.

But my training in Zen, my understanding (no matter how superficial) of Krishnamurti, of Shankara and Sri Ramana Maharshi, of Saint Dionysus to Eckhart—all had told me that the ultimate state was *not an experience*. It was not a particular experience among other experiences, but the very nature and ground of all experiences, high or low. It was the vast background or Abyss (Ruysbroeck) out of which spring various experiential realities. *In itself*, therefore, it was not experiential at all; it had nothing to do with changes of state, with knowing this or that, with seeing this or that, with feeling this or that, because it was prior to all that, the very nature of this and every moment before I try to grasp it. The ultimate state is what I am before I am anything else; it is what I see before I see anything else, and what I feel before I feel anything else. That is why the Tao is said to be beyond knowing *or* not knowing, right or wrong.

Chao-Chou asked, "What is the Tao?"

Master Nan-chuan replied, "Your ordinary consciousness is the Tao."

"But how can one return into accord with it?"

"By trying to accord, you already deviate."

"But without trying, how can one know the Tao?"

"The Tao," said the master, "is prior to knowing or to not knowing. Knowing is false understanding; not knowing is simply ignorance. If you really understand the Tao prior to doubt, it's like the empty sky. Why drag in right and wrong?

—Alan Watts, *Tao: The Watercourse Way*
(New York: Pantheon, 1975)

Explain it this way: The Upanishads say that Brahman is not one among many, but one without a second; not a particular object, but the reality of *all* objects. Yet I was trying to grasp the All as a particular experience—a Big Experience, to be sure, but an experience nonetheless—and that is precisely what prevents the discovery (because an experience is a knowing *or* a not-knowing, and not that which is prior to both). This is why Zen calls all higher experiences by a derogatory name: *makyo*, or "subtle illusions." And, according to Zen, many other traditions mistake makyo for the ultimate state, simply because these extraordinary experiences are indeed more real than ordinary states. Nonetheless, all experiences, high or low, fall short of nondual consciousness as such, and thus eventually must be penetrated.

The point is that experiences, whether sacred or profane, high or low, are all based on the duality between subject and object, seer and seen, experiencer and experienced. Even in the soul-sphere, itself incomparably more real then the lower levels of matter, body, and mind, one is merely engineering for a subtler subject, a more extraordinary object. The witness of these divine states still remains intact. The real awakening, however, is the dissolution of the witness itself, and not a change of state in that which is witnessed.

This is why some form of inquiry—"Who am I?" "Who chants the name of Buddha?" "Who desires release?"—has always been held to be the basic path, perhaps the sole path, beyond the witness (and the Vishnu complex). Not, "I must always be aware of the breath," but "*Who* must be?" Not "I hold the koan," but "*Who* holds it?" What inquiry does is to disengage attention from the objective displays in consciousness, and turn it on consciousness itself. More precisely, with inquiry, attention turns on attention itself, on the very *nature* of attention, and its nature is one of subtle contraction or resistance. Any attention is exclusive, because it attends to this by ignoring that. It is, in other words, dualistic, and this includes "passive attention" and any other such subtly motivated awareness. They are all merely subjective contractions in the Field of Consciousness. But with inquiry, this subjective contraction which *is* attention becomes the *object* of attention. That is, the subject becomes object and the object is the subject, so that the boundary between them is broken and both disappear as exclusive and separative entities. There thus remains only radiant, all-pervading, unobstructed, and prior consciousness, which is neither subjective nor objective but merely whole.

The first time this became even fleetingly obvious to me was at a sesshin, or intensive Zen retreat. On the fourth day there appeared, so to speak, the state of the witness, the transpersonal witness that steadily, calmly, clearly witnesses all arising events, moment to moment. Even in dreaming, one merely witnesses: One can see the dream start, proceed, and end (what Charles Tart has called "translucent dreams"). Roshi, however, was thoroughly unimpressed with all this "makyo." "The witness," he said, "is the last stand of the ego."

At that point, the whole stance of the witness absolutely disappeared. There was no subject anywhere in the universe; there was no object anywhere in the universe; there was only the universe. Everything was arising moment to moment, and it was arising in me and as me; yet there was no me. It is very important to realize that this state was not a loss of faculties but a peak-enhancement of them; it was no blank trance but perfect clarity; not depersonalized but transpersonalized. No personal faculties—language, logic, concepts, motor skills—were lost or impaired. Rather, they all functioned, for the first time, it seemed to me, in radical openness, free of the defenses thrown up by a separate-self sense. This radically open, undefended, and perfectly nondual state was both incredible and profoundly ordinary, so extraordinarily ordinary that it did not even register. There was nobody there to comprehend it, until I fell *out* of it (I guess about three hours later).

In other words, while in that state, which was no experience whatsoever, there was *only* that state, which was the totality of everything arising moment to moment. I did not watch or experience all that, I simply *was* all that. I could not see it because it was everything seen; I could not hear it because it was everything heard; I could not know it because it was everything known. That is why it is both the great mystery and the perfectly obvious. But it was only when I realized that I was in that state that I was actually no longer in it. That is, the recognition or experience of that state was much, much less than the state itself. To experience that state, I had to separate myself from it (that is, destroy it).

From that point on, I became profoundly suspicious of any transpersonalist who spoke of the highest states as "experiential realities," even as I had tended to do in *Spectrum*. I also saw the perfect inadequacy of the otherwise extremely useful paradigm of "altered states" to deal with the ultimate spiritual realm, for that realm, that "no-realm," is actually what all states have in common, and what all states have in common is not itself another state, much as the alphabet is not another letter.

But this whole period of touring the subtle realms, grappling with the Vishnu complex, and penetrating the Dharmakaya—however partial, initial, and incomplete they may have been—at least gave me a fairly solid, firsthand introduction to the various higher spheres of consciousness. With that background, I was more easily capable of returning to the literature of the transpersonal traditions and doing a rather exhaustive breakdown and classification of the various higher realms, realms too often merely lumped together and called "transpersonal," "transcendent," or "mystic." This was the point that, as I mentioned earlier, I subdivided the transpersonal realm into at least four or five major levels based on structural analyses. With these subadditions to the spectrum, and those from *Eden*, I finally felt that I had a more complete cartography of consciousness, one that, while far from perfect and occasionally somewhat sloppy, had at least the merit of comprehensiveness. Refinements could come over the years; in the meantime, this cartography was presented in *Atman Project*, with extensive reference tables showing how it fit with the major psychologies East and West.

CW 2: "Odyssey," 41–47

I cannot perceive my own true identity, or my union with Spirit, because my awareness is clouded and obstructed by a certain activity that I am now engaged in. And that activity, although known by many different names, is simply the activity of contracting and focusing awareness on my individual self or personal ego. My awareness is not open, relaxed, and God-centered, it is closed, contracted, and self-centered. And precisely because I am identified with the self-contraction to the exclusion of everything else, I can't find or discover my prior identity, my true identity, with the All. My individual nature, "the natural man," is thus fallen, or lives in sin and separation and alienation from Spirit and from the rest of the world. I am set apart and isolated from the world "out there," which I perceive as if it were entirely external and alien and hostile to my own being. And as for my own being itself, it certainly does not seem to be one with the All, one with everything that exists, one with infinite Spirit; rather, it seems completely boxed up and imprisoned in this isolated wall of mortal flesh.

CW 5: *Grace and Grit*, 99

Love at first touch. We hadn't said five words to each other. And I could tell by the way she was looking at my shaved head that it definitely was not going to be love at first sight. I, like almost everybody, found Treya quite beautiful, but I really didn't even know her. But when I put my arm around her, I felt all separation and distance dissolve; there was some sort of merging, it seemed. It was as if Treya and I had been together for lifetimes. This seemed very real and very obvious, but I didn't know quite what to make of it. Treya and I still hadn't even talked to each other, so neither of us knew the same thing was happening to the other. I remember thinking, Oh great, it's four in the morning and I'm having some sort of weird mystical experience right in the kitchen of one of my best friends, merely by touching a woman I've never met before. This is not going to be easy to explain. . . .

I couldn't sleep that night; images of Treya poured over me. She was indeed beautiful. But what exactly was it? There was an energy that seemed literally to radiate from her in all directions; a very quiet and soothing energy, but enormously strong and powerful; an energy that was very intelligent and suffused with exceptional beauty, but mostly an energy that was *alive*. This woman said LIFE more than anybody I had ever known. The way she moved, the way she held her head, the ready smile that graced the most open and transparent face I had ever seen—God, she was alive!

Her eyes looked at, and through, everything. It wasn't that she had a penetrating glance—that's much too aggressive—it was simply that she seemed to see through things, and then perfectly accept what she saw, a kind of gentle and compassionate x-ray vision. Eyes committed to truth, I finally decided. When she looked directly at you, you could tell unmistakably that this was a person who would never lie to you. You trusted her immediately; an enormous integrity seemed to permeate even her smallest movements and mannerisms.

She appeared the most self-confident person I had ever met, yet not proud or boastful in the least. I wondered if she ever got flustered; it was hard to imagine. Yet behind the almost intimidating solidness of her character, there were the dancing eyes, seeing everything, not ponderously, but wanting rather to play. I thought, this woman is game for anything; I don't think anything scares her. There was a lightness surrounding her, sincere but not serious; with her super-abundance of life, she could afford to play, she could shed density and float all the way to the stars, if she wanted.

I finally drifted off, only to awaken with a start: I've found her. That's all I kept thinking: I've found her.

CW 5: *Grace and Grit*, 10–11

Worked all morning; decided to go jogging down behind my house. If you remain as the Witness while you run, you don't move, the ground does. You, as the Witness, are immobile—more precisely, you have no qualities at all, no traits, no motion and no commotion, as you rest in the vast Emptiness that you are. You are aware of movement, therefore you as the Witness are not movement. So when you run, it actually feels as if you are not moving at all—the Witness is free of motion *and* stillness—so the ground simply moves along. It's like you're sitting in a movie theater, never moving from your seat, and yet seeing the entire scenery move around you.

(This is easy to do when you're driving down the highway. You can simply sit back, relax, and *pretend* that you are not moving, only the scenery is. This is often enough to flip people into the actual Witness, at which point you will simply rest as choiceless awareness, watching the world go by, and you won't move at all. This *motionless* center of your own pure awareness is in fact the *center* of the *entire* Kosmos, the eye or I-I of the Kosmic cyclone. This motionless center—there is only one in the entire world and it is identical in all beings, the circle whose center is everywhere and whose circumference, nowhere—is also the center of gravity of your soul.)

This is why Zen will say, "A man in New York drinks vodka, a man in Los Angeles gets drunk." The *same* Big Mind is timelessly, spacelessly, present in both places. So drinking in New York and getting drunk in L.A. are the same to the motionless, *spaceless* Witness. This is why Zen will say, "Without moving, go to New York." The answer: "I'm already there."

As the Witness, I-I do not move through time, time moves through me. Just as clouds float through the sky, time floats through the open space of my primordial awareness, and I-I remain untouched by time and space and their complaints. Eternity does not mean living forever in time—a rather horrible notion—but living in the *timeless* moment, prior to time and its turmoils altogether. Likewise, infinity does not mean a really big space, it means completely *spaceless*. As the Witness, I-I am spaceless; as the Witness, I-I am timeless. I-I live in eternity and inhabit infinity, simply because the Witness is free of time and space. And *that* is why I can drink vodka in New York and get drunk in L.A.

So this morning I went jogging, and nothing moved at all, except the scenery in the movie of my life.

CW 8: *One Taste*, 383–384

Love is a time-honored way to transcend the separate-self sense and leap into the sublime; Treya and I held hands, closed our eyes, and jumped.

CW 5: *Grace and Grit*, 27

I knew Treya had cancer when I saw Peter come down and ask the duty nurse for a private conference room. . . .

Strange things happen to the mind when catastrophe strikes. It felt like the universe turned into a thin paper tissue, and then someone simply tore the tissue in half right in front of my eyes. I was so stunned that it was as if absolutely nothing had happened. A tremendous strength descended on me, the strength of being both totally jolted and totally stupefied. I was clear, present, and very determined. As Samuel Johnson drily commented, the prospect of death marvelously concentrates the mind. I felt marvelously concentrated, all right; it was only that our universe had just been torn right down the middle. The rest of the afternoon and all of that evening unfolded in slow-motion freeze-frames, one clear and exquisitely painful frame after the next, no filters, no protection.

CW 5: *Grace and Grit*, 41–42

Worked all morning, research and reading, while watching the sunlight play through the falling snow. The sun is not yellow today, it is white, like the snow, so I am surrounded by white on white, alone on alone. Sheer Emptiness, soft clear light, is what it all looks like, shimmering to itself in melancholy murmurs. I am released into that Emptiness, and all is radiant on this clear light day.

cw 8: *One Taste*, 279

"Listen to me very carefully" the sky now says to me. "I am Prakriti, doorway to all space, the womb in which all manifestation arises, fleshy entrance to that Spirit which is always already here and now, a Spirit that is about to descend on the unwilling world at large, racing through the evolving waves of carbon and silicon at the speed of light. You wish to enter my body, be one with my desire, sexually unite with my flesh, find the ultimate release—that is what you really want, yes?—to fuck to infinity, find an orgasm so immense it releases the entire cosmos—to be totally Free, radically Released, one with the All. This is what you really want, so why be one with only a single female body, when you can be one with the entire cosmos, an orgasmic release beyond your wildest dreams? Why settle for this pound of flesh, when infinity is yours? Ken, are you listening to me? Ken?"

"Yes, yes, I hear you."

"Reach out and touch my breasts, all you will feel are the clouds. Enter my body, all you will find is the earth. Be one with me, that is what you want. Have intercourse with the entire universe, dear soul, and disappear into that bliss. Do you understand?"

Boomeritis, 334 (Note that *Boomeritis* is a *fictional* work by Ken Wilber.)

As for Treya and me, our favorite activity was still very simple: sitting on the sofa, our arms around each other, feeling the dancing energies in our body. So often we were taken beyond ourselves to that place where death is a stranger and love alone shines, where souls unite for all eternity and a single embrace lights up the spheres—the simplest way to discover that God most definitely is embodied, love of the two-armed form.

And yet this brought its own dilemma for me: the more I loved Treya, the more I feared and was obsessed with her death. This was a constant reminder of one of the central tenets of Buddhism (and mysticism in general): everything is impermanent, everything passes, nothing remains, nothing lasts. Only the whole endures eternally; all parts are doomed to death and decay. In meditative or mystical awareness, beyond the prison of individuality, one can taste the whole and escape the fate of a part; one is released from suffering and from the terror of mortality.

CW 5: *Grace and Grit*, 80

The world arises quietly this morning, shimmering on a radiant sea of transparent Emptiness. There is only *this*, vast, open, empty, clear, nakedly luminous. All questions dissolve in this single Answer, all doubts resolve in this single Shout, all worries are a ripple on this Sea of equanimity.

CW 8: *One Taste*, 376

But what moved Treya and me to tears, literally, was Notre Dame. One foot inside and you knew immediately you were in sacred space; the profane world of cancer, illness, poverty, hunger, and woes, all checked at the magnificent doors. The lost art of sacred geometry was everywhere apparent, inviting your awareness to assume the same divine contours. Treya and I attended Mass there one day, holding on to each other as if God Almighty, this time as a Benevolent Father figure, might actually reach down, miraculously, and strike the cancer from her body just like that, due to no other reason than that even He Himself would be compelled to act in a space that sacred, that far removed from what His children had done with the rest of His creation. The sun through the stained-glass windows alone seemed curative; we sat for hours in awe.

CW 5: *Grace and Grit*, 344

From the top of this tower I could see for perhaps a hundred miles in all directions. My eyes swept right: the tower at Bad Godesberg, the Bonn cathedral, the great Dom of Cologne, seventy kilometers north. I looked up: Heaven; I looked down: Earth. Heaven, Earth; Heaven, Earth. And that's what started me thinking of Treya. In the past few years she had returned to her roots in the Earth, to her love of nature, to the body, to making, to her femininity, to her grounded openness and trust and caring. While I had remained where I wanted-ed to be, where I myself am at home—in Heaven, which, in mythology, does not mean the world of Spirit but the Apollonian world of ideas, of logic, of concepts and symbols. Heaven is of the mind, Earth is of the body. I took feelings and related them to ideas; Treya took ideas and related them to feelings. I moved from the particular to the universal, constantly; Treya moved from the universal to the concrete, always. I loved thinking, she loved making. I loved culture, she loved nature. I shut the window so I could hear Bach; she turned off Bach so she could hear the birds.

In the traditions, Spirit is found neither in Heaven nor in Earth, but in the Heart. The Heart has always been seen as the integration or the union point of Heaven and Earth, the point that Earth grounded Heaven and Heaven exalted the Earth. Neither Heaven nor Earth alone could capture Spirit; only the balance of the two found in the Heart could lead to the secret door beyond death and mortality and pain.

CW 5: *Grace and Grit*, 358–359

The sunlight is playing off the remnants of snow, scattered everywhere in patches, snuggling under the dark green pines that cozy up against the house. It all arises in the luminous clearing of Emptiness, the spaciousness of Godhead, the unqualifiable expanse of All Space, which is not other than one's own choiceless awareness, moment to moment. There is *just this*. It blinds me into submission, takes my breath away, forces me to surrender to my own deepest state, where I am totally undone in the Beauty of it all.

That is exactly why Beauty takes on such a profound meaning. In that choiceless awareness, in the utter simplicity of One Taste, all realms—from causal formlessness to subtle luminosity to gross body, mind, and nature—take on a painful beauty, a truly painful beauty. Aesthetics takes on an entirely new importance, aesthetics in all domains—the beauty of the body, the beauty of the mind, the beauty of the soul, the beauty of spirit. When all things are seen as perfect expressions of Spirit, just as they are, all things become deeply, painfully beautiful.

Yesterday I sat in a shopping mall for hours, watching people pass by, and they were all as precious as green emeralds. The occasional joy in their voices, but more often the pain in their faces, the sadness in their eyes, the burdenous slowness of their paces—I registered none of that. I saw only the glory of green emeralds, and radiant buddhas walking everywhere, and there was no I to see any of this, but the emeralds were there just the same. The dirt on the sidewalk, the rocks in the street, the cries of the children, here and there— a paradise in a shopping mall, and who would ever have suspected?

CW 8: One Taste, 354–355

"If you want to be one with the cosmos, Ken, instead of one with only a single female body, then don't see the mountain, be it. Like this: Feel my naked body. Now feel the same way about the entire world in front of you. Erotically unite with everything that is arising."

Boomeritis, 371 (Note that Boomeritis is a fictional work by Ken Wilber.)

Chloe and I are making love, when suddenly her body transforms into the cosmos; one with her, I am everything that is arising: I clutch frantically the entire world and dissolve into no-boundary bliss. Walking is one continuous orgasm, so is sitting, standing, laughing, loving, as ecstasy escapes from the insides of infinity and rains on a welcoming world. The love I have . . . spills out of my being and into the Kosmos at large in ever-expanding waves of care. . . .

Boomeritis, 346 (Note that Boomeritis is a fictional work by Ken Wilber.)

Germany is closed on Sunday. I began walking the back streets of Godesberg feeling sorrier and sorrier for myself. At this point I wasn't so much thinking of Treya as I was wallowing in me. My whole fucking life is a shambles, I've given it all up for Treya, and now Treya, I'll kill her, is going to die.

As I walked and emoted, pissed that no pubs seemed to be open, I heard polka music coming from several blocks away. It must be a pub, I thought; even on Sunday you can't keep good Germans away from Kolsch and Piers. I followed the music to a cute little pub about six blocks out of town. Inside were perhaps a dozen men, all of them somewhat elderly, maybe in their late sixties, rosy cheeks from years of starting the day with Kolsch. The music was lively, not what Americans think of as polka, which is a kind of schmaltzy Lawrence Welk mush, but more like authentic German bluegrass music; I loved this music. About half of the men—there were no women, and no younger men—were dancing together in a semicircle, arms over each others' shoulders, a type of Zorba-the-Greek dance, it looked like to me, every now and then kicking their legs up in unison.

I sat down at the bar, by myself, and put my head in my arms. A Kolsch appeared in front of me, and, without wondering where it came from, I drank it at one pull. Another appeared. I drank it. I guess they think I'm running a tab, I thought.

About four beers later I started crying again, though now I try to hide it. I don't ever remember crying this much, I think. Crying for myself, anyway. I am starting to get slightly tipsy by now. A few of the men dance in my direction and gesture for me to join them. No, thank you, no, I gesture back. A few beers later they gesture again, only this time one of them takes me by the arm, in a friendly way, and tugs.

"*Ich spreche kein Deutsch*," I say, the one phrase I have memorized. They keep tugging and gesturing, smiling, looking concerned, looking like they want to help. I think seriously about bolting for the door, but I haven't paid for the beer. Awkwardly, very self-consciously, I join the men dancing, arms around those on both sides of me, moving back and forth, kicking our legs up every now and then. I start laughing, then I start crying, then laughing, then crying. I would like to turn away, to hide what is happening to me, but I am locked arm-and-shoulder into the semicircle. For about fifteen minutes I seem to lose all control over my emotions. Fear, panic, self-pity, laughter, joy, terror, feeling sorry for myself, feeling happy about myself—they all come rushing through me and show on my face, which embarrasses me, but the men keep nodding their heads, and smiling, as if to tell me it's all OK, young man, it's all OK. Just keep dancing, young man, just keep dancing. You see? Like this. . . .

I stayed in that pub for two hours, dancing and drinking Kolsch. I never wanted to leave. Somehow, in that short period, it all seemed to come to a head, to rise up and wash through my system, to be exposed and to be accepted. Not totally; but I did seem to come to some sort of peace about it all; enough, at any rate, to carry on. I finally got up to go, and gestured goodbye to all the men. They waved and kept dancing. Nobody ever charged me for the beer.

I later told Edith this story, and she said, "Ah, now you know what the real Germany is like."

I would like to claim that my big satori about accepting Treya's condition, that my coming to terms with her likely death, that my becoming finally responsible for my own choices about setting aside my interests and doing anything to support her—I would like to claim that all of that came from some powerful meditation session with blazing white light and spontaneous insights pouring over me, that I grabbed a handful of Zen courage and plunged back into the fight, that I reached high for some transcendental epiphany that set me straight at once. But it happened in a little pub with a bunch of kindly old men whose names I do not know and whose language I did not speak.

CW 5: *Grace and Grit*, 361–363

It's taken almost a week for any sort of meditative awareness to return, including lucid dreaming. The entire time I was in New York I lost all access to pure witnessing, and I had no subject permanence during the dream and deep sleep state. That is, I was not conscious during the dreaming and deep sleep state—a consciousness, a kind of current, that has been with me off and on for the last three or four years.

This constant consciousness through all states—waking, dreaming, and sleeping—tends to occur after many years of meditating; in my case, about twenty-five years. The signs are very simple: you are conscious during the waking state, and then, as you fall asleep and start to dream, you still remain conscious of the dreaming. This is similar to lucid dreaming, but with a slight difference: usually, in lucid dreaming, you start to manipulate the dream—you choose to dream of sex orgies or great food or flying over mountains or whatnot. But with constant witnessing consciousness, there is no desire to change anything that arises: you simply and innocently witness it. It's a choiceless awareness, a mirrorlike awareness, which equally and impartially reflects whatever arises. So you remain conscious during the dream state, witnessing it, not changing it (although you can if you want; usually you don't want).* Then, as you pass into deep, dreamless sleep, you still remain conscious, but now you are aware of nothing but vast pure emptiness, with no content whatsoever. But "aware of" is not quite right, since there is no duality here. It's more like, there is simply pure consciousness itself, without qual-

---

* I call this "pellucid dreaming" to distinguish it from lucid dreaming. Throughout many entries I simply use the well-known term "lucid dreaming." Nonetheless, I almost always mean pellucid dreaming. I also refer to pellucid deep sleep, or tacit witnessing in the deep dreamless state.

ities or contents or subjects or objects, a vast pure emptiness that is not "nothing" but is still unqualifiable.

Then, as you come out of the deep sleep state, you see the mind and the dream state arise and take form. That is, out of causal emptiness there arises the subtle mind (dreams, images, symbols, concepts, visions, forms), and you witness this emergence. The dream state continues for a while, and then, as you begin to wake up, you can see the entire gross realm, the physical realm—your body, the bed, the room, the physical universe, nature—arise directly out of the subtle mind state.

In other words, you have just taken a tour of the Great Chain of Being—gross body to subtle mind to causal spirit—in both its *ascending* and *descending* movements (evolution and involution). As you fall asleep, you pass from gross body (waking) to subtle mind (dreaming) to causal emptiness (deep sleep)—that's evolution or ascent—and then, as you awaken, you move down from causal to subtle to gross—that's involution or descent. (The actual order of states can vary, but the entire cycle is generally present.) Everybody moves through this cycle every twenty-four hours. But with constant consciousness or unbroken witnessing, you remain aware during all these changes of state, even into deep dreamless sleep.

Since the ego exists mostly in the gross state, with a few remnants in the subtle, then once you identify with constant consciousness—or that which exists in all three states—you break the hold of the ego, since it barely exists in the subtle and does not exist at all in causal emptiness (or in the deep sleep state, which is one type of emptiness). You cease identifying with ego, and you identify with pure formless consciousness as such, which is colorless, spaceless, timeless, formless—pure clear emptiness. You identify with nothing in particular, and therefore you can embrace absolutely everything that arises. Gone to the ego, you are one with the All.

You still have complete access to the waking-state ego, but you are no longer *only* that. Rather, the very deepest part of you is one with the entire Kosmos in all its radiant glory. You simply *are* everything that is arising moment to moment. You do not see the sky, you are the sky. You do not touch the earth, you are the earth. You do not hear the rain, you are the rain. You and the universe are what the mystics call "One Taste."

This is not poetry. This is a *direct realization*, as direct as a glass of cold water in the face. As a great Zen Master said upon his enlightenment: "When I heard the sound of the bell ringing, there was no bell and no I, just the ringing." And in that nondual ringing is the entire Kosmos, where subject and object become One Taste and infinity happily surrenders its secrets. As researchers from Aldous Huxley to Huston Smith have reminded us, One Taste or "cosmic consciousness"—the sense of oneness with the Ground of all creation—is the deepest core of the nearly universal consensus of the world's great wisdom traditions. One Taste is not a hallucination, fantasy, or product of a disturbed psyche, but the direct realization and testament of countless yogis, saints, and sages the world over.

It is very simple, very obvious, very clear—concrete, palpable, unmistakable.

CW 8: *One Taste*, 329–331

In addition to slowly getting back into writing, I have also returned to meditation, the whole point of which is really just to learn how to die (to die to the separate-self sense, or ego), and Treya's facing a potentially lethal disease is an extraordinary spur to meditative awareness. The sages say that if you maintain this choiceless awareness, this bare witnessing, moment to moment, then death is just a simple moment like any other, and you relate to it in a very simple and direct way. You don't recoil from death or grasp at life, since fundamentally they are both just simple experiences that pass.

The Buddhist notion of "emptiness" has also helped me a great deal. Emptiness (*shunyata*) doesn't mean blank or void; it means unobstructed or unimpeded or spontaneous; it also is roughly synonymous with impermanence or fleetingness (*anicca*). And the Buddhists say that reality is empty—there is nothing permanent or absolutely enduring that you can hold on to for security or support. As the Diamond Sutra says, "Life is like a bubble, a dream, a reflection, a mirage." The whole point is not to try to grasp the mirage, but rather to "let go," since there's really nothing to hang on to anyway. And again, Treya's cancer is a constant reminder that death is a great letting go, but you needn't wait for actual physical death to profoundly let go of your own grasping and clinging in this moment, and this moment, and this.

And finally, to bring this all back home, the mystics maintain that the type of action that one performs in this world, *if one lives by choiceless awareness*, is an action devoid of ego or devoid of self-centeredness. If you are going to die to (or transcend) the separate-self sense, then you have to die to self-centered and self-serving actions. In other words, you have to perform what the mystics call *selfless service*. You have to serve others, without thought of self or hope for praise; you simply love and serve—as Mother Teresa says, "Love until it hurts."

In other words, you become a good wife. In other words, here I am, cooking dinner and washing dishes. Don't get me wrong, I'm still far from Mother Teresa status, but I increasingly see my support-person activity as being a major part of selfless service and therefore of my own spiritual growth, a type of meditation in action, a type of compassion. Nor does this mean that I have perfected the art; I still bitch and moan, I still get angry, I still blame circumstances; and Treya and I still half-kid (half-not) about holding hands, jumping off the bridge, and putting an end to this whole joke.

And all in all, I'd rather be writing.

CW 5: *Grace and Grit*, 429–430

Sitting here on the porch, watching the sun go down. Except there is no watcher, just the sun, setting, setting. From purest Emptiness, brilliant clarity shines forth. The sound of the birds, over there. Clouds, a few, right up there. But there is no "up," no "down," no "over," and no "there"—because there is no "me" or "I" for which these directions make sense. There is just *this*. Simple, clear, easy, effortless, ever-present *this*.

CW 8: *One Taste*, 342

And so began the most extraordinary forty-eight hours of our life together. Treya had decided to die. There was no medical reason for her to die at this point. With medication and modest supports, her doctors felt she could live another several months at least, albeit in a hospital, and yes, then she would die. But Treya had made up her mind. She was not going to die like that, in a hospital, with tubes coming out of her and continuous IV morphine drip and the inevitable pneumonia and slow suffocation—all the horrible images that had gone through my mind at Drachenfels. And I had the strangest feeling that, whatever else her reasons, Treya was going to spare all of us that ordeal. She would simply bypass all that, thank you very much, and die peacefully now. But whatever her reasons, I knew that once Treya had made up her mind, then it was done.

I put Treya in bed that evening, and sat down next to her. She had become almost ecstatic. "I'm going, I can't believe it, I'm going. I'm so happy, I'm so happy, I'm so happy." Like a mantra of final release, she kept repeating, "I'm so happy, I'm so happy. . . ."

Her entire countenance lit up. She glowed. And right in front of my eyes her body began to change. Within one hour, it looked to me as if she lost ten pounds. It was as if her body, acquiescing to her will, began to shrink and draw in on itself. She began to shut down her vital systems; she began to die. Within that hour, she was a different being, ready and willing to leave. She was very determined about this, and she was very happy. Her ecstatic response was infectious, and I found myself sharing in her joy, much to my confusion.

Then, rather abruptly, she said, "But I don't want to leave you. I love you so much. I can't leave you. I love you so much." She began crying, sobbing, and I began crying, sobbing, as well. I felt like I was crying all the tears of the past five years, deep tears I had held back in order to be strong for Treya. We talked at length of our love for each other, a love that had made both of us—it sounds corny—a love that had made both of us stronger, and better, and wiser. Decades of growth had gone into our care for each other, and now, faced with the conclusion of it all, we were both overwhelmed. It sounds so dry, but it was the tenderest moment I have ever known, with the only person with whom I could ever have known it.

cw 5: *Grace and Grit*, 464–465

I became extremely serious about meditation practice when I read the following line from the illustrious Sri Ramana Maharshi: "That which is not present in deep dreamless sleep is not real."

That is a shocking statement, because basically, there is nothing—literally nothing—in the deep dreamless state. That was his point. Ultimate reality (or Spirit), Ramana said, cannot be something that pops into consciousness and then pops out. It must be something that is constant, permanent, or, more technically, something that, being *timeless*, is *fully present* at every point in time. Therefore, ultimate reality must also be fully present in deep dreamless sleep, and anything that is not present in deep dreamless sleep is NOT ultimate reality.

This profoundly disturbed me, because I had had several *kensho* or *satori*-like experiences (glimpses of One Taste), but they were all generally confined to the waking state. Moreover, most of the things I cared for existed in the waking state. And yet clearly the waking state is not permanent. It comes and goes every twenty-four hours. And yet, according to the great sages, there is something in us that is *always conscious*—that is literally conscious or aware at all times and through all states, waking, dreaming, sleeping. And that *ever-present awareness is Spirit in us*. That underlying current of constant consciousness (or nondual awareness) is a direct and unbroken ray of pure Spirit itself. It is our connection with the Goddess, our pipeline straight to God.

Thus, if we want to realize our supreme identity with Spirit, we will have to plug ourselves into this current of constant consciousness, and follow it through all changes of state—waking, dreaming, sleeping—which will (1) strip us of an exclusive identification with any of those states (such the body, the mind, the ego, or the soul); and (2) allow us to recognize and identify with that which is constant—or timeless—through all of those states, namely, Consciousness as Such, by any other name, timeless Spirit.

I had been meditating fairly intensely for around twenty years when I came across that line from Ramana. I had studied Zen with Katagiri and Maezumi; Vajrayana with Kalu and Trungpa; Dzogchen with Pema Norbu and Chagdud; plus I had studied—sometimes briefly, sometimes for extended periods—Vedanta, TM, Kashmir Shaivism, Christian mysticism, Kabbalah, Daism, Sufism . . . well, it's a long list. When I ran across Ramana's statement, I was on an intensive Dzogchen retreat with my primary Dzogchen teacher, Chagdud Tulku Rinpoche. Rinpoche also stressed the importance of carrying the mirror-mind into the dream and deep sleep states. I began having flashes of this constant nondual awareness, through all states, which Rinpoche confirmed. But it wasn't until a year later, during a very intense eleven-day period—in which the separate self seemed to radically, deeply, thoroughly die—that it all seemed to come to fruition. I slept not at all during those eleven days; or rather, was conscious for eleven days and nights, even as the body and mind went through waking, dreaming, and sleeping: I was unmoved in the midst of changes; there was no I to be moved; there was only unwavering empty consciousness, the luminous mirror-mind, the witness that as one with everything witnessed. I simply reverted to what I am, and it has been so, more or less, ever since.

The moment this constant nondual consciousness is obvious in your case, a new destiny will awaken in the midst of the manifest world. You will have discovered your own Buddha Mind, your own Godhead, your own formless, spaceless, timeless, infinite Emptiness, your own Atman that is Brahman, your Keter, Christ consciousness, radiant Shekhinah—in so many words, One Taste. It is unmistakably so. And just that is your true identity—pure Emptiness or pure unqualifiable Consciousness as Such—and thus you are released from the terror and the torment that necessarily arise when you identify with a little subject in a world of little objects.

Once you find your formless identity as Buddha-mind, as Atman, as pure Spirit or Godhead, you will take that constant, nondual, ever-present consciousness and reenter the lesser states, subtle mind and gross body, and reanimate them with radiance. You will not remain merely Formless and Empty. You will Empty yourself of Emptiness: you will pour yourself out into the mind and world, and create them in the process, and enter them all equally, but especially and particularly that specific mind and body that is called you (that is called, in my case, Ken Wilber); this lesser self will become a vehicle of the Spirit that you are.

And then all things, including your own little mind and body and feelings and thoughts, will arise in the vast Emptiness that you are, and they will self-liberate into their own true nature just as they arise, precisely because you no longer identify with any one of them, but rather let them play, let them all arise, in the Emptiness and Openness that you now are. You then will awaken as radical Freedom, and sing those songs of radiant release, beam an infinity too obvious to see, and drink an ocean of delight. You will look at the moon as part of your body and bow to the sun as part of your heart, and all of it is just so. For eternally and always, eternally and always, there is only *this*.

But you have not found this Freedom, or in any way *attained* it. It is in fact the same Freedom that has lived in the house of the pure Witness from the very start. You are merely recognizing the pure and empty Self, the radical I-I, that has been your natural awareness from the beginning and all along, but that you didn't notice because you had become lost in the intoxicating movie of life.

CW 8: *One Taste*, 342–344

We put her to bed that night—Sunday night—and again I slept on her acupuncture table so I could be there if anything happened. Something extraordinary seemed to be going on in that house, and we all knew it.

About 3:30 that morning, Treya awoke abruptly. The atmosphere was almost hallucinogenic. I awoke immediately, and asked how she was. "Is it morphine time?" she said with a smile. In her entire ordeal with cancer, except for surgery, Treya had taken a sum total of four morphine tablets. "Sure, sweetie, whatever you want." I gave her a morphine tablet and a mild sleeping pill, and we had our last conversation.

"Sweetie, I think it's time to go," she began.

"I'm here, honey."

"I'm so happy." Long pause. "This world is so weird. It's just so weird. But I'm going." Her mood was one of joy, and humor, and determination.

I began repeating several of the "pith phrases" from the religious traditions that she considered so important, phrases that she had wanted me to remind her of right up to the end, phrases she had carried with her on her flash cards.

"Relax with the presence of what is," I began. "Allow the self to uncoil in the vast expanse of all space. Your own primordial mind is unborn and undying; it was not born with this body and it will not die with this body. Recognize your own mind as eternally one with Spirit."

Her face relaxed, and she looked at me very clearly and directly.

"You'll find me?"

"I promise."

"Then it's time to go."

There was a very long pause, and the room seemed to me to become entirely luminous, which was strange, given how utterly dark it was. It was the most sacred moment, the most direct moment, the simplest moment I have ever known. The most obvious. The most perfectly obvious. I had never seen anything like this in my life. I did not know what to do. I was simply present for Treya.

She moved toward me, trying to gesture, trying to say something, something she wanted me to understand, the last thing she told me. "You're the greatest man I've ever known," she whispered. "You're the greatest man I've ever known. My champion . . ." She kept repeating it: "My champion." I leaned forward to tell her that she was the only really enlightened person I had ever known. That enlightenment made sense to me because of her. That a universe that had produced Treya was a sacred universe. That God existed because of her. All these things went through my mind. All these things I wanted to say. I knew she was aware how I felt, but my throat had closed in on itself; I couldn't speak; I wasn't crying, I just couldn't speak. I croaked out only, "I'll find you, honey, I will. . . ."

Treya closed her eyes, and for all purposes, she never opened them again.

My heart broke. Da Free John's phrase kept running through my mind: "Practice the wound of love . . . practice the wound of love." Real love hurts; real love makes you totally vulnerable and open; real love will take you far beyond yourself; and therefore real love will devastate you. I kept thinking, if love does not shatter you, you do not know love. We had both been practicing the wound of love, and I was shattered. Looking back on it, it seems to me that in that simple and direct moment, we both died.

It was at that moment that I began to notice that the atmosphere had become very turbulent. It took me several minutes to realize that it wasn't my distress or my grief that seemed to be so disturbing. It was the wind blowing wildly outside the house. And not just blowing. The wind began whipping up a ferocious storm; our ordinarily rock-solid house was shaking and rattling in the gale-force winds that hammered the house at exactly that moment. In fact, the newspapers reported the next day that at exactly four o'clock that morning, record-breaking winds—reaching up to an incredible 115 miles an hour—began to whip through Boulder (though inexplicably, no place else in Colorado). The winds overturned cars—and even an airplane!—all of which was duly reported in the headlines of the papers the next day.

The winds, I suppose, were coincidence. Nonetheless, the constant rattling and shaking of the house simply added to the feeling that something unearthly was happening. I remember trying to go back to sleep, but the house was rattling so hard I got up and put some blankets around the windows in the bedroom, fearing they would shatter. I finally drifted off, thinking, "Treya is dying, nothing is permanent, everything is empty, Treya is dying. . . ."

The next morning, Treya settled into the position in which she would die—propped up on pillows, arms at her sides, mala in her hand. The night before she had begun repeating silently to herself "Om Mani Padme Hung," the Buddhist mantra of compassion, and

"Surrender to God," her favorite Christian prayer. I believe she continued to do so. . . .

The afternoon stretched on; the winds continued rattling the house and contributing to the eeriest atmosphere. For hours I held Treya's hand and kept whispering in her ear: "Treya, you can go now. Everything here is complete and finished. Just let go, just let it happen. We're all here, honey, just let it happen." . . .

I stepped out to get a drink of water, and suddenly Tracy was there, saying, "Ken, get up there immediately." I ran upstairs, jumped on the bed, grabbed Treya's hand. The entire family—every single member, and good friend Warren—made it into the room. Treya opened her eyes, looked very softly at everybody there, looked directly at me, closed her eyes, and quit breathing.

Everybody in the room was completely there and present for Treya. Then the entire room began to cry. I was holding her hand, with my other hand over her heart. My body began to shake violently. It had finally happened. I could not stop shaking. I whispered in her ear the few key phrases from the Book of the Dead ("Recognize the clear light as your own primordial Mind, recognize you are now one with Enlightened Spirit"). But mostly we all cried.

The best, the strongest, the most enlightened, the most honest, the most beautiful, the most inspiring, the most virtuous, the most cherished person I had ever known, had just died. Somehow, I felt that the universe would never be the same.

Exactly five minutes after her death, Michael said, "Listen. Listen to that." The gale-force winds had completely ceased blowing, and the atmosphere was a perfect calm.

This, too, was dutifully noted in the next day's papers, right to the exact minute. The ancients have a saying: "When a great soul dies, the winds go wild." The greater the soul, the greater the wind necessary to carry it away. Perhaps it was all coincidence, but I couldn't help thinking: A great, great soul had died, and the wind responded. . . .

I had arranged for Treya's body to remain undisturbed for twenty-four hours. About an hour after her death, we all left the room, mostly to compose ourselves. . . .

Everybody went up and said goodbye to her that evening. I stayed up that night and read to her until three that morning. I read her favorite religious passages (Suzuki Roshi, Ramana Maharshi, Kalu, Saint Teresa, Saint John, Norbu, Trungpa, the *Course*); I repeated her favorite Christian prayer ("Surrender to God"); I performed her

favorite sadhana or spiritual practice (Chenrezi, the Buddha of compassion); and most of all I read to her the essential pointing-out
instructions from *The Book of the Dead*. (These I read to her forty-
nine times. The essence of these instructions is that, to put it in Christian terms, the time of death is the time that you shed your physical
body and individual ego, and become one with absolute Spirit or
God. Recognizing the radiance and luminosity that naturally dawns
at the time of death is thus to recognize your own awareness as eternally enlightened, or one with Godhead. You simply repeat these instructions to the person, over and over again, with the very likely
assumption that their soul can still hear you. And so this I did.)

I may be imagining all this, but I swear that, on the third reading
of the essential instructions for recognizing that your soul is one with
God, something audibly clicked in the room. I actually ducked. I had
the distinct and palpable feeling, at that utterly dark 2:00 A.M., that
she directly recognized her own true nature and burned clean. In
other words, that she acknowledged, upon hearing, the great liberation or enlightenment that had always been hers. That she had dissolved cleanly into All Space, mixing with the entire universe, just
like in her experience as a thirteen-year-old, just like in her medita-
tions, just like she hoped she would upon final death.

I don't know, maybe I'm imagining this. But knowing Treya,
maybe I'm not.

Some months later I was reading a highly revered text of Dzogchen
which describes the stages of dying. And it listed two physical signs
that indicated that the person had recognized their own True Nature
and had become one with luminous Spirit—that they had dissolved
cleanly into All Space. The two signs?

> If you remain in the Ground Luminosity,
> As a sign of that, your complexion will be nice . . .
> And it is taught also that your mouth will be smiling.

I stayed in Treya's room that night. When I finally fell asleep, I had
a dream. But it wasn't a dream, it was more of a simple image: a raindrop fell into the ocean, thus becoming one with the all. At first I
thought that this meant Treya had become enlightened, that Treya
was the drop that had become one with the ocean of enlightenment.
And that made sense.

But then I realized it was more profound than that: I was the drop, and Treya the ocean. She had not been released—she was already so. Rather, it was I who had been released, by the simple virtue of serving her.

And there, there it was: that was exactly why she had so insistently asked me to promise that I would find her. It wasn't that she needed me to find her; it was that, through my promise to her, she would therefore find me, and help me, yet again, and again, and again. I had it all backwards: I thought my promise was how I would help her, whereas it was actually how she would reach and help me, again, and again, and forever again, as long as it took for me to awaken, as long as it took for me to acknowledge, as long as it took for me to realize the Spirit that she had come so clearly to announce. And by no means just me: Treya came for all her friends, for her family, and especially for those stricken with terrible illness. For all of this, Treya was present.

Twenty-four hours later, I kissed her forehead, and we all said goodbye. Treya, still smiling, was taken for cremation. But "goodbye" is the wrong word. Perhaps *au revoir*—"till we meet again"— or *aloha*—"goodbye/hello"—would be better.

cw 5: *Grace and Grit*, 466–476

"Everybody starts out living in a fragmented, broken, dualistic, brutalized state. The world is divided into subject versus object, self versus other, me in here versus the world out there. Once the world is broken in two, the world knows only pain, suffering, torment, terror. In the gap between subject and object lies the entire misery of humankind."

"That's the gap between the Seer and the Seen," Joan softly adds.

"Yes. So you can find the ultimate state of oneness, of cosmic consciousness, or radiant love, by going through the Seer or the Seen, since they both end up coming together as one. Men generally find it easier to pursue the Seer, and women generally find it easier to go through the Seen. But men and women can do both, it's just a matter of personal choice."

"I do not understand a single word you said."

"It's not that hard, young Ken, honest. Let us start with the Seer, and follow me just one more time, because you have heard these words before, haven't you?:

"Let your mind relax. Let your mind relax and expand, mixing with the sky in front of it. Then notice: the clouds float by in the sky, and you are effortlessly aware of them. Feelings float by in the body, and you are effortlessly aware of them, too. Thoughts float by in the mind, and you are aware of them as well. Nature floats by, feelings float by, thoughts float by . . . and you are aware of all of them.

"So tell me: *Who are you?*

"You are not your thoughts, for you are aware of them. You are not your feelings, for you are aware of them. You are not any objects that you can see, for you are aware of them too.

"Something in you is aware of all these things. So tell me: What is it in you that is conscious of everything?

"What in you is always awake? Always fully present? Something in you right now is effortlessly noticing everything that arises. What is that?

"That vast infinite witnessing awareness, don't you recognize it?

"What is that Witness?"

The voice pauses. "You are that Witness, aren't you? You are the pure Seer, pure awareness, the pure Spirit that impartially witnesses everything that arises, moment to moment. Your awareness is spacious, wide-open, empty and clear, and yet it registers everything that arises.

"That very Witness is God within, looking out on a world that it created."

Boomeritis, 448–449 (Note that *Boomeritis* is
a *fictional* work by Ken Wilber.)

Another Christmas party, this time for the staff and residents of the Developmental Disabilities Center. Marci and I were some of the main dance partners for the residents, and we spent about three hours dancing, if that's the right word. Allen stood in the middle of the floor and didn't move a muscle; but he was smiling. Tavio spun his wheelchair in circles. Sandy bobbed back and forth at a terrifying rate; I tried to keep up with her, but she was too fast for me. Tom jumped up and down, swirling his arms like helicopter blades, also too fast for me. There were perhaps one hundred residents present, about half of whom danced, often simultaneously. Holding hands in a circle and kicking up our feet seemed to be the group dance of choice, when we could get everybody facing the same direction.

I have often written about what I think are the three main types of value in the world: intrinsic value, extrinsic value, and Ground value. Intrinsic value is the value a thing has in itself. Extrinsic value is the value a thing has for others. And Ground value is the value that all things have by virtue of being manifestations of Spirit. . . .

Intrinsic and extrinsic are relative values; Ground value is absolute. Ground value is the value that each and every holon has by virtue of being a radiant manifestation of Spirit, of Godhead, of Emptiness. All holons, high or low, have the *same* Ground value— namely, One Taste. Holons can have greater or lesser intrinsic value (the greater the depth, the greater the value), but all holons have absolutely equal Ground value: they all share equal Suchness, Thusness, Isness, which is the face of Spirit as it shines in manifestation, One Taste in all its wonder.

Whenever I am with dear people who have been disadvantaged in their own growth and development—crippled in their own depth—I am so much more easily reminded of their Ground value, green emeralds each and all, perfect in their glory. I am reminded that intrinsic and extrinsic fall away in One Taste, where all Spirit's children equally shine in the infinity that they are. I know this for a fact, because last night I spent three hours dancing with buddhas, and who would dare deny that?

cw 8: *One Taste*, 600–602

SCOTT WARREN: How long does it take to write a book?

KEN WILBER: My usual pattern of writing is, I read hundreds of books during the year, and a book forms in my head—I write the book in my head. Then I sit down and enter it on computer, which usually takes a month or two, maybe three.

SCOTT WARREN: So all these books took a few months to write?

KEN WILBER: Yes, except *Sex, Ecology, Spirituality*. That book took me three years, really excruciating years. But the amount of actual writing time itself was still fairly short, several months.

SCOTT WARREN: Why excruciating? What happened?

KEN WILBER: Well, if you think about a book like *The Spectrum of*

Consciousness or *The Atman Project*, those were difficult books to conceive because you're trying to fit together dozens of different schools of psychology. But those books only covered the Upper-Left quadrant [subjectivity]. In SES I was trying to pull together dozens of disciplines in all four quadrants [domains of knowledge], and this was a seemingly unending nightmare. So I really closed in on myself, and for three years I lived exactly the type of life that many people think I live all the time—namely, I really became a hermit. In fact, apart from grocery shopping and such, I saw exactly four people in three years. It turned out to be very close to a traditional three-year silent retreat. It was by far the most difficult voluntary thing I've ever done.

SCOTT WARREN: Didn't you go nuts?

KEN WILBER: The worst part came about seven months into the retreat. I found that what I missed most was not sex, and not talking, but skin contact—simple human touch. I ached for simple touching, I had what I started calling "skin hunger." My whole body seemed to ache with skin hunger, and for about three or four months, each day when I finished work, I would sit down and just start crying. I'd cry for about half an hour. It just really hurt. But what can you do in these cases except witness it? So eventually a type of meditative equanimity started to develop toward this skin hunger, and I found that this very deep need seemed to burn away, at least to some degree, precisely because of the awareness I was forced to give it. After that, my own meditation took a quantum leap forward—it was shortly thereafter that I started having glimpses of constant consciousness, or a mirrorlike awareness that continued into the dream state and the deep sleep state. All of this came about, I think, because I was not allowed to act on this skin hunger, I was forced to be aware of it, to bring consciousness to it, to witness it and not merely act it out. This skin hunger is a very primitive type of grasping, a very deep type of desire, of subjective identity, and by witnessing it, making it an object, I ceased identifying with it, I transcended it to some degree, and that released my own consciousness from this most ancient of biological drives. But it was a very rocky roller-coaster ride for a while.

CW 8: *One Taste*, 392-393

So my promise to Treya—the only promise that she made me repeat over and over—my promise that I would find her again really meant that I had promised to find my own enlightened Heart.

And I know, in those last six months, that I did so. I know that I found the cave of enlightenment, where I was married, by grace, and where I died, by grace. This was the change that had come over me that Treya had noticed, and about which she kept saying, "What is it?" The fact is, she knew exactly what it was. She simply wanted to know if I did. ("And as for the Heart, it is Brahman, it is All. And the couple, now one, having died to themselves, live life eternal.")

And I know, in those last few moments of death itself, and during the night that followed, when Treya's luminosity overwhelmed my soul, and outshone the finite world forever, that it all became perfectly clear to me. There are no lies left in my soul, because of Treya. And Treya, honey, dear sweet Treya, I promise to find you forever and forever and forever in my Heart, as the simple awareness of what is.

CW 5: *Grace and Grit*, 477

Raindrops are beating, a large puddle is forming, there on the balcony. It all floats in Emptiness, in purest Transparency, with no one here to watch it. If there is an I, it is all that is arising, right now and right now and right now. My lungs are the sky; those mountains are my teeth; the soft clouds are my skin; the thunder is my heart beating time to the timeless; the rain itself, the tears of our collective estate, here where nothing is really happening at all.

CW 8: *One Taste*, 429

3

Spirit-in-Action

One thing that characterizes Ken Wilber's integral vision is his skill in articulating the evolutionary dynamics of Spirit's unfolding in time and through space. In the following selections, Wilber traces the choreography of the dance in which Heaven and Earth are engaged: how Heaven throws itself out of the Abyss creating Earth, and how Earth reaches ever upward toward Heaven.

Wilber refers to the process of Spirit coming into Matter as involution (the process of folding into) and the telos of Matter becoming Spirit as evolution (the process of unwinding). These selections reveal a dedicated exploration and straightforward explanation of this ebb and flow of the Divine cascading into and out of form. Wilber masterfully describes the interlocking relationship of the manifest realm with the sacred luminosity of openness, thus demonstrating how Spirit interacts with Matter, angels dance with rocks, and emptiness is form (and vice-versa).

In an effort to highlight its multivalent nature, Wilber describes this dynamism in various ways. Whether discussing Ascent into the sky and Descent toward soil or Eros's drive toward wholeness and Agape's embrace of the many, Wilber always poetically describes the relationship between development and stillness: Spirit's Longing to incarnate and Matter's desire to be God.

EVOLUTION is best thought of as *Spirit-in-action*, God-in-the-making, where Spirit unfolds itself at every stage of development, thus manifesting more of itself, and realizing more of itself, at every unfolding. Spirit is not some particular stage, or some favorite ideology, or some specific god or goddess, but rather the entire process of unfolding itself, an infinite process that is completely present at every finite stage, but becomes more available to itself with every evolutionary opening.

cw 7: *A Brief History of Everything*, 61

Emptiness alone, only and all, with an edge of extremely faint yet luminous bliss. That is how the subtle feels when it emerges from the causal. So it was early this morning. As the gross body then emerges from this subtle luminous bliss it's hard to tell, at first, exactly where its boundaries are. You have a body, you know that, but the body seems like the entire material universe. Then the bedroom solidifies, and slowly, very slowly, your awareness accepts the conventions of the gross realm, which dictate that *this* body is *inside* this room. And so it is. And so you get up. And so goes involution, yet again.

But the Emptiness remains, always.

cw 8: *One Taste*, 410

To say that matter, body, mind, soul, and Spirit are evolutionary potentials is to say both quite a lot and not very much.

cw 2: *Introduction*, 11

Being and consciousness exist as a spectrum, reaching from matter to body to mind to soul to Spirit. And although Spirit is, in a certain sense, the highest dimension or level of the spectrum of existence, it is also the ground or condition of the entire spectrum. It is as if Spirit were both the highest rung on the ladder of existence *and* the wood out of which the entire ladder is made—Spirit is both totally and completely immanent (as the wood) and totally and completely transcendent (as the highest rung). Spirit is both Ground and Goal.

In its immanent aspect, Spirit is the Condition of all conditions, the Being of all beings, the Nature of all natures. As such, it neither evolves nor involves, grows or develops, ascends or descends. It is the simple suchness or isness—the perfect isness—of all that is, of each and every thing in manifestation. There is no contacting immanent Spirit, no way to reach It, no way to commune with It, for there is nothing It is not. Being completely and totally present at every single point of space and time, It is fully and completely present here and now, and thus we can no more attain immanent Spirit than we could, say, attain our feet.

In its transcendental aspect, however, Spirit is the highest rung on our own ladder of growth and evolution. It is something we must work to comprehend, to understand, to attain union with, to identify with. The realization of our Supreme Identity with Spirit dawns only after much growth, much development, much evolution, and much inner work—only then do we understand that the Supreme Identity was there, from the beginning, perfectly given in its fullness. In other words, it is only from the highest rung on the ladder that we can realize the wood out of which the entire ladder is made.

It is this paradox of Spirit—both fully present (as the Ground of Being) and yet to be realized (as our highest Goal)—that lies behind such paradoxical Zen sayings as:

> If there is any discipline toward reaching Spirit, then the completion of that discipline means the destruction of Spirit. But if there is no discipline toward Spirit, one remains an ignoramus.

In other words, while in its immanent aspects Spirit simply *is*, in its transcendental aspects Spirit evolves or develops. The entire manifest world, while remaining fully and completely grounded in Spirit, is also struggling to awaken Spirit in itself, struggling to realize Spirit *as* Spirit, struggling to arouse from the nightmare of time and stand strong in eternity. This struggle of growth and development appears in the world at large as evolution, and in individual men and women as the growth and development of their own consciousness (which is simply the arena of cosmic evolution in human beings). Evolution is the movement of Spirit, toward Spirit, as Spirit, the conscious resurrection, in all men and women, of the Supreme Identity, an Identity present all along, but an Identity seemingly obscured by manifestation, seemingly obscured by the limited view from a lower rung on the ladder. As one intuits the higher and highest rungs of the ladder of existence, Spirit sees Itself as Spirit, sees Itself everywhere, sees there was never a time that It wasn't—and then, but only then, is the entire ladder thrown away, now having served its manifest purpose. And one understands, in the entire process, that not a single thing has been attained.

CW 1: *The Spectrum of Consciousness*, 43–44

According to the perennial philosophy—or the common core of the world's great wisdom traditions—Spirit manifests a universe by "throwing itself out" or "emptying itself" to create soul, which condenses into mind, which condenses into body, which condenses into matter, the densest form of all. Each of those levels is still a level of Spirit, but each is a reduced or "stepped-down" version of Spirit. At the end of that process of *involution*, all of the higher dimensions are enfolded, as potential, in the lowest material realm. And once the material world blows into existence (with, say, the Big Bang), then the reverse process—or evolution—can occur, moving from matter to living bodies to symbolic minds to luminous souls to pure Spirit itself. In this developmental or evolutionary unfolding, each successive level does not jettison or deny the previous level, but rather includes and embraces it, just as atoms are included in molecules, which are included in cells, which are included in organisms. Each level is a whole that is also part of a larger whole (each level or structure is a whole/part or holon). In other words, each evolutionary unfolding transcends but includes its predecessor(s), with Spirit transcending and including absolutely everything.

This arrangement—Spirit transcends but includes soul, which transcends but includes mind, which transcends but includes body, which transcends but includes matter—is often referred to as the Great Chain of Being, but that is clearly a very unfortunate misnomer. Each successive level is not a link but a nest, which includes, embraces, and envelops its predecessor(s). The Great Chain of Being is really the Great Nest of Being—not a ladder, chain, or one-way hierarchy, but a series of concentric spheres of increasing holistic embrace.

cw 2: Introduction, 10

The different levels of the spectrum are something like the various waves of the ocean—each wave is certainly different from all others. Some waves, near the shore, are strong and powerful; while others, farther out, are weaker and less powerful. But each wave is still different from all the others, and if you were surfing you could select a particular wave, catch it, ride it, and work it according to your ability. You couldn't do any of this if the waves weren't different. Each level of the spectrum is like a particular wave, and thus we can "catch" any of them with the right technique and enough practice.

Unity consciousness, however, is not so much a particular wave as it is the *water* itself. And there is no boundary, no difference, no separation between water and any of the waves. That is, the water is equally present in *all* waves, in the sense that no wave is wetter than another.

So if you are looking for "wetness" itself—the *condition* of all waves—nothing whatsoever will be gained by jumping from one wave to another. In fact, there is much to lose, for as long as you are wave-jumping in search of wetness, you obviously will never discover that wetness exists in its purity on whatever wave you're riding now. Seeking unity consciousness is like jumping from one wave of experience to another in search of water. And that is why "there is neither path nor achievement."

cw 1: *No Boundary*, 559

Have you ever wondered why life comes in opposites? Why everything you value is one of a pair of opposites? Why all decisions are between opposites? Why all desires are based on opposites?

Notice that all spatial and directional dimensions are opposites: up vs. down, inside vs. outside, high vs. low, long vs. short, North vs. South, big vs. small, here vs. there, top vs. bottom, left vs. right. And notice that all things we consider serious and important are one pole of a pair of opposites: good vs. evil, life vs. death, pleasure vs. pain, God vs. Satan, freedom vs. bondage.

So also, our social and esthetic values are always put in terms of opposites: success vs. failure, beautiful vs. ugly, strong vs. weak, intelligent vs. stupid. Even our highest abstractions rest on opposites. Logic, for instance, is concerned with the true vs. the false; epistemology, with appearance vs. reality; ontology, with being vs. non-being. Our world seems to be a massive collection of opposites.

This fact is so commonplace as to hardly need mentioning, but the more one ponders it the more it is strikingly peculiar. For nature, it seems, knows nothing of this world of opposites in which people live. Nature doesn't grow true frogs and false frogs, nor moral trees and immoral trees, nor right oceans and wrong oceans. There is no trace in nature of ethical mountains and unethical mountains. Nor are there even such things as beautiful species and ugly species—at least not to Nature, for it is pleased to produce all kinds. Thoreau said Nature never apologizes, and apparently it's because Nature doesn't know the opposites of right and wrong and thus doesn't recognize what humans imagine to be "errors."

It is certainly true that some of the things which we call "opposites" appear to exist in Nature. There are, for instance, big frogs and small frogs, large trees and small trees, ripe oranges and unripe oranges. But it isn't a problem for them, it doesn't throw them into paroxysms of anxiety. There might even be smart bears and dumb bears, but it doesn't seem to concern them very much. You just don't find inferiority complexes in bears.

Likewise, there is life and death in the world of nature, but again it doesn't seem to hold the terrifying dimensions ascribed to it in the world of humans. A very old cat isn't swept with torrents of terror over its impending death. It just calmly walks out to the woods, curls up under a tree, and dies. A terminally ill robin perches comfortably on the limb of a willow, and stares into the sunset. When finally it can see the light no more, it closes its eyes for the last time and drops gently to the ground. How different from the way humans face death:

> Do not go gentle into that good night
> Rage, rage against the dying of the light.

While pain and pleasure do appear in the world of nature, they are not problems to worry over. When a dog is in pain, it yelps. When not, it just doesn't worry about it. It doesn't dread future pain nor regret past pain. It seems to be a very simple and natural affair.

CW 1: *No Boundary*, 448–449

Now, there is indeed a *falling away* from Godhead, from Spirit, from the primordial Ground, and this is the truth the Romantics are trying to get at, before they slip into their pre/trans fallacies. This falling away is called *involution*, the movement whereby all things fall away from a consciousness of their union with the Divine, and thus imagine themselves to be separate and isolated monads, alienated and alienating. And once involution has occurred—and Spirit becomes unconsciously involved in the lower and lowest forms of its own manifestation—then *evolution* can occur: Spirit unfolds . . . from the Big Bang to matter to sensation to perception to impulse to image to symbol to concept to reason to psychic to subtle to causal occasions, on the way to its own shocking self-recognition, Spirit's own self-realization and self-resurrection. And in each of those stages—from matter to body to mind to soul to spirit—evolution becomes more and more conscious, more and more aware, more and more realized, more and more awake—with all the joys and all the terrors inherently involved in that dialectic of awakening.

At each stage of this process of Spirit's return to itself, we—you and I—nonetheless remember, perhaps vaguely, perhaps intensely, that we were once consciously one with the very Divine itself. It is there, this memory trace, in the back of our awareness, pulling and pushing us to realize, to awaken, to remember who and what we always already are.

In fact, all things, we might surmise, intuit to one degree or another that their very Ground is Spirit itself. All things are driven, urged, pushed and pulled to manifest this realization. And yet, prior to that divine awakening, all things seek Spirit in a way that actually prevents the realization: or else we would be realized right now! We seek Spirit in ways that prevent it.

We seek for Spirit in the world of time; but Spirit is timeless, and cannot there be found. We seek for Spirit in the world of space; but Spirit is spaceless, and cannot there be found. We seek for Spirit in this or that object, shiny and alluring and full of fame or fortune; but Spirit is not an object, and it cannot be seen or grasped in the world of commodities and commotion.

In other words, we are seeking for Spirit in ways that prevent its realization, and force us to settle for substitute gratifications, which propel us through, and lock us into, the wretched world of time and terror, space and death, sin and separation, loneliness and consolation.

And that is the Atman project.

The Atman project: the attempt to find Spirit in ways that prevent it and force substitute gratifications. And . . . the entire structure of the manifest universe is driven by the Atman project, a project that continues until we—until you and I—awaken to the Spirit whose substitutes we seek in the world of space and time and grasping and despair. The nightmare of history is the nightmare of the Atman project, the fruitless search in time for that which is finally timeless, a search that inherently generates terror and torment, a self ravaged by repression, paralyzed by guilt, beset with the frost and fever of wretched alienation—a torture that is only undone in the radiant

Heart when the great search itself uncoils, when the self-contraction relaxes its attempt to find God, real or substitute: the movement in time is undone by the great Unborn, the great Uncreate, the great Emptiness in the Heart of the Kosmos itself.

And so, as you read this book, try to remember: remember the great event when you breathed out and created this entire Kosmos; remember the great emptying when you threw yourself out as the entire World just to see what would happen. Remember the forms and forces through which you have traveled thus far: from galaxies to planets, to verdant plants reaching upward for the sun, to animals stalking day and night, restless with their weary search; through primal men and women, yearning for the light, to the very person now holding this book: remember who and what you have been, what you have done, what you have seen, who you actually are in all those guises, the masks of God and the Goddess, the masks of your own Original Face.

Let the great search wind down; let the self-contraction uncoil in the immediateness of present awareness; let the entire Kosmos rush into your being, since you are its very Ground; and then you will remember that the Atman project never really occurred, and you have never moved, and it is all exactly as it should be, when the robin sings on a glorious morning, and raindrops beat on the temple roof.

CW 2: *The Atman Project*, 59–61

The movement of descent and discovery begins at the moment you consciously become dissatisfied with life. Contrary to most professional opinion, this gnawing dissatisfaction with life is not a sign of "mental illness," nor an indication of poor social adjustment, nor a character disorder. For concealed within this basic unhappiness with life and existence is the embryo of a growing intelligence, a special intelligence usually buried under the immense weight of social shams. A person who is beginning to sense the suffering of life is, at the same time, beginning to awaken to deeper realities, truer realities. For suffering smashes to pieces the complacency of our normal fictions about reality, and forces us to become alive in a special sense— to see carefully, to feel deeply, to touch ourselves and our worlds in ways we have heretofore avoided. It has been said, and truly I think, that suffering is the first grace. In a special sense, suffering is almost a time of rejoicing, for it marks the birth of creative insight.

But only in a special sense. Some people cling to their suffering as a mother to its child, carrying it as a burden they dare not set down. They do not face suffering with awareness, but rather clutch at their suffering, secretly transfixed with the spasms of martyrdom. Suffering should neither be denied awareness, avoided, despised, nor glorified, clung to, dramatized. The emergence of suffering is not so much good as it is a good sign, an indication that one is starting to realize that life lived outside unity consciousness is ultimately painful, distressing, and sorrowful. The life of boundaries is a life of battles—of fear, anxiety, pain, and finally death. It is only through all manner of numbing compensations, distractions, and enchantments that we agree not to question our illusory boundaries, the root cause of the endless wheel of agony. But sooner or later, if we are not rendered totally insensitive, our defensive compensations begin to fail their soothing and concealing purpose. As a consequence, we begin to suffer in one way or another, because our awareness is finally directed toward the conflict-ridden nature of our false boundaries and the fragmented life supported by them.

Suffering, then, is the initial movement of the recognition of false boundaries. Correctly understood, it is therefore liberating, for it points beyond boundaries altogether. We suffer, then, not because we are sick, but because intelligent insight is emerging. The correct understanding of suffering, however, is necessary in order that the birth of insight is not aborted. We must correctly interpret suffering in order to enter into it, live it, and finally live beyond it. If we do not correctly understand suffering, we simply get stuck in the middle of it—we wallow in it, not knowing what else to do.

CW 1: *No Boundary*, 508–509

Evolution—wherever it appears—manifests itself as a series of transcendences, of ascents, of emergences—and emergences of higher-order *wholes*. For to remember is really to re-member, or join again in unity, and that is just why evolution consists of a series of ever-higher wholes until there is only Wholeness. Evolution is holistic because it is nature's remembrance of God.

CW 2: *The Atman Project*, 267

The notion of evolution as Eros, or Spirit-in-action, performing, as Whitehead put it, throughout the world by gentle persuasion toward love, goes a long way to explaining the inexorable unfolding from matter to bodies to minds to souls to Spirit's own Self-recognition. Eros, or Spirit-in-action, is a rubber band around your neck and mine, pulling us all back home.

cw 2: *Introduction*, 12

Look at the course of evolution to date: from amoebas to humans! Now, what if that ratio, amoebas to humans, were applied to future evolution? That is, amoebas are to humans as humans are to—what? Is it ridiculous to suggest that the "what" might indeed be omega, *geist*, supermind, spirit? That Brahman is not only the *ground* of evolution but the *goal* as well?

cw 3: *A Sociable God*, 446

And so proceeds meditation, which is simply higher development, which is simply higher evolution—a transformation from unity to unity until there is simple Unity, whereupon Brahman, in an unnoticed shock of recognition and final remembrance, grins silently to itself, closes its eyes, breathes deeply, and throws itself outward for the millionth time, losing itself in its manifestations for the sport and play of all. Evolution then proceeds again, transformation by transformation, remembering more and more, unifying more and more, until every soul remembers Buddha, as Buddha, in Buddha—whereupon there is then no Buddha and no soul. And that is the final transformation. When Zen master Fa-ch'ang was dying, a squirrel screeched on the roof. "It's just this," he said, "and nothing more."

cw 3: *Eye to Eye*, 263

Mysticism is transrational and thus lies in our collective future, not our collective past. Mysticism is evolutionary and progressive, not devolutionary and regressive, as Aurobindo and Teilhard de Chardin realized. And science, in my opinion, is stripping us of our infantile and adolescent views of spirit, is stripping us of our prerational views, in order to make room for the genuinely transrational insights of the higher stages of development, the transpersonal stages of genuine mystical or contemplative development. It is stripping magic and mythic in order to make room for psychic and subtle. In that sense science (and rationality) is a very healthy, very evolutionary, very necessary step toward real spiritual maturity. Rationality is a movement *of* spirit *toward* spirit.

cw 5: *Grace and Grit*, 234

By centering on the fact that temporary satori-like experiences are indeed available to virtually anybody ("fluid access"), we tend to miss the crucial fact that, once the experiential fireworks have subsided, the arc of consciousness returns to its structural patterns, which themselves evolve and develop in intersubjective formative processes.

cw 6: *Sex, Ecology, Spirituality*, 773

Any general stage/level *not objectified* will remain *as a hidden subject* (a hidden self-sense), obscuring no-self or pure nondual awareness.

cw 6: *Sex, Ecology, Spirituality*, 637

Every stage of development liberates the Witness from a previous identification: symbols witness images, concepts witness symbols, rules witness concepts, and so forth.

cw 6: *Sex, Ecology, Spirituality*, 637

The Great Goddess is best conceived, not as any particular structure or epoch or nature, horticultural or otherwise, but as the overall movement of Efflux, of Creative Descent and Superabundance, of Agape and Goodness and Compassion. She is not Gaia, not nature, not planting mythology (although She embraces all of those in Her divinely Creative Matrix). She even embraces the patriarchy and was every bit as much behind that structure as any other. (Likewise, true God is not the Great Father figure, but the overall movement of Reflux and Ascent and Eros . . .)

By confusing the Great Goddess with the horticultural Great Mother mythic corpus—which was indeed *superseded* with the coming of the patriarchy—it appears that male culture destroyed the Goddess (a handful of males on a small planet destroyed the Creative Efflux of the entire Kosmos?), and that what is required is a recovery and resurrection of the Great Mother mythos.

The same Zoroastrian dualism, the same assumption that the Goddess *could* be banished, when all that was banished was a poorly differentiated mythos that many ecofeminists have reinterpreted to fit their ideology. When the Great Goddess is instead seen to be the entire movement of Creative Descent and Efflux (at each and every epoch), then the cure is no longer regression to horticultural mythology, but progression to Goddess embodiment in the forms of today's integrations (Agape).

The Great Goddess is not a victim, nor could She be banished without destroying the entire manifest universe. But by claiming that She was banished, and by purporting to know how and why it happened, these ecofeminists are then in possession of a certain type of power, the power to tell the world what it must do in order to recapture an ethos of which these theorists are now the primary possessors. The Goddess is shackled to a horticultural planting mythology that ensures that She could never be integrated with modernity, and sees Her only as our Lady of the Eternal Victim. The very framing of the Goddess in those terms denies Her ever-present creative attributes and buries them in rhetoric.

That which one can deviate from is not the true Tao. Not only is modernity not devoid of the Goddess, her Goodness and Agape and Compassion are written all over it, with its radically new and emergent stance of worldcentric pluralism, universal benevolence, and multicultural tolerance, something that no horticultural society could even conceive, let alone implement. Her Grace grows stronger and more obvious with every gain in the liberation movements, and that we ourselves have not always lived up to her new Grace that was modernity's Enlightenment, shows only that we are still surly children not on speaking terms with our own divine parents.

cw 6: *Sex, Ecology, Spirituality*, 692–693

Q: So this causal unmanifest—is it the absolute end point? Is this the end of time, the end of evolution, the end of history? The final Omega point?

KW: Well, many traditions take this state of cessation to be the ultimate state, the final end point of all development and evolution, yes. And this end state is equated with full Enlightenment, ultimate release, pure nirvana.

But that is not the "final story," according to the Nondual traditions. Because at some point, as you inquire into the Witness, and
rest in the Witness, the sense of being a Witness "in here" completely vanishes itself, and the Witness turns out to be everything
that is witnessed. The *causal* gives way to the *Nondual*, and formless mysticism gives way to nondual mysticism. "Form is Emptiness
and Emptiness is Form."

Technically, you have dis-identified with even the Witness, and
then integrated it with all manifestation . . .

And this is the second and most profound meaning of
Emptiness—it is not a *discrete* state, but the reality of *all* states, the
Suchness of all states. You have moved from the causal to the
Nondual.

Q: Emptiness has two meanings?

KW: Yes, which can be very confusing. On the one hand, as we just
saw, it is a discrete, identifiable state of awareness—namely, unmanifest absorption or cessation (nirvikalpa samadhi, ayn, jnana
samadhi, nirodh, classical nirvana). This is the causal state, a discrete state.

The second meaning is that Emptiness is not merely a particular
state among other states, but rather the reality or suchness or condition of *all* states. Not a particular state apart from other states,
but the reality or condition of all states, high or low, sacred or profane, ordinary or extraordinary.

CW 7: *A Brief History of Everything*, 257–258

Human beings are born and begin their evolution through the great
spiral of consciousness, moving from archaic to magic to mythic to
rational to . . . perhaps integral, and perhaps from there into genuinely transpersonal domains. But for every person that moves into
integral or higher, dozens are born into the archaic. The spiral of
existence is a great unending flow, stretching from body to mind to
soul to spirit, with millions upon millions constantly flowing through
that great river from source to ocean.

CW 7: *A Brief History of Everything*, 35

The overall Romantic view: one starts out in unconscious Heaven, an unconscious union with the Divine; one then *loses* this unconscious union, and thus plunges into conscious Hell; one can then regain the Divine union, but now in a higher and conscious fashion.

The only problem with that view is that the first step—the loss of the unconscious union with the Divine—is an absolute impossibility. All things are one with the Divine Ground—it is, after all, the Ground of all being! To lose oneness with that Ground is to cease to exist.

Follow it closely: there are only two general stances you can have in relation to the Divine Ground: since all things are one with Ground, you can either be aware of that oneness, or you can be unaware of that oneness. That is, you can be conscious or unconscious of your union with the Divine Ground: those are the only two choices you have.

And since the Romantic view is that you start out, as an infant, in an unconscious union with Ground, you *cannot then lose that union*! You have *already* lost consciousness of the union; you cannot then further lose the union itself or you would cease to be! So if you are unconscious of your union, it can't get any worse, ontologically speaking. That is already the pits of alienation. You are already living in Hell, as it were; you are already immersed in samsara, only you don't realize it—you haven't the awareness to recognize this burning fact. And so that is more the actual state of the infantile self: unconscious Hell. The infant self already suffers hunger, pain, rudimentary fear, and thirst—all the signs of samsara. But it registers them dimly.

What does start to happen, however, is that you begin to wake up to the alienated world in and around you. You go from unconscious Hell to *conscious* Hell, and being conscious of Hell, of samsara, of lacerating existence, is what makes growing up—and being an adult—such a nightmare of misery and alienation. The infant self is relatively peaceful, not because it is living in Heaven, but because it isn't aware enough to fully register the flames of Hell all around it. The infant is most definitely immersed in samsara, it just doesn't know it, it isn't aware enough to realize it, and enlightenment is certainly not a return to this infantile state! Or a "mature version" of this state! Neither the infant self nor my dog writhes in guilt and angst and agony, but enlightenment does not consist in recapturing dog-consciousness (or a "mature form" of dog consciousness!).

As the infant self grows in awareness and consciousness, it slowly becomes aware of the intrinsic pain of existence, the torment inherent in samsara, the mechanism of madness coiled inherently in the manifest world: it begins to suffer. It is introduced to the first Noble Truth, a jolting initiation into the world of perception, whose sole mathematics is the torture-inducing fire of unquenched and unquenchable desire. This is not a desire-ridden world that was lacking in the infant's previous "wonderful" immersion state, but simply a world that dominated that state unconsciously, a world which the self now slowly, painfully, tragically becomes aware of.

And so, as the self grows in awareness, it moves from unconscious Hell to conscious Hell, and there it may spend its entire life, seeking above all else the numbing consolations that will blunt its raw and ragged feelings, blur its etchings of despair. Its life becomes a map of morphine, and folding itself into the anesthetic glow of all its compensations, it might even manage to convince itself, at least for an endearing blush of rose-tinted time, that the dualistic world is an altogether pretty thing.

But alternatively, the self might continue its growth and development into the genuinely spiritual domains: transcending the separate-self sense, it uncoils in the very Divine. The union with the Divine— a union or oneness that had been present but unconscious since the start—now flares forth in consciousness in a brilliant burst of illumination and a shock of the unspeakably ordinary: it realizes its Supreme Identity with Spirit itself, announced, perhaps, in nothing more than the cool breeze of a bright spring day, this outrageously obvious affair.

And thus the actual course of human ontogeny: from unconscious Hell to conscious Hell to conscious Heaven. *At no point does the self lose its union with the Ground,* or it would utterly cease to be! In other words, the Romantic agenda is right about the second and third steps (the conscious Hell and the conscious Heaven), but utterly confused about the infantile state itself, which is not unconscious Heaven but unconscious Hell.

cw 7: *The Eye of Spirit,* 465–467

It is flat-out strange that something—that *anything*—is happening at all. There was nothing then a Big Bang, then here we all are. This is extremely weird.

cw 6: *Sex, Ecology, Spirituality,* 3

The Masculine Face of Spirit—or God—is preeminently Eros, the Ascending and *transcendental* current of the Kosmos, ever-striving to find greater wholeness and wider unions, to break the limits and reach for the sky, to rise to unending revelations of a greater Good and Glory, always rejecting the shallower in search of the deeper, rejecting the lower in search of the higher.

And the Feminine Face of Spirit—the Goddess—is preeminently Agape, or Compassion, the Descending and *immanent* and manifesting current of the Kosmos, the principle of embodiment, and bodily incarnation, and relationship, and relational and manifest embrace, touching each and every being with perfect and equal grace, rejecting nothing, embracing all. Where Eros strives for the Good of the One in transcendental wisdom, Agape embraces the Many with Goodness and immanent care.

cw 7: *A Brief History of Everything,* 284

[Idealism], truly, was a stunning vision, the likes of which humankind has rarely seen: evolution as Spirit's temporal unfolding of its own timeless potentials. Grounded in the pragmatic facts and actual history of consciousness, yet at the same time wedded to an all-pervading spiritual reality glorious in its grace and grand in its splendor, this Idealist vision brought Heaven down to awaken the Earth and brought Earth up to exalt its Heaven.

cw 8: *The Marriage of Sense and Soul,* 176

If we look at the various types of human attempts to comprehend the Divine—both East and West, North and South—what we find are two very different types of spirituality, which I call *Ascending* and *Descending.*

The Ascending path is purely transcendental and otherworldly. It is usually puritanical, ascetic, yogic, and it tends to devalue or even deny the body, the senses, sexuality, the Earth, the flesh. It seeks its salvation in a kingdom not of this world; it sees manifestation or samsara as evil or illusory; it seeks to get off the wheel entirely. And, in fact, for the Ascenders, any sort of Descent tends to be viewed as illusory or even evil. The Ascending path glorifies the One, not the Many; Emptiness, not Form; Heaven, not Earth.

The Descending path counsels just the opposite. It is this-worldly

to the core, and it glorifies the Many, not the One. It celebrates the
Earth, and the body, and the senses, and often sexuality. It even identifies Spirit with the sensory world, with Gaia, with manifestation,
and sees in every sunrise, every moonrise, all the Spirit a person
could ever want. It is purely immanent and is often suspicious of anything transcendental. In fact, for the Descenders, any form of Ascent
is usually viewed as evil.

CW 7: *A Brief History of Everything*, 61–62

KW: . . . The Path of Ascent from the Many to the One is the *path of
wisdom*. Wisdom sees that behind all the multifarious forms and
phenomena there lies the One, the Good, the unqualifiable Emptiness, against which all forms are seen to be illusory, fleeting, impermanent. Wisdom is the return of the Many to the One. In the East:
Prajna, or wisdom, sees that Form is Emptiness.

The Path of Descent, on the other hand, is the *path of compassion*. It sees that the One actually manifests as the Many, and so all
forms are to be treated equally with kindness, compassion, mercy.
Compassion or Goodness is, in fact, the very mechanism of manifestation itself. The One manifests as the Many through an infinite
act of compassion and charity, and we embrace the Many with that
same compassion and care. Compassion touches all manifestation
with concern and gentle wonderment. In the East: Karuna, or compassion, sees that Emptiness is Form.

So we have: Wisdom sees that the Many is One, and Compassion
sees that the One is the Many. Or in the East: Prajna sees that Form
is Emptiness, Karuna sees that Emptiness is Form.

Q: Wisdom and Compassion—this is also Eros and Agape.

KW: Yes, ascending Eros and descending Agape, transcendence and
immanence, the love that reaches up and the love that reaches
down. . . .

The central historical point in all of this is that with the great
Nondual systems, from Plotinus in the West to Nagarjuna in the
East, we see an emphasis on *balancing and integrating these two
movements*. The *Ascending* or *transcendental* current of wisdom
or Eros or prajna is to be balanced with the *Descending* or *immanent* current of compassion or Agape or karuna; and the union of

these two, the union of the One and the Many, of Emptiness and Form, of Wisdom and Compassion—their union in the nondual Heart of One Taste is the source and goal and ground of genuine spirituality.

                    CW 7: *A Brief History of Everything*, 283

Because Spirit manifests equally in all four quadrants, or equally in the Big Three, then we can describe Spirit *subjectively* as one's own Buddha-mind—the "I" of Spirit, the Beauty. And we can describe Spirit *objectively* as Dharma—the "It" of Spirit, the ultimate Truth. And we can describe Spirit *culturally* as Sangha—the "We" of Spirit, the ultimate Good.

These four quadrants, or the Big Three, are all facets of Spirit, facets of Emptiness. When Emptiness manifests, it does so as subject and object, each of which can be singular or plural. And that gives us the four quadrants, or simply the Big Three. So Spirit can be described—and must be described—with all three languages, I and we and it.

Each of those domains evolves. Which means, each unfolds its spiritual nature more and more, and thus realizes its spiritual nature more and more. And in the uppermost reaches of that evolution, the I and the We and the It increasingly become transparent to their own true nature. They each radiate the glory of the Ground that they are.

And in that radiant awareness, every I becomes a God, and every We becomes God's sincerest worship, and every It becomes God's most gracious temple.

                    CW 7: *A Brief History of Everything*, 174

All such attempts [at formulating a theory of everything], of course, are marked by the many ways in which they fail. The many ways in which they fall short, make unwarranted generalizations, drive specialists insane, and generally fail to achieve their stated aim of holistic embrace. It's not just that the task is beyond any one human mind; it's that the task itself is inherently undoable: knowledge expands faster than ways to categorize it. The holistic quest is an ever-receding dream, a horizon that constantly retreats as we approach it, a pot of gold at the end of a rainbow that we will never reach.

So why even attempt the impossible? Because, I believe, a little bit of wholeness is better than none at all, and an integral vision offers considerably more wholeness than the slice-and-dice alternatives. We can be more whole, or less whole; more fragmented, or less fragmented; more alienated, or less alienated—and an integral vision invites us to be a little more whole, a little less fragmented, in our work, our lives, our destiny.

A Theory of Everything: xii

Pathways [magazine]: Why does Spirit bother to manifest at all, especially when that manifestation is necessarily painful and requires that It become amnesiac to Its true identity? Why does God incarnate?

KEN WILBER: Oh, I see you're starting with the easy questions. Well, I'll give you a few theoretical answers that have been offered over the years, and then I'll give you my personal experience, such as it is.

I have actually asked this same question of several spiritual teachers, and one of them gave a quick, classic answer: "It's no fun having dinner alone."

That's sort of flip or flippant, I suppose, but the more you think about it, the more it starts to make sense. What if, just for the fun of it, we pretend—you and I—blasphemously pretend, just for a moment—that we are Spirit, that Tat Tvam Asi? Why would you, if you were God Almighty, why would *you* manifest a world? A world that, as you say, is *necessarily* one of separation and turmoil and pain? Why would you, as the One, ever give rise to the Many?

Pathways: It's no fun having dinner alone?

KEN WILBER: Doesn't that start to make sense? Here you are, the One and Only, the Alone and the Infinite. What are you going to do next? You bathe in your own glory for all eternity, you bask in your own delight for ages upon ages, and then what? Sooner or later, you might decide that it would be fun—just *fun*—to pretend that you were not you. I mean, what else are you going to do? What else can you do?

Pathways: Manifest a world.

KEN WILBER: Don't you think? But then it starts to get interesting. When I was a child, I used to try to play checkers with myself. You ever tried that?

Pathways: Yes, I remember doing something like that.

KEN WILBER: Does it work?

Pathways: Not exactly, because I always knew what my "opponent's" move was going to be. I was playing both sides, so I couldn't "surprise" myself. I always knew what I was going to do on both sides, so it wasn't much of a game. You need somebody "else" to play the game.

KEN WILBER: Yes, exactly, that's the problem. You need an "other." So if you are the only Being in all existence, and you want to *play*—you want to play any sort of game—you have to take the role of the other, and then *forget* that you are playing both sides. Otherwise the game is no fun, as you say. You have to pretend you are the other player with such conviction that you forget that you are playing all the roles. If you don't forget, then you've got no game, it's just no fun.

Pathways: So if you want to play—I think the Eastern term is *lila*—then you have to forget who you are. Amnesis.

KEN WILBER: Yes, I think so. And that is exactly the core of the answer given by the mystics the world over. If you are the One, and—out of sheer exuberance, plenitude, superabundance—you want to play, to rejoice, to have fun, then you must first, manifest the Many, and then second, forget it is you who are the Many. Otherwise, no game. Manifestation, incarnation, is the great Game of the One playing at being the Many, for the sheer sport and fun of it.

Pathways: But it's not always fun.

KEN WILBER: Well, yes and no. The manifest world is a world of opposites—of pleasure versus pain, up versus down, good versus evil, subject versus object, light versus shadow. But if you are going to play the great cosmic Game, that is what you yourself set into motion. How else can you do it? If there are no parts and no players and no suffering and no Many, then you simply remain as the One and Only, Alone and Aloof. But it's no fun having dinner alone.

Pathways: So to start the game of manifestation is to start the world of suffering.

KEN WILBER: It starts to look like that, doesn't it? And the mystics seem to agree. But there is a way out of that suffering, a way to be free of the opposites, and that involves the overwhelming and direct realization that Spirit is not good versus evil, or pleasure versus pain, or light versus dark, or life versus death, or whole versus part, or holistic versus analytic. Spirit is the great Player that gives rise to *all* those opposites equally—"I the Lord make the Light to fall on the good and the bad alike; I the Lord do all these things"— and the mystics the world over agree. Spirit is not the good half of the opposites, but the ground of *all* the opposites, and our "salvation," as it were, is not to find the good half of the dualism but to find the Source of both halves of the dualism, for that is what we are in truth. We are both sides in the great Game of Life, because we—you and I, in the deepest recesses of our very Self—have created *both* of these opposites in order to have a grand game of cosmic checkers.

That, anyway, is the "theoretical" answer that the mystics almost always give. "Nonduality" means, as the Upanishads put it, "to be freed of the pairs." That is, the great liberation consists in being freed of the pairs of opposites, freed of duality—and finding instead the nondual One Taste that gives rise to both. This is *liberation* because we cease the impossible, painful dream of spending our entire lives trying to find an up without a down, an inside without an outside, a good without an evil, a pleasure without its inevitable pain.

Pathways: You said that you had a more personal response as well.

KEN WILBER: Yes, such as it is. When I first experienced, however haltingly, "nirvikalpa samadhi"—which means, meditative absorption in the formless One—I remember having the vague feeling—

very subtle, very faint—that I didn't want to be alone in this wonderful expanse. I remember feeling, very diffusely but very insistently, that I wanted to share this with somebody. So what would
one do in that state of loneliness?

Pathways: Manifest the world.

KEN WILBER: That's how it seems to me. And I knew, however ama-
teurishly, that if I came out of that formless Oneness and recognized the world of the Many, that I would then *suffer*, because the
Many always hurt each other, as well as help each other. And you
know what? I was glad to surrender the peace of the One even
though it meant the pain of the Many. Now this is just a little
tongue taste of what the great mystics have seen, but my limited
experience seems to conform to their great pronouncement: You
are the One freely giving rise to the Many—to pain and pleasure
and all the opposites—because you choose not to abide as the
exquisite loneliness of Infinity, and because you don't want to have
dinner alone.

Pathways: And the pain that is involved?

KEN WILBER: Is *freely* chosen as part of the necessary Game of Life.
You cannot have a manifest world without all the opposites of
pleasure and pain. And to get rid of the pain—the sin, the suffering, the duhkha—you must *remember* who and what you really
are. This remembrance, this recollection, this anamnesis—"Do this
in Remembrance of Me"—means, "Do this in Remembrance of
the Self that You Are"—Tat Tvam Asi. The great mystical religions
the world over consist of a series of profound practices to quiet the
small self that we pretend we are—which *causes* the pain and suffering that you feel—and awaken as the Great Self that is our own
true ground and goal and destiny—"Let this consciousness be in
you which was in Christ Jesus."

Pathways: Is this realization an all-or-nothing affair?

KEN WILBER: Not usually. It's often a series of glimpses of One
Taste—glimpses of the fact that you are one with absolutely all
manifestation, in its good and bad aspects, in all its frost and fever,

its wonder and its pain. You are the Kosmos, *literally*. But you tend to understand this ultimate fact in increasing glimpses of the infinity that you are, and you realize exactly why you started this wonderful, horrible Game of Life. But it is absolutely not a cruel Game, not ultimately, because you, and you alone, instigated this Drama, this Lila, this Kenosis.

Pathways: But what about the notion that these experiences of "One Taste" or "Kosmic Consciousness" are just a by-product of meditation, and therefore aren't "really real"?

KEN WILBER: Well, that can be said of any type of knowledge that depends on an instrument. "Kosmic consciousness" often depends on the instrument of meditation. So what? Seeing the nucleus of a cell depends on a microscope. Do we then say that the cell nucleus isn't real because it's only a by-product of a microscope? Do we say the moons of Jupiter aren't real because they depend on a telescope? The people who raise this objection are almost always people who don't want to look through the instrument of meditation, just as the Churchmen refused to look through Galileo's telescope and thus acknowledge the moons of Jupiter. Let them live with their refusal. But let us—to the best of our ability, and hopefully driven by the best of charity or compassion—try to convince them to look, just once, and see for themselves. Not coerce them, just invite them. I suspect a different world might open for them, a world that has been abundantly verified by all who look through the telescope, and microscope, of meditation.

Pathways: Could you tell us . . .

KEN WILBER: If I could interrupt, do you mind if I give you one of my favorite quotes from Aldous Huxley?

Pathways: Please.

KEN WILBER: This is from *After Many a Summer Dies the Swan*:

"I like the words I use to bear some relation to facts. That's why I'm interested in eternity—psychological eternity. Because it's a fact."

"For you perhaps," said Jeremy.

"For anyone who chooses to fulfill the conditions under which it can be experienced."

"And why should anyone wish to fulfill them?"

"Why should anyone choose to go to Athens to see the Parthenon? Because it's worth the bother. And the same is true of eternity. The experience of timeless good is worth all the trouble it involved."

"Timeless good," Jeremy repeated with distaste. "I don't know what the words mean."

"Why should you?" said Mr. Propter. "You've never bought your ticket for Athens."

Pathways: So contemplation is the ticket to Athens?

KEN WILBER: Don't you think?

> "A Ticket to Athens," interview with *Pathways: A Magazine of Psychological and Spiritual Transformation*, in cw 8, *One Taste*, 470–476

The great and rare mystics of the past (from Buddha to Christ, from al-Hallaj to Lady Tsogyal, from Hui-neng to Hildegard) were, in fact, ahead of their time, and still ahead of ours. In other words, they most definitely are not figures of the past. They are figures of the future.

In their spirituality, they did not tap into yesterday, they tapped into tomorrow. In their profound awareness, we do not see the setting sun, but the new dawn. They absolutely did not inherit the past, they inherited the future. . . .

We are yet the bastard sons and daughters of an evolution not yet done with us, caught always between the fragments of yesterday and the unions of tomorrow, unions apparently destined to carry us far beyond anything we can possibly recognize today, and unions that, like all such births, are exquisitely painful and unbearably ecstatic. And with yet just the slightest look—once again, within—new marriages unfold, and the drama carries on.

> cw 6: *Sex, Ecology, Spirituality*, 261–262

At the subtle level, the process of "interiorization" or "within-and-beyond" intensifies—a new transcendence with a new depth, a new embrace, a higher consciousness, a wider identity—and the soul and

God enter an even deeper interior marriage, which discloses at its summit a divine union of Soul and Spirit, a union *prior* to any of its manifestations as matter or life or mind, a union that outshines any conceivable nature, here or anywhere else. Nature-nation mysticism gives way to Deity mysticism, and the God within announces itself in terms undreamt of in gross manifestation, with a Light that blinds the sun and a Song that thunders nature and culture into stunned and awestruck silence.

Nature lovers here scream "Foul!," as if beyond the glories of nature there should be no other glory, as if the visible and tangible scene exhausted the wonders of the Kosmos, as if in all the worlds and possible worlds through all eternity, their beloved nature alone should be allowed to shine.

But nature, dear sweet nature, is mortal and finite. It was born, it will remain a bit, and it will pass. It was created, it will be undone. And in all cases, it is bounded, and limited, and doomed to the decay that marks all manifest worlds. "I am somehow receptive of the great soul, and thereby I do overlook the sun and the stars and feel them to be the fair accidents and effects which change and pass," as Emerson said.

We are, of course, perfectly free to identify with nature, and to find a geocentric earth-religion that consoles us in our passing miseries. We are free to identify with a finite, limited, mortal Earth; we are not free to call it infinite, unlimited, immortal, eternal.

That Spirit which is within and beyond the Earth, which is prior to the Earth but not other to the Earth, that Spirit which is source and support and goal of all—that Spirit is intuited at the psychic and comes to the fore in the subtle stage of consciousness evolution, utterly including the previous stages, utterly outshining them. Let the Earth and Cosmos and Worlds dissolve, and see Spirit still shining in the Emptiness, never arising, never dissolving, never blinking once in the worlds of created time. "That joy," says [Saint] Teresa [of Ávila], "is greater than all the joys of earth, and greater than all its delights, and all its satisfactions; and they are apprehended, too, very differently, as I have learned by experience."

CW 6: *Sex, Ecology, Spirituality*, 301–302

And so the question remains: . . . is there still any sense in which a collective humanity would eventually evolve into an Absolute Omega Point, a pure Christ Consciousness (or some such) for all beings? Are we heading for the Ultimate End of History, the Omega of all omegas? Does It even exist?

And the answer is that It does exist, and we are not heading toward it. Or away from It. Or around It. Uncreate Spirit, the causal unmanifest, is the nature and condition, the source and support, of this and every moment of evolution. It does not enter the stream of time at a beginning or exit at the end. It upholds all times and supports all places, with no partiality at all, and thus exerts neither push nor pull on history.

As the utterly Formless, it does not *enter* the stream of form at *any* point. And yet, as Ramana said, there is a sense in which it is indeed the *summum bonum*, the ultimate Omega Point, in the sense that no finite thing will rest short of release into this Infinity. The Formless, in other words, is indeed an ultimate Omega, an ultimate End, but an End that is never reached *in* the world of form. Forms continue endlessly, ceaselessly, holarchically forever (unless the universe collapses in on itself, retreating back along the path it came—to start anew, one presumes).

Thus, in the world of Form, the ultimate Omega appears as an ever-receding horizon of fulfillment (the ever-receding horizon of the totality of manifestation), forever pulling us forward, forever retreating itself, thus always conferring wholeness and partialness in the same breath: the wholeness of this moment is part of the whole of the next moment: the world is always complete and incomplete in any given moment, and thus condemned to a fulfillment that is never fulfilled: the forms rush and run forward to a reward that retreats with the run itself.

But at any sufficiently developed point in an individual's development, a radical leap (Eckhart's "breakthrough") into the Formless can occur. The higher the development, the easier and more likely the jump will occur. Yet the Formless itself is not the result of that jump, nor does it then come to be. It is there, from the start, as one's own Original Face, the Face one had before the Big Bang, the Face that looks out from each and every sentient being in each and every universe, calling out to each and all for mutual Self-, and not just self-, recognition.

Abide as Emptiness, embrace all Form: the liberation is in the Emptiness, never finally in the Form (though never apart from it). And thus even if I realize the *summum bonum*, even if I cut abruptly off the path of endless form and find myself in the Formless, still, still, and still the world of form goes on—into the psychic, into the subtle, into the billions and billions of universes of form available and available and available, endlessly, ceaselessly, dramatically.

Evolution seeks only this Formless *summum bonum*—it wants *only* this ultimate Omega—it rushes forward always and solely in search of *this*—and it will *never* find it, because evolution unfolds in the world of form. The Kosmos is driven forward endlessly, searching in the world of time for that which is altogether timeless. And since it will *never* find it, it will *never cease* the search. Samsara circles endlessly, and that is always the brutal nightmare hidden in its heart.

cw 6: *Sex, Ecology, Spirituality,* 323–325

We can therefore summarize Plato's overall position in words that would apply to any Nondual stance wherever it appears: flee the Many, find the One; having found the One, embrace the Many *as* the One.

Or, in short: Return to One, embrace Many. . . .

Indeed, wherever the Nondual traditions would appear—traditions uniting and integrating the Ascending and Descending paths, in the East and in the West—we find a similar set of themes expressed so constantly as to border on mathematical precision. From Tantra to Zen, from the Neoplatonists to Sufism, from Shaivism to Kegon, stated in a thousand different ways and in a hundred different contexts, nonetheless the same essential word would ring out from the Nondual Heart: the Many returning to and embracing the One is Good, and is known as *wisdom*; the One returning to and embracing the Many is Goodness, and is known as *compassion*.

Wisdom knows that behind the Many is the One. Wisdom sees through the confusion of shifting shapes and passing forms to the groundless Ground of all being. Wisdom sees beyond the shadows to the timeless and formless Light (in Tantra, the self-luminosity of Being). Wisdom, in short, sees that the Many is One. Or, as in Zen, wisdom or *prajna* sees that Form is Emptiness (the "solid" and "substantial" world of phenomena is really fleeting, impermanent, insubstantial—"like a bubble, a dream, a shadow," as *The Diamond Sutra* puts it). Wisdom sees that "this world is illusory; Brahman alone is real."

But if wisdom sees that the Many is One, *compassion* knows that the One is the Many; that the One is expressed *equally* in each and every being, and so each is to be treated with compassion and care, not in any condescending fashion, but rather because each being, exactly as it is, is a perfect manifestation of Spirit. Thus, compassion sees that the One is the Many. Or, as in Zen, compassion or *karuna* sees that Emptiness is Form . . . Compassion sees that "Brahman is the world," and that, as Plato put it, the entire world is a "visible, sensible God."

And it was further maintained, in East and West alike, that the *integration* of Ascent and Descent is the *union* of wisdom (which sees that Many is One) and compassion (which sees that One is Many). The love we have for the One is extended to the Many, since they are ultimately not-two, thus uniting wisdom and compassion in every moment of perception.

cw 6: *Sex, Ecology, Spirituality*, 336–337

For Plotinus, "Ascent" does not mean a change of place or a change in location or a change from "this world" to an "other world." It means a change in perception so that more and more of this world is perceived *as* the other world—more and more of this world is perceived as Perfectly Divine, until there is *only* the Perfectly Divine in *all* perception, "this world" and "that world" being utterly irrelevant, and the way up and the way down meeting *in every single act* of loving and choiceless and nondual awareness.

cw 6: *Sex, Ecology, Spirituality*, 371

The God that was to come. The Descent of the all-pervading World Soul. The coming of the Over-human, the Over-Soul, the transpersonal dawn, *Homo universalis*. And not merely in rare, individual, isolated cases, but as a *center of social organizing forces*—just as magic and mythic and mental had previously emerged in large and organized cultures around the world according to their basic patterns. The coming of the World Soul, blessing each and all with intuitions of the Over-Soul, joined each and all in the council and communion of all sentient beings, the community of all souls, likewise institutionalized in structures that guard its preciousness the way the worldcentric rationality is now institutionalized and guarded in law and education and government and community. The integration of the physiosphere and the biosphere and noosphere in each and every compound individual, not as a theory but as a *central identity in consciousness* (just as the ego or person is the central identity institutionalized in rational cultures of today).

The coming of the Over-Soul that is the World Soul, touching each and all with its Goodness and its Glory, baptizing each with its Brilliance and its Blessing. The coming of the World Soul, trailing clouds of wonderment, singing songs of liberation, dancing madly and divine in splendor and salvation. The long-sought coming of the World Soul, changing every "it" and every "we" and every "I" it touches: in a moment, in the twinkling of an eye, we will be changed, we all will be changed.

The loveless, beaten, battered self will let go the torment and the torture of its self-embracing ways, tire of that marriage to a special misery that it had chosen over loneliness, to nurse it through the long brutality of a life that doesn't care, surrender the murderous love affair with its own perplexed reflection, which had itself pretended to the throne of the Divine, and find instead its soul in Grace and drenched throughout with a luminous God that is its own true Being—its always and only Original Face, smiling now from the radiant Abyss, unreasonably happy in the face of every sight, set helplessly afloat on the Sea of Intimacy, adrift in currents of Compassion and caressed in unrelenting Care, one with each and one with all in mutual Self-recognition, dancing in the dawn that heralds now the Self of all that truly is, and the Community of all that well might be, and the State of all that is to come.

And every I will sing of the Self, and every We will resonate with worship of the Divine, and every It will radiate the light of a Spirit happy to be seen, with dialogue the abode of the Gods and perception the home of Grace, and gone the lonely loveless self, the god of its own perception, and gone the Godless destiny of time and separation.

The blessed, blessed Descent of the World Soul: in a moment, in the twinkling of an eye, we will be changed, we all will be changed.

Perhaps it will happen after all.

And perhaps it will not. I believe that the intuition of the Over-Soul, the World Soul, is indeed increasing in frequency and in intensity in more and more individuals around the globe . . .

But as always, we have to *make* the future that is *given* to us. And it is my strongest conviction that the Descent of the all-pervading

World Soul is facilitated, or hindered, to precisely the degree that we unpack its intuition adequately.

cw 6: *Sex, Ecology, Spirituality*, 520–522

In Spirit I am not a whole/part, but the *infinity* in which all whole/ parts arise, remain a bit, and pass. And thus, by *developing* from nature to mind to Spirit, I can embrace the entire Kosmos in a free and complete fashion, for I-I am that Kosmos for all eternity: which is to say: *right now*, when seen in the eye of Spirit, for which both mind and nature are simply integral chapters in my own continuing story.

United in Spirit without erasing differences—there is the One-in-the-Many as my truest Self (the ultimate I or Buddha), and as the highest Truth (the ultimate It or Dharma), and as the all-encompassing Community of all sentient beings (the ultimate We or Sangha).

Further, according to the Idealists (and nondual sages everywhere), the extraordinary and altogether paradoxical secret is that the Final Release is always already accomplished. The "last step" is to step off the cycle of time altogether and find the Timeless there *from the start*, ever-present from the very beginning and at *every point* along the way. The great far-off spectacular climax . . . is right now. "The Good," says Hegel, "the absolutely Good, is eternally accomplishing itself in the world; and the result is that it need not wait upon us, but is *already in full actuality accomplished*."

cw 6: *Sex, Ecology, Spirituality*, 535–536

Grace is Agape, and is given freely to all; it shines on all as the omega pull of the Source-Goal, urging Eros to return, to reflux, to that Source. (This doctrine of grace is also extensively found in the East, even—I would say especially—in Buddhism, where it is behind all forms of guru yoga.)

In Japanese Buddhism, a distinction is made between self-power (Eros) and other-power (grace or Agape), as represented respectively in Zen and Shin, but both schools agree that the distinction is ultimately based on the subject-object dualism, that there is neither self nor other, neither eros nor agape—again, Eros and Agape united only in the nondual Heart.

cw 6: *Sex, Ecology, Spirituality*, 663

If by "One" we mean the infinite, by "All" we mean the sum total of finite manifestation, and by "Each" we mean each particular manifestation, the Nondual "stance" is: One-in-Each, Each-is-One, Each-in-All, All-in-Each, One-in-All. The pantheistic stance as popularly advanced is: One-is-All, Each-in-All. The holographic "paradigm" is: Each-in-All, All-in-Each; as an overall worldview, this is magical syncretism (which is why it is often hooked up with foraging worldviews).

When the Nondual traditions speak of the One-in-the-Many and the Many-in-the One, they mean the One-in-Each-and-All and Each-and-All-is-the-One.

The realization of One-in-Many and Many-in-One, is, of course, common and definitive for all Nondual schools, whether of the East or the West. D. T. Suzuki, for example, maintained that the essence of Zen realization is contained in the *Avatamsaka Sutra*, where the interpenetration of the Absolute (*li*) and the relative (*shih*)—One-in-Each (*shih li wu ai*)—allows the complete interpenetration of the Each with Each and All (*shih shih wu ai*)—precisely Plotinus's point.

At the same time, the "final" philosophical position of Zen, and all of Mahayana, is expressed in the *Vimalakirti-Nirdesha Sutra*, which is a discourse on Nonduality. Each of the assembled sages gives his or her definition of Nonduality: it is the not-twoness of nirvana and samsara, it is the not-twoness of enlightenment and passions, it is the not-twoness of the many and the one, and so forth. The "correct" answer is finally given by Vimalakirti, who responds with "a thunderous silence."

cw 6: *Sex, Ecology, Spirituality*, 665

The world has got to do what the world has got to do. Just as we had to farm the physical—by learning agriculture and then industry—before we could collectively move to the mental, so now we have to farm the mental—information and computers and technology—before we go beyond it to the spiritual. All in its own time. Frankly, I think the world is moving along at a handsome clip.

cw 4: "Paradigm Wars," 179

Physics, in short, deals with—and can only deal with—the world of shadow-symbols, not the light of reality beyond the shadowy cave. . .

Both the old and the new physics were dealing with shadow-symbols, *but the new physics was forced to be aware of that fact*—forced to be aware that it was dealing with shadows and illusions, not reality. . . .

There is the great difference between the old and new physics—both are dealing with shadows, but the old physics didn't recognize that fact. If you are *in* the cave of shadows and don't even know it, then of course you have no reason or desire to try to escape to the light beyond. The shadows appear to be the whole world, and no other reality is acknowledged or even suspected—this tended to be the philosophic effect of the old physics. But with the new physics, the shadowy character of the whole enterprise became much more obvious, and sensitive physicists by the droves began to look beyond the cave (and beyond physics) altogether. . .

To put it in a nutshell: according to this view, physics deals with shadows; to go beyond shadows is to go beyond physics; to go beyond physics is to head toward the metaphysical or mystical—and *that* is why so many of our pioneering physicists were mystics. The new physics contributed nothing positive to this mystical venture, except a spectacular failure, from whose smoking ruins the spirit of mysticism gently arose.

CW 4: *Quantum Questions*, 252–255

Spirit or Godhead, when apprehended by the mind, is a paradox: both Goal and Ground, Source and Summit, Alpha and Omega. *From the view of Ground*, history *is* pure illusion. Since God is equally and wholly present at every point of time, then history can neither add to nor subtract from God's omnipresence. *From the view of Summit or Goal*, however, history *is* the unfolding of God to Itself, or the movement from subconscious to selfconscious to superconscious modes; only the latter or superconscient mode can *directly realize* an everpresent unity with God-as-Ground, and thus the latter *alone*, of all the modes, is the direct realization *of* God *by* God. From that point of view, history is the unfolding of God to Itself, an unfolding that appears to us, through a glass darkly, as evolution. From this side of the paradox, history is no mere illusion, *it is the very substance of this drama and the very means of its enactment.*

CW 4: "Sociocultural Evolution," 337

Most [meditative paths] follow a similar, general, overall course of unfolding. There is the initial rising above the gross ego, experienced as a release from the confines of the separate-self sense and its obsessive sufferings. This initial release—depending on the specifics of the path and the person—might be experienced as a type of cosmic consciousness or nature mysticism, as an initial arousal of kundalini energy beyond the conventional realm, as an awakening of paranormal powers, or as an interior experience of blissful luminosity, to name a common few. If consciousness continues to move through the subtle and into the causal, all of those experiences continue to intensify, to the point that they are all dissolved or reduced to pure formlessness, to the causal unmanifest, to an Emptiness prior to all form, a Silence prior to all sounds, an Abyss prior to all being, a Godhead prior to God. The soul reverts to spirit and is released into formless infinity, timeless eternity, unmanifest absorption, radiant emptiness. Consciousness resides as the unmoved Witness, the formless mirror-mind, impartially reflecting all that arises, utterly indifferent to the play of its own patterns, thoroughly quiet in the face of its own sounds, wholly nonattached to the forms of its own becoming. And then, in the final mystery, the Witness dies into everything that is witnessed, Emptiness is realized not other than Form, the mirror mind and its reflections are not two, Consciousness awakens as the entire World. The sound of a waterfall on the distant horizon, the sight of a gentle misty fog, the crack of lightning in a late night storm, somehow say it all. The subject and object, the human and divine, the inner and the outer, by any other names, are simply and only One Taste.

CW 4: "Death, Rebirth, and Meditation," 355

We dig within in order to go beyond, not back.

CW 4: *Integral Psychology*, 534

Evolution in all forms has started to become conscious of itself. Evolution, as Spirit-in-action, is starting to awaken on a more collective scale. Kosmic evolution is now producing theories and performances of its own integral embrace. This Eros moves through you and me, urging us to include, to diversify, to honor, to enfold. The Love that moves the sun and other stars is moving theories such as this, and it will move many others, as Eros connects the previously unconnected, and pulls together the fragments of a world too weary to endure.

Some would call these integral endeavors "powerful glimmers of a true Descent of the all-pervading World Soul." Others would simply say the time is ripe for such. But this much seems certain: less comprehensive endeavors are starting to lose their appeal; the allure of flatland, the call of fragmentation, the regressive pull of reductionism, are becoming much less fascinating. Their power to enthrall the mind becomes weaker every day, as Eros works its subtle wonders in and through us all.

If we can believe the collective wisdom of the many ages of humankind, we can perhaps say:

This Eros is the same Spirit-in-action that originally threw itself outward to create a vast morphogenetic field of wondrous possibilities (known as the Great Nest). Out of itself, as matter, it began; out of itself, as life, it continued; out of itself, as mind, it began to awaken. The same Spirit-in-action differentiated itself into modes of the good and the true and the beautiful, as it continued its evolutionary play. And it is now the same Spirit-in-action, starting to become collectively conscious of itself, that has initiated an era of integral embrace—global village to communications internet to integral theories to network society—as it slowly binds together the fragments of a world that has forgotten how to care.

Just so, the same Spirit-in-action has written this book, and it is the very same Spirit-in-action who is now reading it. From subconscious to self-conscious to superconscious, the great Play continues and the grand River flows, with all of its glorious streams rushing to the ocean of One Taste, never really lost, never really found, this sound of the rain on the temple roof, which only alone is.

CW 4: *Integral Psychology*, 625–626

With Spirit's shocking Self-recognition, Forms continue to arise and evolve, but the secret is out: they are all Forms of Emptiness in the universe of One Taste, endlessly transparent and utterly Divine. There is no end limit, no foundation, no final resting place, only Emptiness and endless Grace. So the luminous Play carries on with insanely joyous regard, timeless gesture to timeless gesture, radiant in its wild release, ecstatic in its perfect abandon, endless fullness beyond endless fullness, this miraculously self-liberating Dance, and there is no one anywhere to watch it, or even sing its praises.

CW 7: *A Brief History of Everything*, 276

God does not lie in our collective past, God lies in our collective future; the Garden of Eden is tomorrow, not yesterday; the Golden Age lies down the road, not up it.

CW 7: *The Eye of Spirit*, 475

Creativity is part of the basic ground of the universe. Somehow, some way, miraculously, new holons emerge. I say out of Emptiness, but you can call that creative ground whatever you want. Some would call it God, or Goddess, or Tao, or Brahman, or Keter, or Rigpa, or Dharmakaya, or Maat, or Li. The more scientifically oriented tend to prefer to speak simply of the "self-transcending" capacity of the universe, as does Jantsch. That's fine. It doesn't matter. The point is, stuff emerges. Amazing!

CW 7: *A Brief History of Everything*, 256

There is a new koan for our age, and only the neoperennial philosophy can answer it: Does a computer have Buddha-nature?

CW 7: *The Eye of Spirit*, 475

The past has the Great Religions. The future will have the Greater Religions.

CW 7: *The Eye of Spirit*, 477

There is, in other words, an important distinction between Truth and *forms* of Truth. Radical Truth itself is formless, timeless, spaceless, changeless; its various forms, however, the various ideas, symbols, images, and thoughts we use to represent it, ceaselessly change and evolve. Radical Truth is timeless; its various forms exist in the world of time, and are subject to time's laws. Radical Truth is spaceless, whereas its various forms are space-bound, finite, and contingent. Radical Truth is not one condition among other conditions, but the very Condition of all conditions, the Nature of all natures, the suchness or thatness or isness of all phenomena and all forms, and is therefore not itself any particular phenomenon or form.

Now we can never know *all* the forms of Truth—psychological truth, sociological truth, economic truth, biological truth, and so on. These forms ceaselessly advance and evolve, alter and complexify. And although we can never know all these forms of Truth, we can know Truth itself, or the absolute reality of which all these forms are but partial and approximate reflections. In other words, although we can never know all the facts of existence, we can know the Fact of Existence which underlies and grounds all possible and relative facts, just as, once we know the ocean is wet, we know all waves are wet, even though we may never know each and every wave.

cw 7: *The Eye of Spirit*, 473

Spirit knows itself objectively as Nature; knows itself subjectively as Mind; and knows itself absolutely as Spirit—the Source, the Summit, the Ground, and the Process of the entire ordeal.

cw 8: *The Marriage of Sense and Soul*, 175

Spirit is *unfolding* itself in each new transcendence, which it also *enfolds* into its own being at the new stage. Transcends and includes, brings forth and embraces, creates and loves, Eros and Agape, unfolds and enfolds—different ways of saying the same thing.

So we can summarize all this very simply: because evolution *goes beyond* what went before, but because it must *embrace* what went before, then its very nature is to transcend and include, and thus it has an inherent directionality, a secret impulse, toward increasing depth, increasing intrinsic value, increasing consciousness. In order for evolution to move at all, it must move in those directions—there's no place else for it to go!

cw 7: *A Brief History of Everything*, 89–90

Because [the] Nondual condition is the nature or suchness of any and all states—because this Emptiness is one with whatever Forms arise—then the world of Form will continue to arise, and you will continue to relate to Form. You will not try to get out of it, or away from it, or suspend it. You will enter it fully.

And since Forms continue to arise, then you are *never* at an *end point* where you can say, "Here, I am fully Enlightened." In these traditions, Enlightenment is an ongoing process of new Forms arising, and you relate to them as Forms of Emptiness. You are one with all these Forms as they arise. And in that sense, you are "enlightened," but in another sense, this enlightenment is *ongoing*, because new Forms are arising all the time. You are never in a *discrete* state that has no further development. You are always learning new things about the world of Form, and therefore your overall state is always evolving itself.

So you can have certain breakthrough Enlightenment experiences—satori, for example—but these are just the *beginning* of an *endless* process of riding the new waves of Form as they ceaselessly arise. So in this sense, in the Nondual sense, you are never "fully" Enlightened, any more than you could say that you are "fully educated." It has no meaning.

CW 7: *A Brief History of Everything*, 267–268

In a sense, the nondual realization for a fair number of people right around the turn of the century, including Sri Aurobindo, is still unfolding. I mean, the world of form keeps unfolding, keeps evolving—spirit's own self-expression keeps unfolding—and it happens, as far as we can tell, to build on what it did yesterday, which is why evolution is indeed an unfolding event in the world of form. So as this incarnational nonduality, this ultimately ecstatic tantric nonduality itself, began to unfold, and its forms of manifestation began to unfold, you find that by the time you get to people like Sri Aurobindo, there's such a full-bodied understanding of this process. Even though some of the earlier sages were ultimately enlightened for their time, there's a richness, an unfolding, a resonance of spirit's own incarnational understanding in some of these recent sages that just gives you goosebumps.

If we talk about enlightenment as the union of emptiness and form, the pure emptiness doesn't change because it doesn't enter the stream of time, but the form does change, and the two of those are inextricably united. And therefore, there is, in that sense, an evolution of enlightenment.

"The Guru and the Pandit," *What Is Enlightenment?* no. 21: 48–49

But every time new types of realization come into being—and that means, again, whenever the world of form has so evolved and changed that you need a different type of evolutionary enlightenment or incarnational nonduality—you've got to rewrite the instruction manual.

"The Guru and the Pandit," *What Is Enlightenment?* no. 21: 136

Humans can end their alienated and unhappy consciousness, not primarily by going back to Nature but by going forward to nondual Spirit. Not preconventional Nature but postconventional Spirit holds the key to overcoming alienation and dissociation, and that Spirit is contacted, not by spiraling regression to a preconventional slumber, but by evolutionary progression to a radiant Nonduality.

cw 8: *The Marriage of Sense and Soul,* 175

Because the universe has direction, we ourselves have direction. There is meaning in the movement, intrinsic value in the embrace. As Emerson put it, we lie in the lap of immense intelligence, which by any other name is Spirit. There is a theme inscribed on the original face of the Kosmos. There is a pattern written on the wall of Nothingness. There is a meaning in its every gesture, a grace in its every glance.

We—and all beings as such—are drenched in this meaning, afloat in a current of care and profound value, ultimate significance, intrinsic awareness. We are part and parcel of this immense intelligence, this Spirit-in-action, this God-in-the-making. We don't have to think of God as some mythic figure outside of the display, running the show. Nor must we picture it as some merely immanent Goddess, lost in the forms of her own production. Evolution is both God and Goddess, transcendence and immanence. It is immanent in the process itself, woven into the very fabric of the Kosmos; but it everywhere transcends its own productions, and brings forth anew in every moment.

cw 7: *A Brief History of Everything,* 90

Thus evolution, far from being an antispiritual movement—as so many Romantics and antimodernists and virtually all premodern cultures imagined—is actually the concrete unfolding, holarchical integration, and self-actualization of Spirit itself. Evolution is the mode and manner of Spirit's creation of the entire manifest world, not one item of which is left untouched by its all-encompassing embrace.

cw 8: The Marriage of Sense and Soul, 177

"I believe that what we see in all these attempts to find a spiritual paradise—to find the beach beneath the pavement—is often a genuine intuition of a very real Spirit, but an intuition distorted and misplaced from the timeless Present onto a fantasized past, and reduced from the All to a mere sensory slice. Spirit, if it has any meaning at all, is surely an infinite Ground and not merely the sum total of finite things, and thus it ought not be reduced to the biosphere, even though it embraces and includes the biosphere. And surely it is a timeless Presence and not merely a past reality, and thus it ought not to be equated with any particular historical epoch, even though it embraces and includes all history.

"I believe that the evidence shows that there is a real Spirit, a real Beach, but it is beneath no pavement whatsoever, for all pavements arise within it: Spirit is all-encompassing. It transcends everything, it includes everything. But looking for Spirit under a pavement saddles boomeritis with a vicious dualism—biosphere vs. patriarchy, feelings vs. rationality, tribal vs. modern—so that Spirit is imagined to be found in just one-half of that dualism, with the other half then thought to be malignant, so that true wholeness and redemption can then *never* be found."

Boomeritis, 297–298

This, then, is the message of Jung; the message of Maslow, Assagioli, and the whole Fourth Force; and more, of the saints, sages, and mystics, whether Amerindian, Taoist, Hindu, Buddhist, or Christian: at the bottom of your soul is the soul of humanity itself, but a divine, uncreate soul, leading from time to eternity, from death to immortality, from bondage to liberation, from enchantment to awakening. To salvation in this life go those who comprehend the supreme identity. Listen to Kabir:

> O Friend, hope for Him whilst you live, know whilst
> you live, understand whilst you live; for in life
> deliverance abides.
> If your bonds be not broken whilst living, what hope
> of deliverance in death?
> It is but an empty dream that the soul shall have
> union with Him because it has passed from the
> body;
> If he is found now, He is found then;
> If not, we do but go to dwell in the City of Death.

At this point, we can hardly speak of potentials. What could one say, when the deepest potentials of *your* soul are already the very ones that move the planets and radiate as light from the stars; that explode as the thunderous crack of lightning and echo as the rain through the mists; that hurl the comets through the skies and suspend the moon in blackness of night? The little potentials of the persona, ego, and centaur which we nurture so carefully and of which we are so pleased, dare to stand up as candles in the sunlight. Dame Julian of Norwich cried out in her enlightenment: "See! I am God; see! I am all things; see! I do all things; see! I never lift mine hands off my works, nor ever shall, without end; see! I lead all thing to the end I ordained it to from without beginning, by the same Might, Wisdom, and Love whereby I made it. How should anything be amiss?"

Nevertheless we have to be careful how we understand this ultimate potential, this divine and cosmic potential. It is not that the deepest I (or I-I) stands back from the cosmos and orders it around. It is not that this I has the potentials of the entire cosmos because this I can personally control the cosmos, but because this I *is* the cosmos. For as the very depths of the transpersonal self are pushed through, the transpersonal self gives way to the ultimate or universal self—the Self that *is* all realms of existence, manifest and unmanifest, in all directions and all dimensions.

For as the intuition of the transpersonal self begins to mature and deepen, it slowly—no, instantly!—dawns on you why you can't see the Seer anywhere in the universe. You cannot see the Seer anywhere in the universe because the Seer *is all* of the universe. You cannot see the Seer because it is everything which is seen, and thus could never be perceived as a separate entity apart from something else. Everything you are looking at is you who are looking at it. When this is understood, the seer and the seen collapse as each other; *all boundaries between all I's and all Its dissolve* in what has been called cosmic consciousness. Even the transpersonal witness crashes apart and falls into *everything* that is witnessed. No longer do you perceive objects or Its, because you *are* all objects and all Its. There is no separate subject standing apart from the entire field of awareness. As Zen puts it, everywhere you look you see only your own Original Face, "the face you had before your parents were born." (So, after all, it doesn't matter if you had different parents.) "The awakened one," explains Ramana Maharshi, "does not see the universe as different from himself."

Look at it this way: if you now close your eyes and attend very carefully to everything you hear, you will hear an extraordinary flux of sounds crashing around you: birds singing, cars honking, children playing, TV blaring, people chatting, crickets chirping; but notice that even now—just as you are—there is one thing that you cannot hear, no matter how hard you try, how long you try, how much you strain. Of all the sounds you can hear, you cannot hear—the hearer.

Now you cannot hear the hearer for a simple reason. As William James pointed out, you cannot hear the hearer because the hearer is nothing but the entire stream of sounds heard. You cannot hear the hearer because it is everything you hear! You do not hear the sound of thunder, you are the sound of thunder. Likewise, you cannot taste the taster—because what we have long thought of as a separate or subjective taster is really just the sum of present, "objective" tastes. There is no subject—the "taster"—that "tastes" special objects—the "tasted." There is just the present stream of tastes, with no split into subject and object. In just the same way, you cannot really see the seer because the seer is everything seen. What you are looking out of is what you are looking at. A famous Zen master exclaimed upon his enlightenment, "When I heard the temple bell ring, suddenly there was no bell and no I, just the ringing."

At that point, the whole realm of the transcendent collapses into the immanent. The supernatural world and the natural world turn out to be the same world. The extraordinary is finally only ordinary. Because there is no place that the Ultimate is not, the Ultimate is only present. Thus the ultimate potential is the very suchness of things as they exist now. The greatest human potential is not that you personally can make the sun move around in the sky, but that your own true Self is already the movement of the sun as it is now. All the activities of the cosmos now occurring are already activities of your own deepest I. That is why the absolutely ordinary is already the absolutely extraordinary. That is why the greatest potential of your cosmic self is already manifest all around you. It is already the case in every direction. And finally, that is why the Zen masters say that Layman P'ang had the final word on the ultimate human potential:

> How marvelous, how supernatural this!
> I draw water, I carry fuel.

When your real self is the cosmos, then all the activities of the cosmos are already manifesting your greatest potentials: the birds sing in springtime; in fall the leaves turn yellow. To look elsewhere is to miss the point. Dogen hit it:

> This slowly drifting cloud is pitiful!
> What dreamwalkers we all are!
> Awakened, the one great potential:
> Black rain on the temple roof.

Yasutani Roshi used to explain enlightenment as—and these are his words—"the direct awareness that you are more than this puny body or limited mind. Stated negatively, it is the realization that the universe is not external to you. Positively, it is experiencing the universe as yourself" [in P. Kapleau, *The Three Pillars of Zen*]. As R. H. Blyth put it, "The experience by the universe of the universe." Says Dogen Zenji, quoting an old Zen Master:

> I came to realize clearly that Mind
> Is no other than mountains and rivers and
>   the great wide earth,
> The sun and the moon and the stars.

How incredible! For the entire universe has become the I. *The entire universe—that is the ultimate It.* Recall what the body and the shadow looked like before they were re-membered (or turned back into I). The shadow, for instance, really and truly appeared as an object-out-there; the persecutors (in our shadow example) appeared in every way to be *out there, not-self, alien*. Something that was really a part of the self was seen as not-self. Something that should have been I was felt and perceived as an It out there. Now, at the bottom of the soul, there lies around us the great and ultimate It: the universe appears as object-out-there; as really and truly not-self. *The cosmos is the ultimate It.*

Thus, the mystics have come with the great message, the message that unlocks the greatest and deepest potential of the human soul: *that ultimate It can become I.* That It can be *re-membered*—can indeed, like all the other Its we have studied, become I. *Tat tvam asi*— That art Thou: where It was, I shall become. Like all our projections, the cosmos itself is a part of I that is erroneously felt and perceived as an It. The trees, the stars, the cars and lakes, the tables, dogs, frogs, and rocks—these "environmental objects" or Its are just as much a part of our real self as the shadow is of our egoic self and the body is of our centauric self. And when that ultimate It, the universe, finally returns to I, then It is no longer It, and I am no longer I.

A Zen text:

> Without outer forms, without inner self, spring still
>   arrives;
> Unstopped, unhindered, the moon traverses the sky.
> Many born of the same branch, but
> Few who die of the same branch.
> The last word is, "just this";
> A wind-boat, having loaded the moon,
> Bobs on autumn waters.

Could Freud have ever guessed? Could he even have suspected? "Aside from the 'I,'" we heard him say at the beginning of this paper, "we perceive another region of the soul, much more extensive, much more impressive, and much more obscure than the 'I,' which we designate the 'It.'" The It: Freud stumbled onto the very tip of the It, but an It that stretched down so much more deeply and profoundly than he ever surmised—an It that swirls down through the shadow to the ego, through the body to the centaur, through the cosmos to the true Self. Each of the levels of this incredible It can be *re-membered*, or joined again with, to disclose deeper I's. For *all* our projections can be re-membered and taken back. And every time an It is returned to I, then greater potentials are released, for the capacities and energies of the Its are given unto I. Then, at the very bottom of an individual's soul, the final anamnesis: looking at the cosmos, he sees his Original Face; gazing into the firmament, he sees his own true nature; and of all the vast expanses of this marvelous universe, which he manifests with the clarity of a silver mirror, he truly and innocently knows within: where It was, I have become.

CW 1: "Where It Was, There I Shall Become," 629–633

It is true that, in individuals, spirit can awaken as spirit ("spirit-as-spirit," traditional enlightenment). And it is true that this is in some important ways a *developmental* or *evolutionary* process. That is, certain developments clear the way for this timeless realization: both humans and rocks are equally spirit, but only humans can consciously realize that fact, and between the rock and the human lies evolution.

This is behind the Buddhist prayer of thanks "for this precious human body"—only in a human body can enlightenment be attained. Not gods, not animals, not demons, not angels: only with this human body can I awaken to the empty Ground that is equally present in all other sentient beings. This, too, is Aurobindo's and Murphy's emphasis on *The Future of the Body*, the precious human body. And that human body is, among many other things, the product of evolution.

And *that* means that Spirit has evolved the vehicle for its own self-realization. Because Spirit is involved with and as this world, this world evolves with and as Spirit, to the point that Spirit superconsciously realizes its own Original Face. The possibility of that realization is a product of Spirit's own evolutionary unfolding, and in that sense, this realization has a very strong developmental aspect.

But it is not the whole story. Evolution occurs in the world of time and space and form, whereas Spirit's primordial nature is finally timeless and Formless, prior to the world of evolution but not other to it. We do not find Spirit or Emptiness by reaching some evolutionary Omega point in time, but rather by stepping off the cycle of time and evolution altogether (or ceasing to contract into it).

In other words, a certain amount of evolution is required before you can step off of evolution, out of time, and into the timeless itself—into that shocking re-cognition of your own True Self, the Self that was prior to the Big Bang, prior to the temporal world altogether, eternally shining in this and every moment, untouched by the ravages of time and the motion sickness of space: your own primordial awareness is not the Omega point of the show but the Emptiness of the show, radiant in all directions, full beyond what time or space could ever do for it, yet embracing all time and all space for no other reason than that Eternity is in love with the productions of time and Infinity those of space.

Once you learn to count, you don't have to count to a million to get the point. Once you profoundly recognize Emptiness, you don't have to watch its endless displays in order to awaken. Emptiness is fully present at every point of evolution; it is not merely the end point of evolution. The game is undone in that primal Glance, and all that remains is the radiance itself, perfectly obvious in the singing of a robin, early on a bright spring dawn.

cw 7: *The Eye of Spirit*, 670–671

4

Immediate Awareness

It has been said that in finding the doorway to Spirit, one must first abandon time. That is, to recognize one's true nature means to abandon the notions of past and future. For it is only in the present moment that we may discover our own Original Face.

From our accustomed hideouts of past and future, of history and anticipation, Wilber flushes us into the open space of the present moment. It is in the naked awareness of here and now that we become truly alive, capable of seeing ourselves and the world directly.

LET US BEGIN with our senses. Do we ever sense time? That is, do we ever directly sense a past or a future? Start again with hearing. For the moment concentrate your attention on just your auditory field, and notice the flux of sounds kaleidoscoping through your awareness. You might be able to hear people talking, dogs barking, kids playing; perhaps wind blowing, rain splashing, faucet dripping; maybe you can hear the house creaking, or cars honking, or someone laughing. But notice: *all* these sounds are *present* sounds. You cannot hear past sounds, nor can you hear future sounds. *The only thing you ever hear is the present.* You do not and cannot hear a past or future.

Just as all sounds are only present sounds, so all tastes are only present tastes, all smells are present smells, and all sights are present sights. You cannot touch, see, or feel anything resembling a past or a future. In other words, in your direct and immediate awareness, there is no time—no past, no future, only an endlessly changing present, shorter than a minisecond yet never coming to an end. All direct awareness is timeless awareness.

CW 1: *No Boundary*, 493

[There are many] ways to dissolve the boundary between the mind and body so as to discover again this unity of opposites lying asleep in the depths of our being. "This split cannot be overcome," says Lowen, "by a knowledge of the energetic processes in the body. Knowledge itself is a surface phenomenon and belongs to the realm of the ego. One has to feel the flow and sense the course of the excitation in the body. To do this, however, one must give up the rigidity of one's ego control so that the deep body sensations can reach the surface."

Simple as it sounds, that is the very difficulty almost every person faces as he tries to connect with his body. He won't really feel his legs, stomach, or shoulders, but, out of habit, he thinks about his legs, stomach, and shoulders. He pictures them to himself and thus avoids giving feeling-attention to them directly. This is, of course, one of the very mechanisms responsible for the dissociation of the body in the first place. Special attention should be given this tendency to conceptualize our feelings, and a special effort made to suspend, at least temporarily, this habitual translation of feeling-attention into thoughts and pictures.

One way to begin connecting with the body is by lying down on your back, outstretched, on a rug or mat. Simply close your eyes, breathe deeply but easily, and begin to explore your bodily feelings. Don't *try* to feel anything, don't force feelings, just let your attention flow through your body and note if any feeling, positive or negative, is present in the various parts of the body. Can you, for example, feel your legs? your stomach? your heart? eyes? genitals, buttocks, scalp, diaphragm, feet? Notice which parts of the body seem alive with feeling, full and strong and vital, and which parts seem dull, heavy, lifeless, dimmed, tight, or painful. Try this for at least three minutes, and notice how often your attention might leave the body and wander into daydreams. Does it strike you as odd that it might be very difficult to stay in your body for three minutes? If you're not in the body, where are you?

After this preliminary, we can move to the next step: still lying with your arms alongside and legs slightly parted, eyes closed, breathe very deeply but slowly, *drawing the inhalation from the throat to the abdomen*, eventually filling up your entire midsection. Imagine, if you like, that your entire chest and stomach are lined with a large balloon and that with each inhalation you are totally filling the balloon. The "balloon" should softly extend into the chest and bulge out fully and strongly in the abdomen. If you can't feel the gentle force of the expanded balloon in any of these areas, simply let the balloon fill out a little more, extending itself into that particular area. Then exhale slowly and smoothly, allowing the balloon to empty completely. Repeat this seven or eight times, maintaining the gentle but firm pressure inside the balloon so it bulges the abdomen and reaches the pelvic basin. Note especially which areas feel tight, tense, painful, or numb.

Can you feel that the entire ballooned area is one piece, or does it seem divided and segmented into chest, abdomen, and pelvic floor, each segment separated from the others by areas or bands of tightness, tension, or pain? In spite of these minor pains and discomforts, you might begin to notice that the feeling which extends throughout the balloon is one of subtle pleasure and joy. You are literally breathing in pleasure and radiating it throughout your bodymind. Upon exhalation, do not lose or exhaust the breath, but release it as pleasure to permeate the entire body. In this way, subtle pleasure flows through your bodymind and becomes fuller with each cycle. If you are not sure of this, complete another three or four total expansion breaths, yielding to the pleasure involved.

Perhaps you can start to understand why yogis call the breath a *vital force*—not in the philosophical sense, but in the feeling sense. Upon inhalation, you draw in a vital force from the throat to the abdomen, charging the body with energy and life. Upon exhalation, you release and radiate this force as subtle pleasure and joy throughout the bodymind itself.

You might continue the total expansion balloon breathing, inhaling vital force *from* the throat *to* the navel-abdomen (the "hara"), but start to feel the exhalation as a vital force radiating outward from the abdomen to all parts of the body. With each inhalation from the throat, charge the hara with vitality. Then, upon exhalation, see how far down and into each leg you can feel (or follow) the vital force or pleasure radiate—into the thighs? knees? feet? It eventually should go literally to the tips of the toes. Continue this for several breaths, and then try the same thing with the upper extremities. Can you feel the vitality being released into your arms? fingers? head, brain, and scalp? Then, upon exhalation, allow this subtle pleasure to pass through your body and *into the world at large*. Release your breath, through the body, to infinity.

Putting all these components together, we arrive at a complete breathing cycle: Upon inhalation, draw the breath *from* the throat *to* the hara, charging it with vital force. Upon exhalation, release this subtle pleasure *through* the entire bodymind *to* the world, to the cosmos, to infinity. Once this cycle becomes full, then start to allow all thinking to dissolve in the exhalation and pass to infinity. Do the same with all distressful feelings, with disease, with suffering, with pain. Allow feeling-attention to pass through all present conditions and then beyond them to infinity, moment to moment to moment.

We come now to the specifics of this type of exercise. More than likely you were able to feel vital pleasure and feeling-attention circulate easily throughout your bodymind. But in each aspect of this exercise you might also have felt some area of numbness, lack of feeling, or deadness on the one hand, or tightness, tension, rigidity, or pain on the other. You felt, in other words, blocks (mini-boundaries) to the full flow of feeling-attention. Most people invariably feel tightness and tension in the neck, eyes, anus, diaphragm, shoulders, or lower back. Numbness is often found in the pelvic area, genitals, heart, lower abdomen, or the extremities. It's important to discover, as best you can, just where your own particular blocks exist. For the moment, *don't try to get rid of them.* At best, that won't work and at worst it will tighten them. Just find out where they seem to be, and mentally note the locations.

Once you have pinpointed these blocks, you can begin the process of dissolving them. But first we might consider just what these blocks and resistances mean—these areas of bands of tightness, pressure, and tension anchored throughout the body. We saw that on the ego level a person could resist and avoid an impulse or emotion by denying ownership of it. Through the mechanism of egoic projection, a person could prevent the awareness of a particular shadow tendency in himself. If he actually felt very hostile, but denied his own hostility, he would project it and thus feel that the world was attacking him. In other words, he would feel anxiety and fear, the result of projected hostility.

What is happening in the body when this hostility is projected? Mentally, a projection has occurred, but physically something else must happen simultaneously, since mind and body are not two. What happens in the body when you repress hostility? How, on the body level, do you suppress a strong emotion which seeks discharge in some activity?

If you get very hostile and angry, you might discharge this emotion in the activities of screaming, yelling, and striking out with the arms and fists. These muscular activities are the very essence of hostility itself. Thus, if you are to suppress hostility, you can only do so by phys-ically suppressing these *muscular* discharge activities. You must, in other words, use your muscles to hold back these discharge activities. Rather, you must use *some* of your muscles to hold back the action of *some* of your other muscles. What results is a war of muscles. Half of your muscles struggle to discharge the hostility by striking out, while the other half strain to prevent just that. It's like stepping on the gas with one foot and the brake with the other. The conflict ends in stale-mate, but a very tense one, with large amounts of energy expended with a net movement of zero.

In the case of suppressing hostility, you will probably clamp the muscles of your jaw, throat, neck, shoulders, and upper arms, for this is the only way you can physically "hold in" hostility. And hostility denied, as we have seen, usually floats into your awareness as fear. Thus, the next time you are in the grip of an irrational fear, notice that your whole shoulder area is pulled in and up, the sign that you are holding in hostility, and therefore feeling fear. But in your shoul-ders themselves you will *no longer feel* the tendency to reach out and attack; you will no longer feel hostility; you will only feel a strong tension, tightness, pressure. You have a block.

This is precisely the nature of the blocks which you located throughout your body during the breathing exercises. Every block, every tension or pressure in the body, is basically a *muscular* holding-in of some taboo impulse or feeling. That these blocks are muscular is an extremely important point, a point to which we will return very shortly. For now, we need only note that these blocks and bands of tension are the result of two sets of muscles fighting each other (across a mini-boundary), one set seeking to discharge the impulse, one set seeking to hold it in. And this is an active holding in, an "in-holding" or inhibiting. You literally crush yourself in certain areas instead of letting-out the impulse associated with that area.

Thus, if you find a tension around the eyes, you might be in-hold-ing a desire to cry. If you find a tension-ache in your temples, you may be clamping your jaws together unknowingly, perhaps trying to prevent screaming, yelling, or even laughing. A tension in the shoul-der and neck indicates suppressed or in-held anger, rage, or hostility, while a tension in the diaphragm indicates that you chronically re-strict and in-hold your breathing in an attempt to control the display of wayward emotions or feeling-attention in general. (During any act of self-control, most people will hold their breath.) Tension through the lower abdomen and pelvic floor usually means you have cut off all awareness of your sexuality, that you stiffen-up and in-hold that area to prevent the vital force of breath and energy from flowing through. Should this occur—for whatever reason—you will also shut off most feeling in your legs. And a tension, rigidity, or lack of strength in your legs usually indicates lack of rootedness, stability, groundedness, or balance in general.

Thus, as we have just seen, one of the best ways to understand the general *meaning* of a particular block is by noting where it occurs in the body. Particular body areas usually discharge particular emotions. You probably don't scream with your feet, cry with your knees, or have orgasms in your elbows. So if there is a block in a particular body area, we can assume the corresponding emotion is being suppressed and in-held. . . . Assuming you have now more or less located your major blocks to feeling, you can proceed to the really interesting endeavor: releasing and dissolving the blocks themselves. Although the basic procedure is simple to comprehend and easy enough to perform, the fruition of conscious results takes much hard work, effort, and patience. You probably have spent at least 15 years building up a specific block, so you shouldn't be surprised if it doesn't vanish permanently after 15 minutes of work. Like all boundaries, these take time to dissolve in conscious awareness.

If you have encountered these blocks before, you will realize that the most annoying aspect of them is that no matter how hard you try, you can't seem to relax them, at least not permanently. Through conscious effort you might succeed in going limp for a few minutes, but the tension (in your neck, back, chest, etc.) returns with a vengeance the moment you forget this "forced relaxation." Some blocks and tensions—perhaps most—refuse to relax at all. And yet the only remedy we habitually apply is the futile attempt to consciously relax these tensions (an approach, paradoxically enough, which itself demands a rather exhausting effort).

It seems, in other words, that these blocks happen to us, that they occur against our will, that they are wholly involuntary and uninvited. We seem to be their uncomfortable victims. Let us see, then, just what is involved in the persistence of these uninvited guests.

The first thing to notice is that these blocks are all muscular, as we mentioned earlier. Each block is actually a contraction, a tightening, a locking of some muscle or group of muscles. Some group of *skeletal* muscles, that is, and *every skeletal muscle is under voluntary con-*

trol. The same voluntary muscles you use to move an arm, to chew, to walk, to jump, to make a fist, or to kick—just these same muscles are operating in every body block.

But that means that these blocks are not—indeed, they physically *cannot*—be involuntary. They do not happen to us. They are and must be something we are actively doing to ourselves. In short, we have deliberately, intentionally, and voluntarily created these blocks, since they consist solely of voluntary muscles.

Yet, curiously enough, we *don't know* that we are creating them. We are tightening these muscles, and although we know that they are tight and tense, we do not know that *we* are actively tensing them. Once this type of block occurs, we can't relax these muscles, simply because we don't know we are contracting them in the first place. It then appears that these blocks happen all by themselves (just like all other unconscious processes), and we seem helpless victims crushed by forces "beyond" our control.

This whole situation is almost exactly as if I were pinching myself but didn't know it. It is as if I intentionally pinched myself, but then forgot it was I who was doing the pinching. I feel the pain of the pinching, but cannot figure out why it won't stop. Just so, all of these muscular tensions anchored in my body are deep-seated forms of self-pinching. So the important question is *not*, "How can I stop or relax these blocks?" but rather, "How can I see that *I* am actively producing them?" If you are pinching yourself but don't know it, to ask somebody else to stop the pain does no good. To ask how to stop pinching yourself implies that *you aren't* doing it yourself. On the other hand, as soon as you see that you are actively pinching yourself, then, and only then, do you spontaneously stop. You don't go around asking how to stop pinching yourself, any more than you ask how to raise your hand. They are both voluntary actions.

The crux, therefore, is getting the direct feel of how I actively tense these muscles, and therefore the one thing I *don't* do is try to relax them. Rather, I must, as always, play my opposites. I must do what I would have never thought of doing before: I must actively and consciously attempt to *increase* the particular tension. By deliberately increasing the tension, I am making my self-pinching activity conscious instead of unconscious. In short, I start to remember how *I* have been pinching myself. I see how I have literally been attacking myself. That understanding felt through-and-through releases energy from the war of muscles, energy which I can then direct outward toward the environment instead of inward on myself. Instead of squeezing and attacking myself, I can "attack" a job, a book, a good meal, and thus learn afresh the correct meaning of the word aggression: "to move toward."

But there is a second and equally important aspect of dissolving these blocks. We have just seen that the first is to deliberately increase the pressure or tension by further tightening the muscles involved. In this way we do consciously what we have heretofore been doing unconsciously. But remember that these tension blocks were serving a most significant function—they were initially introduced to choke off feelings and impulses that at one time seemed dangerous, taboo, or unacceptable. These blocks were, and still are, forms of *resistance* to particular emotions. Thus, if these blocks are to be permanently dissolved, you will have to open yourself to the emotions which lie buried beneath the muscular cramp.

It should be emphasized that these "buried feelings" are not some sort of wildly insatiable and totally overpowering orgiastic demands, nor some form of demonically possessing and bestial urges to wipe out your father and mother and siblings. They are most often rather mild, although they might seem dramatic because you have muscularly in-held them so long. They usually involve a release of tears, a good scream or two, ability for uninhibited orgasm, a good old-fashioned temper tantrum, or a temporary but enraged attack upon pillows set up for that purpose. Even if some fairly strong negative emotion surges up—some full-blown rage—it need not cause great alarm, for it does not constitute a major portion of your personality. In a live theatre play, when a minor two-line character walks on stage for the first time, all eyes in the audience turn to this minor player, even though he is an insignificant part of the total cast. Likewise, when some negative emotion first walks into the stage of your awareness, you might become temporarily transfixed with it, even though it too is but a fragment of the total cast of your emotions. Much better to have it up front than rambling around back stage.

In any case, this emotional release, this upsurge of some type of in-held emotion, will usually happen of itself as you begin to consciously take responsibility for increasing the tightening of the muscles in the various blocks of the body. As you deliberately begin to contract the muscles involved, you tend to remember what it is you are contracting your muscles against. For example, if you see a friend about to cry, and you say, "Whatever you do, fight it!" she will probably burst into tears. At that moment she is deliberately trying to in-hold something natural to the organism, and she knows that she is trying to block it, so the emotion cannot easily go underground. In the same way, as you deliberately take charge of your blocks while trying to increase them, the inhibited emotion may start to surface and exhibit itself.

The entire procedure for this type of body awareness experiment might run as follows: After locating a specific block—let's say a tenseness in the jaw, throat, and temples—you give it your full awareness, feeling out just where the tension is and what muscles seem to be involved. Then, slowly but deliberately begin to increase that tension and pressure; in this case, by tightening your throat muscles and clamping your teeth together. While you are experimenting with increasing the muscular pressure, remind yourself that you are not just clamping muscles, *you are actively trying to hold something in*. You can even repeat to yourself (out loud if your jaws aren't involved), "No! I won't! I'm resisting!" so that you truly feel that part of yourself that is doing the pinching, that is trying to in-hold some feeling. Then you can slowly release the muscles—and at the same time open yourself totally to whatever feeling would like to surface. In this case, it might be a desire to cry, or to bite out, or to vomit, or to laugh, or to scream. Or it might only be a pleasurable glow where the block used to be. To allow a genuine release of blocked emotions requires time, effort, openness, and some honest work. If you have a typically persistent block, daily "workouts" of 15 minutes or so for upwards of a month will almost certainly be necessary for significant results. The block is released when feeling-attention can flow through that area in a full and perfectly unobstructed fashion on its way to infinity.

An important change in one's sense of self and reality results from this simple healing of the split between the mind and body, the voluntary and involuntary, the willed and the spontaneous. To the extent you can feel your involuntary body processes as *you*, you can begin to *accept* as perfectly natural all manner of things which you cannot *control*. You may more readily accept the uncontrollable and rest easily in the spontaneous, with faith in a deeper self which goes beyond the superficial will and ego rumblings. You may learn you needn't control yourself in order to accept yourself. In fact your deeper self, your centaur, lies beyond your control. It is voluntary *and* involuntary, both perfectly acceptable as manifestations of *you*.

CW 1: *No Boundary*, 529–537

Since the opposites cannot exist without each other, if you aren't aware of both of them, you will send the rejected pole underground. You will render it unconscious, and thus project it. You will, in short, create a boundary between the opposites, and thus generate a battle. But this is a battle that can never be won, only perpetually lost in way after painful way, because the two sides are actually aspects of each other.

The shadow, then, is simply your unconscious opposites. Thus, a simple way to contact your shadow is to assume the very opposite of whatever you now consciously intend, wish, or desire. That will show you exactly how your shadow looks at the world, and it is this view which you will want to befriend. This does not mean to *act* on your opposites, merely to be aware of them. If you feel you intensely dislike someone, be aware of the side of you that likes the person. If you are madly in love, be aware of the part of you that couldn't care less. If you hate a particular feeling or symptom, be aware of that aspect of yourself which secretly enjoys it. The moment you are truly aware of your opposites, of both the positive and negative feelings toward any situation, then many tensions connected with that situation drop out, because the battle of opposites which created that tension is dissolved. On the other hand, the moment you lose the unity of opposites, the awareness of both sides in yourself, then you split the opposites apart, erect a boundary between them, and thus render the rejected pole unconscious where it returns to plague you as symptom. Since the opposites are always a unity, the only way they can be separated is by unconsciousness—selective inattention.

As you begin to explore your opposites, your shadow, your projections, you will begin to find that you are assuming responsibility for your own feelings and your own states of mind. You will start to see that most battles between you and other people are really battles between you and your projected opposites. You will start to see that your symptoms are not something that the environment is doing to you, but something you are doing to yourself as an exaggerated substitute for what you would really like to do to others. You will find that people and events don't cause you to be upset, but are merely the occasions for you to upset yourself. It is a tremendous relief when you first understand that you yourself are producing your own symptoms, because that also means you can *stop* producing those symptoms by translating them back to their original form. You become the cause of your own feelings, and not the effect.

CW 1: *No Boundary*, 522–523

To re-own the body might initially strike one as a peculiar notion. The boundary between ego and flesh is so deeply embedded in the average person's unconscious that he responds to the proposed task of healing this split with a curious mixture of puzzlement and boredom. He has come to believe that the boundary between the mind and body is unalterably real, and thus he can't figure out why anyone would want to tamper with it, let alone dissolve it.

As it turns out, few of us have lost our minds, but most of us have long ago lost our bodies, and I'm afraid we must take that literally. It seems, in fact, that "I" am almost sitting on my body as if I were a horseman riding on a horse. I beat it or praise it, I feed and clean and nurse it when necessary. I urge it on without consulting it and I hold it back against its will. . . .

Indeed, my body seems to just dangle along under me. I no longer approach the world *with* my body but *on* my body. I'm up here, it's down there, and I'm basically uneasy about just what it is that *is* down there. My consciousness is almost *exclusively* head consciousness—*I am* my head, but I *own* my body. The body is reduced from self to property, something which is "mine" but not "me." The body, in short, becomes an object or a projection, in just the same way the shadow did. A boundary is erected upon the total organism so that the body is projected as not-self. This boundary is a split, a fissure, or, in the words of Lowen, a *block*: "The block also operates to separate and isolate the psychic realm from the somatic realm. Our consciousness tells us that each acts upon the other, but because of the block it does not extend deep enough for us to sense the underlying unity. In effect the block creates a split in the unity of the personality. Not only does it dissociate the psyche from the soma, but it also separates surface phenomena from their roots in the depths of the organism."

What fundamentally concerns us here is the *disruption of the total organism*, the centaur, of which the loss of the body is only the most visible and sensible sign. The loss of the body is not precisely synonymous with the disruption of the centaur, "the underlying unity," but is merely one of the manifestations that this disruption may take. Nevertheless, it is the one to which we will confine our attention in this chapter, inasmuch as it is the easiest to grasp and the simplest to communicate. Please remember, however, that I am not saying that the body per se—what we call the "physical body"—is a deeper reality than the mental-ego. In fact, the simple body itself is the lowest of all modes of consciousness . . . The body is not a "deeper reality" than the ego, as many somatologists think, but the *integration* of the body *and* the ego is indeed a deeper reality than either alone . . .

There are, as one would expect, all sorts of reasons why we abandon our bodies, and why we now fear to reclaim them . . . On a superficial level, we refuse to reclaim the body because we just don't think there's any reason to—it seems a big to-do about nothing. On a deeper level, we fear to reclaim the body because it houses, in a particularly vivid and living form, strong emotions and feelings which are socially taboo. And ultimately, the body is avoided because it is the abode of death.

For all these reasons, and more, a generally "adjusted" person has long ago projected her body as an "object out there," or, we might say, as an object "down there." The centaur is abandoned, and the person identifies with the ego as against the body. But, like all projections, this alienation of the body only results in the projected body returning to haunt the individual, clobbering her in the most agonizing of ways, and worse yet, with her own energy. Since the body is for all purposes placed on the *other* side of the self/not-self boundary, since it is not befriended, since it is no longer an ally, it naturally becomes an enemy. The ego and the body square off, and an intense if sometimes subtle war of opposites begins.

cw 1: *No Boundary,* 526–528

It is this primal resistance to unity consciousness that we must approach, and not unity consciousness itself. For until you see precisely how you resist unity consciousness, all your efforts to "achieve" it will be in vain, because what you are trying to achieve is also what you are unconsciously resisting and trying to prevent. We secretly resist unity consciousness, we covertly manufacture the "symptoms" of nonenlightenment, just as we secretly produced all our other symptoms on the different levels of the spectrum. What on the surface we fervently desire, in the depths we successfully prevent. And this resistance is our real difficulty. Thus, we won't move *toward* unity consciousness, we will simply understand how we are always moving *away* from it. And that understanding itself might allow a glimpse of unity consciousness, *for that which sees resistance is itself free of resistance.*

CW 1: *No Boundary*, 568

Meditation, whether Christian, Buddhist, Hindu, Taoist, or Muslim, was invented as a way for the soul to venture inward, there ultimately to find a supreme identity with Godhead. "The Kingdom of Heaven is within"—and meditation, from the very beginning, has been the royal road to that Kingdom. Whatever else it does, and it does many beneficial things, meditation is first and foremost a search for the God within.

CW 5: *Grace and Grit*, 91

After one has developed a strong foundation practice in vipassana, one moves on to the practice of tonglen. This practice is so powerful and so transformative it was kept largely secret until just recently in Tibet. . . . The practice is as follows:

In meditation, picture or visualize someone you know and love who is going through much suffering—an illness, a loss, depression, pain, anxiety, fear. As you breathe in, imagine all of that person's suffering—in the form of dark, black, smokelike, tarlike, thick, and heavy clouds—entering your nostrils and traveling down into your heart. Hold that suffering in your heart. Then, on the outbreath, take all of your peace, freedom, health, goodness, and virtue, and send it out to the person in the form of healing, liberating light. Imagine they take it all in, and feel completely free, released, and happy. Do that for several breaths. Then imagine the town that person is in, and, on the inbreath, take in all of the suffering of that town, and send back all of your health and happiness to everyone in it. Then do that for the entire state, then the entire country, the entire planet, the universe. You are taking in all the suffering of beings everywhere and sending them back health and happiness and virtue.

When people are first introduced to this practice, their reactions are usually strong, visceral, and negative. Mine were. Take that black tar into me? Are you kidding? What if I actually get sick? This is insane, dangerous! When Kalu [Rinpoche] first gave us these tonglen instructions, the practice of which occupied the middle portion of the retreat, a woman stood up in the audience of about one hundred people and said what virtually everybody there was thinking:

"But what if I am doing this with someone who is really sick, and I start to get that sickness myself?"

Without hesitating Kalu said, "You should think, Oh good! It's working!"

That was the entire point. It caught all of us "selfless Buddhists" with our egos hanging out. We would practice to get our own enlightenment, to reduce our own suffering, but take on the suffering of others, even in imagination? No way.

Tonglen is designed exactly to cut that egoic self-concern, self-promotion, and self-defense. It exchanges self for other, and thus it profoundly undercuts the subject/object dualism. It asks us to undermine the self/other dualism at exactly the point we are most afraid: getting hurt ourselves. Not just talking about having compassion for others' suffering, but being willing to take it into our own heart and release them in exchange. This is true compassion, the path of the Mahayana. In a sense it is the Buddhist equivalent of what Christ did: be willing to take on the sins of the world, and thus transform them (and you).

The point is fairly simple: For the true Self, or the one Self, self and other can be easily exchanged, since both are equal, it makes no difference to the only Self. Conversely, if we cannot exchange self for other, then we are locked out of one-Self awareness, locked out of pure nondual awareness. Our unwillingness to take on the suffering of others locks us into our own suffering, with no escape, because it locks us into our self, period. As William Blake put it, "Lest the Last Judgment come and find me unannihilate, and I be seized and given unto the hands of my own selfhood."

A strange thing begins to happen when one practices tonglen for any length of time. First of all, nobody actually gets sick. I know of no bona fide cases of anyone getting ill because of tonglen, although a lot of us have used that fear as an excuse not to practice it. Rather, you find that you stop recoiling in the face of suffering, both yours and others'. You stop running from pain, and instead find that you can begin to transform it by simply being willing to take it into yourself and then release it. The real changes start to happen in *you*, by the simple willingness to get your ego-protecting tendencies out of the way. You begin to relax the self/other tension, realizing that there is only one Self feeling all pain or enjoying all success. Why get envious of others, when there is only one Self enjoying the success? This is why the "positive" side of tonglen is expressed in the saying: I rejoice in the merit of others. It's the same as mine, in nondual awareness. A great "equality consciousness" develops, which undercuts pride and arrogance on the one hand, and fear and envy on the other.

When the Mahayana path of compassion is established, when the exchangeability of self and other is realized, at least to some degree, then one is ready for the Vajrayana path. The Vajrayana is based on one uncompromising principle: There is only Spirit. As one continues to undercut the subject/object duality in all its forms, it increasingly becomes obvious that all things, high or low, sacred or profane, are fully and equally perfect manifestations or ornaments of Spirit, of Buddhamind. The entire manifest universe is recognized as a play of one's own awareness, empty, luminous, clear, radiant, unobstructed, spontaneous. One learns not so much to seek awareness as to delight in it, play with it, since there is *only* awareness. Vajrayana is the path of playing with awareness, with energy, with luminosity, reflecting the perennial wisdom that the universe is a play of the Divine, and you (and all sentient beings as such) *are* the Divine.

cw 5: *Grace and Grit*, 287–290

In vipassana, one simply sits in a comfortable position (lotus or half-lotus if possible, cross-legged if not), and one gives "bare attention" to whatever is arising, externally and internally, without judging it, condemning it, following after it, avoiding it, or desiring it. One simply *witnesses* it, impartially, and then lets it go. The aim of this practice is to see that the separate ego is not a real and substantial entity, but just a series of fleeting and impermanent sensations like anything else. When one realizes just how "empty" the ego is, one ceases identifying with it, defending it, worrying about it, and this in turn releases one from the chronic suffering and unhappiness that comes from defending something that isn't there. As Wei Wu Wei put it:

> Why are you unhappy?
> Because 99.9% of everything you think,
> And everything you do,
> Is for your self,
> And there isn't one.

cw 5: *Grace and Grit*, 286–287

In meditation this morning, instead of resting in choiceless, clear, ever-present awareness—a standard "nonpractice"—I did an old yabyum tantra visualization (technically, anuttaratantra yoga)— "old," because I used to do this a lot—which involves the transformation of sexual energy into radiant bliss and compassionate embrace. These are all mostly subtle-level practices (they start at psychic, lead to subtle, and occasionally dissolve into causal. Rarely do they reach nondual One Taste or *sahaja*, but they are exemplary exercises for the development of the psychic-to-subtle domains). The standard core of this type of practice is summarized as "Bliss cognizing Emptiness arises as compassion."

It goes something like this. In meditation, you visualize yourself in sexual union with your consort. You visualize yourself and your consort as a god or goddess, angel or bodhisattva, buddha or saint— whatever works as a symbol of your deepest or highest nature. But you must visualize very intensely and very clearly you and your consort as transparent radiant divinities, making love. You actually become sexually aroused, and you coordinate this with breathing: on the in-breath, you breathe Light down the front of the body to the genitals, seat of Life; on the out-breath, you breathe Life up the back of the body—up the spine—into Light at and above the crown of the head. (This is just another version of involution/evolution, or the higher entering into the lower, and then the lower returning to the higher, forming a great circle of descending and ascending energy. If you are doing this with an actual partner, you can coordinate breathing.)

Any pleasure that is generated in the genital region is, with the out-breath, directed up the spine and released into the Light at the crown of the head—you simply breathe any pleasure from the body directly into and above the crown of the head, the home of infinite Light and Release. Then, on the in-breath, you directly breathe Light down and into the body—especially down the frontal line of the body, face to throat to chest to stomach to the base of the genitals. And so the cycle goes, bringing heavenly Light down and into earthly Life, and then returning Life to Light—thus uniting downward Agape and upward Eros, Descending and Ascending, Compassion and Wisdom, with every breath you take.

As your entire bodymind becomes full with circulating pleasure-bliss, you simply but directly take any bliss that is present and use it to meditate on Emptiness—or on the absolute Mystery of existence, or on the simple Transparency of the world, or on God as unqualifiable expanse—whatever works for you. In practice, a simple way to do this is to rest as I-I—rest as the great Seer which cannot itself be seen, the pure Witness that is completely open and empty. And then, resting as I-I, allow bliss to expand into that open and empty space that you now are—allow bliss to expand and fill the infinity of the I-I that you are. The sky of your awareness becomes filled with the bliss of the divine union that you are.

When you are in this state of the spacious bliss of I AMness, and you are full to infinity, with no desires and no wants, allow a gentle, small, ripple of a thought to arise: I vow to liberate all sentient beings into this free and open space. And with that, a ripple of compassion arises out of this vast ocean of bliss. That compassion is literally *composed of* this *infinite empty bliss*, it is made of it, as waves are of the ocean. Compassion is infinite empty bliss in action.

And so: bliss cognizing emptiness arises as compassion—in other words, bliss recognizing and reconnecting with its own divine ground (spirit or emptiness) is moved to extend this liberating and ecstatic grace to all beings, and so it arises as compassion in the service of others.

cw 8: *One Taste*, 377–379

Well, a glimmer, a taste, a hint of the nondual—this is easy enough to catch. But for the Nondual traditions, *this is just the beginning*. As you rest in that uncontrived state of pure immediateness or pure freedom, then strange things start to happen. All of the subjective tendencies that you had previously *identified* with—all of those little selves and subjects that held open the gap between the seer and the seen—they all start burning in the freedom of nonduality. They all scream to the surface and die, and this can be a very interesting period.

As you rest in this primordial freedom of One Taste, you are no longer acting on these subjective inclinations, so they basically die of boredom, but it's still a death, and the death rattles from this liberation are very intense. You don't really have to do anything, except hold on—or let go—they're both irrelevant. It's all spontaneously accomplished by the vast expanse of primordial freedom. But you are still getting burned alive, which is just the most fun you can have without smiling.

Fundamentally, it doesn't matter what type of experience arises—the simple, natural, nondual, and uncontrived state is prior to experience, prior to duality, so it happily embraces whatever comes up. But strange things come up, and you have to stay with this "effort-less effort" for quite some time, and die these little deaths constant-ly, and this is where real practice becomes very important.

cw 7: *A Brief History of Everything*, 264–265

And once you taste One Taste, no matter how fleetingly at first, an entirely new motivation will arise from the depths of your very own being and become a constant atmosphere which your every impulse breathes, and that atmosphere is compassion. Once you taste One Taste, and see the fundamental problems of existence evaporate in the blazing sun of obviousness, you will never again be the same per-son, deep within your heart. And you will want—finally, profound-ly, and most of all—that others, too, may be relieved of the burden of their sleep-walking dreams, relieved of the agony of the separate self, relieved of the inherent torture called time and the gruesome tragedy called space.

No matter that lesser motivations will dog your path, no matter that anger and envy, shame and pity, pride and prejudice will remind you daily how much more you can always grow: still, and still, under it all, around it all, above it all, the heartbeat of compassion will resound. A constant cloud of caring will rain on your every parade. And you will be driven, in the best sense of the word, by this ruthless taskmaster, but only because you, eons ago, made a secret promise to let this motiva-tion rule you until all souls are set free in the ocean of infinity.

Because of compassion, you will strive harder. Because of com-passion, you will get straight. Because of compassion, you will work your fingers to the bone, push at the world until you literally bleed, toil till the tears stain your vision, struggle until life itself runs dry. And in the deepest, deepest center of your Heart, the World is already thanking you.

cw 8: *One Taste*, 579

And tell me: is [the] story, sung by mystics and sages the world over, any crazier than the scientific materialism story, which is that the entire sequence is a tale told by an idiot, full of sound and fury, sig-nifying absolutely nothing? Listen very carefully: just which of those two stories actually sounds totally insane?

I'll tell you what I think. I think the sages are the growing tip of the secret impulse of evolution. I think they are the leading edge of the self-transcending drive that always goes beyond what went before. I think they embody the very drive of the Kosmos toward greater depth and expanding consciousness. I think they are riding the edge of a light beam racing toward a rendezvous with God.

And I think they point to the same depth in you, and in me, and in all of us. I think they are plugged into the All, and the Kosmos sings through their voices, and Spirit shines through their eyes. And I think they disclose the face of tomorrow, they open us to the heart of our own destiny, which is also already right now in the timelessness of this very moment, and in that startling recognition the voice of the sage becomes your voice, the eyes of the sage become your eyes, you speak with the tongues of angels and are alight with the fire of a realization that never dawns nor ceases, you recognize your own true Face in the mirror of the Kosmos itself: your identity is indeed the All, and you are no longer *part* of that stream, you *are* that stream, with the All unfolding not around you but in you. The stars no longer shine out there, but in here. Supernovas come into being within your heart, and the sun shines inside your awareness. Because you transcend all, you embrace all. There is no final Whole here, only an endless process, and you are the opening or the clearing or the pure Emptiness in which the entire process unfolds—ceaselessly, miraculously, everlastingly, lightly.

The whole game is undone, this nightmare of evolution, and you are exactly where you were prior to the beginning of the whole show. With a sudden shock of the utterly obvious, you recognize your own Original Face, the face you had prior to the Big Bang, the face of utter Emptiness that smiles as all creation and sings as the entire Kosmos—and it is all undone in that primal glance, and all that is left is the smile, and the reflection of the moon on a quiet pond, late on a crystal clear night.

CW 7: *A Brief History of Everything*, 91

When it comes to spiritual teachers, there are those who are safe, gentle, consoling, soothing, caring; and there are the outlaws, the living terrors, the Rude Boys and Nasty Girls of God-realization, the men and women who are in your face, disturbing you, terrifying you, until you radically awaken to who and what you really are.

And may I suggest?: choose your teachers carefully.

If you want encouragement, soft smiles, ego stroking, gentle caresses of your self-contracting ways, pats on the back and sweet words of solace, find yourself a Nice Guy or Good Girl, and hold their hand on the sweet path of stress reduction and egoic comfort. But if you want Enlightenment, if you want to wake up, if you want to get fried in the fire of passionate Infinity, then, I promise you: find yourself a Rude Boy or a Nasty Girl, the ones who make you uncomfortable in their presence, who scare you witless, who will turn on you in a second and hold you up for ridicule, who will make you wish you were never born, who will offer you not sweet comfort but abject terror, not saccharine solace but scorching angst, for then, just then, you might very well be on the path to your own Original Face.

Most of us, I suspect, prefer our spiritual teachers to be of the Nice-Guy variety. Soft, comforting, non-threatening, a source of succor for a worn and weary soul, a safe harbor in the samsaric storm. There is nothing wrong with that, of course; spirituality comes in all sorts of flavors, and I have known some awfully Nice Guys. But if the flavor tends toward Enlightenment instead of consolation, if it drifts away from soothing dreams toward actually waking up, if it rumbles toward a God realization and not egoic fortification, then that demands a brutal, shocking death: a literal death of your separate self, a painful, frightening, horrifying dissolution—a miraculous extinction you will actually witness as you expand into the boundless, formless, radical Truth that will pervade your every cell and drench your being to the core and expand what you thought was your self until it embraces the distant galaxies. For only on the other side of death lies Spirit, only on the other side of egoic slaughter lies the Good and the True and the Beautiful. "You will come in due course to realize that your true glory lies where you cease to exist," as the illustrious Sri Ramana Maharshi constantly reminded us. Your true glory lies on the other side of your death, and who will show you that?

Not the Nice Guys and not the Good Girls. They don't want to hurt your feelings. They don't want to upset you. They are here to whisper sweet nothings in your ear and place consolation prizes in the outstretched hand of the self-contraction, balm for a war-torn weary ego, techniques to prop it up in its constant battle with the world of otherness. In a sense, it's very easy being a Nice-Guy teacher: no muss, no fuss, no wrestling with egoic resistance and exhausting confrontation. Be nice to the ego, pat it on the back, have it count its breaths, hum a few mantras.

Rude Boys know better. They are not here to console but to shatter, not to comfort but to demolish. They are uncompromising, brutal, laser-like. They are in your face until you recognize your Original Face—and they simply will not back off, they will not back down, they will not let up until you let go—radically, fully, completely, unhesitatingly. They live as Compassion—real compassion, not idiot compassion—and real compassion uses a sword more often than a sweet. They deeply offend the ego (and the greater the offense, the bigger the ego). They are alive as Truth, they are everywhere confronted with egos, and they choose the former uncompromisingly. . . .

So, can you stand the heat? Or would you like more soft and consoling words of comfort, more consolation prizes for an Enlightenment that will continue to elude you? Would you like a pat on the back, or are you ready to be skinned and fried? May I suggest this? If you can stand the heat, you will indeed come to realize that your true glory lies where you cease to exist, where the self-contraction has uncoiled in the vast expanse of all space, where your separate self has been roasted and replaced by infinity resplendent—a radical Release much too obvious to see, much too simple to believe, much too near to be attained—and your real Self will quietly but surely announce its Presence as it calmly embraces the entire universe and swallows galaxies whole. . . .

If you can stand the heat, then enter the real kitchen of your own soul, where you will find nothing other than the radiant God of the entire cosmos. For it is radiant Spirit that is looking out from your eyes right now, speaking with your tongue right now, reading the words on this very page, *right now*. Your real Self is glorious Spirit in this and every moment, and it takes a very, very Rude Boy to point that out and to stay in your face until you recognize your own Original Face, shining even here and now.

Foreword to Living Enlightenment by Andrew Cohen, pp. xiii–xviii

. . . The very desire to seek spiritual enlightenment is in fact nothing but the grasping tendency of the ego itself, and thus the very search for enlightenment prevents it. The "perfect practice" is therefore not to search for enlightenment, but to inquire into the motive for seeking itself. You obviously seek in order to avoid the present, and yet the present alone holds the answer: to seek forever is to miss the point forever. You always already *are* enlightened Spirit, and therefore to *seek* Spirit is simply to deny Spirit. You can no more attain Spirit than you can attain your feet or acquire your lungs. . . .

The authentic spiritual camps have the heart and soul of the great transformative traditions, and yet they will always do two things at once: appreciate and engage the lesser and translative practices (upon which their own successes usually depend), but also issue a thundering shout from the heart that translation alone is not enough.*

And therefore, all of those for whom authentic transformation has deeply unseated their souls must, I believe, wrestle with the profound moral obligation to shout from the heart—perhaps quietly and gently, with tears of reluctance; perhaps with fierce fire and angry wisdom; perhaps with slow and careful analysis; perhaps by unshakable public example—but *authenticity* always and absolutely carries a *demand* and *duty*: you must speak out, to the best of your ability, and shake the spiritual tree, and shine your headlights into the eyes of the complacent. You must let that radical realization rumble through your veins and rattle those around you.

Alas, if you fail to do so, you are betraying your own authenticity. You are hiding your true estate. You don't want to upset others because you don't want to upset yourself. You are acting in bad faith, the taste of a bad infinity.

Because, you see, the alarming fact is that any realization of depth carries a terrible burden: those who are allowed to see are simultaneously saddled with the obligation to *communicate* that vision in no uncertain terms: that is the bargain. You were allowed to see the truth under the agreement that you would communicate it to others (that is the ultimate meaning of the bodhisattva vow). And therefore, if you have seen, you simply must speak out. Speak out with compassion, or speak out with angry wisdom, or speak out with skillful means, but speak out you must.

And this is truly a terrible burden, a horrible burden, because in any case there is no room for timidity. The fact that you might be wrong is simply no excuse: You might be right in your communication, and you might be wrong, but that doesn't matter. What does

---

*On Wilber's notion of translation and transformation, see the selection from *One Taste* on pp. 168-169.

matter, as Kierkegaard so rudely reminded us, is that only by invest-
ing and speaking your vision with *passion* can the truth, one way or
another, finally penetrate the reluctance of the world. If you are
right, or if you are wrong, it is only your passion that will force
either to be discovered. It is your duty to promote that discovery—
either way—and therefore it is your duty to speak your truth with
whatever passion and courage you can find in your heart. You must
shout, in whatever way you can.

The vulgar world is already shouting, and with such a raucous
rancor that truer voices can scarcely be heard at all. The materialis-
tic world is already full of advertisements and allure, screams of
enticement and cries of commerce, wails of welcome and whoops
of come hither. I don't mean to be harsh here, and we must honor
all lesser engagements. Nonetheless, you must have noticed that
the word "soul" is now the hottest item in the title of book sales—
but all "soul" really means, in most of these books, is simply the
ego in drag. "Soul" has come to denote, in this feeding frenzy of
translative grasping, not that which is timeless in you but that which
most loudly thrashes around in time, and thus "care of the soul"
incomprehensibly means nothing much more than focusing intensely
on your ardently separate self. Likewise, "spiritual" is on everybody's lips, but usually all it really means is any intense egoic feeling, just as "heart" has come to mean any sincere sentiment of the
self-contraction.

All of this, truly, is just the same old translative game, dressed up
and gone to town. And even that would be more than acceptable
were it not for the alarming fact that all of that translative jockeying
is aggressively called "transformation," when all it is, of course, is
a new series of frisky translations. In other words, there seems to
be, alas, a deep hypocrisy hidden in the game of taking any new
translation and calling it the great transformation. And the world at
large—East or West, North or South—is, and always has been, for
the most part, perfectly deaf to this calamity.

And so: given the measure of your own authentic realization, you
were actually thinking about *gently whispering* into the ear of that
near-deaf world? No, my friend, you must shout. Shout from the
heart of what you have seen, shout however you can.

But not indiscriminately. Let us proceed carefully with this transformative shout. Let small pockets of radically transformative spirituality, authentic spirituality, focus their efforts and transform their

students. And let these pockets slowly, carefully, responsibly, humbly, begin to spread their influence, embracing an *absolute tolerance* for all views, but attempting nonetheless to advocate a true and authentic and integral spirituality—by example, by radiance, by obvious release, by unmistakable liberation. Let those pockets of transformation gently persuade the world and its reluctant selves, and challenge their legitimacy, and challenge their limiting translations, and offer an awakening in the face of the numbness that haunts the world at large.

Let it start right here, right now, with us—with you and with me—and with our commitment to breathe into infinity until infinity alone is the only statement that the world will recognize. Let a radical realization shine from our faces, and roar from our hearts, and thunder from our brains—this simple fact, this obvious fact: that you, in the very immediateness of your present awareness, are in fact the entire world, in all its frost and fever, in all its glories and its grace, in all its triumphs and its tears. You do not see the sun, you are the sun; you do not hear the rain, you are the rain; you do not feel the earth, you are the earth. And in that simple, clear, unmistakable regard, translation has ceased in all domains, and you have transformed into the very Heart of the Kosmos itself—and there, right there, very simply, very quietly, it is all undone.

Wonder and remorse will then be alien to you, and self and others will be alien to you, and outside and inside will have no meaning at all. And in that obvious shock of recognition—where my Master is my Self, and that Self is the Kosmos at large, and the Kosmos is my Soul—you will walk very gently into the fog of this world, and transform it entirely by doing nothing at all.

And then, and then, and only then—you will finally, clearly, carefully and with compassion, write on the tombstone of a self that never even existed: There is only Spirit.

cw 8: *One Taste*, 309–313

Nobody will save you but you. You alone have to engage your own contemplative development. There is all sorts of help available, and all sorts of good agency to quicken this development, but nobody can do it for you. And if you do not engage this development, and on your deathbed you confess and scream out for help to God, nothing is going to happen. Spiritual development is not a matter of mere belief. It is a matter of actual, prolonged difficult growth, and merely professing belief is meaningless and without impact. It's like smoking for twenty years, then saying, "Sorry, I quit." That will not impress cancer. Reality, in other words, is not interested in your beliefs; it's interested in your actions, what you actually do, your actual karma. And this is why infantile and childish views of God, once appropriate, are so detrimental for mature spirituality.

CW 4: "Paradigm Wars," 189

The essence of Dzogchen (or maha-ati) is radically simple, and is in accord with the highest teachings of other of the world's great wisdom traditions, particularly Vedanta Hinduism and Ch'an (early Zen) Buddhism. In a nutshell:

If Spirit has any meaning, it must be omnipresent, or all-pervading and all-encompassing. There can't be a place Spirit is not, or it wouldn't be infinite. Therefore, Spirit has to be completely present, right here, right now, in your own awareness. That is, your own present awareness, precisely as it is, without changing it or altering it in any way, is perfectly and completely permeated by Spirit.

Furthermore, it is not that Spirit is present but you need to be enlightened in order to see it. It is not that you are one with Spirit but just don't know it yet. Because that would also imply that there is some place Spirit is not. No, according to Dzogchen, you are always already one with Spirit, and that awareness is always already fully present, right now. You are looking directly at Spirit, with Spirit, in every act of awareness. There is nowhere Spirit is not.

Further, if Spirit has any meaning at all, then it must be eternal, or without beginning or end. If Spirit had a beginning in time, then it would be strictly temporal, it would not be timeless and eternal. And this means, as regards your own awareness, that you cannot *become* enlightened. You cannot attain enlightenment. If you could attain enlightenment, then that state would have a beginning in time, and so it would not be true enlightenment.

Rather, Spirit, and enlightenment, has to be something that you are fully aware of right now. *Something you are already looking at right now.* As I was receiving these teachings, I thought of the old puzzles in the Sunday supplement section of the newspaper, where there is a landscape and the caption says, "The faces of twenty famous people are hidden in this landscape. Can you spot them?"

The faces were maybe Walter Cronkite, John Kennedy, that kind of thing. The point is that you are looking right at the faces. You don't need to see *anything* more in order to be looking at the faces. They are completely entering your visual field already, you just don't recognize them. If you still can't find them, then somebody comes along and simply points them out.

It's the same way with Spirit or enlightenment, I thought. We are all already looking directly at Spirit, we just don't recognize it. We have all the necessary cognition, but not the recognition. This is why the Dzogchen teachings don't particularly recommend meditation, useful as that may be for other purposes. Because meditation is an attempt to change cognition, to change awareness, and that is unnecessary and beside the point. Spirit is already completely and fully present in the state of awareness that you have now; nothing needs to be changed or altered. And, indeed, the attempt to change awareness is like trying to paint in the faces in the puzzle instead of simply recognizing them.

And thus, in Dzogchen, the central teaching is not meditation, because meditation aims at a change of state, and enlightenment is not a change of state but the recognition of the nature of *any* present state. Indeed, much of the teaching of Dzogchen centers on why meditation doesn't work, on why enlightenment can never be gained because it is always already present. Trying to get enlightenment would be like trying to attain your feet. The first rule in Dzogchen: There is nothing you can try to do, or try not to do, to get basic awareness, because it already and fully is.

Instead of meditation, then, Dzogchen uses what are called "the pointing-out instructions." Here the Master simply talks to you, and points out that aspect of your awareness that is *already* one with Spirit and has always been one with Spirit, that part of your awareness that is timeless and eternal, that is beginningless, that has been with you even before your parents were born (as Zen would put it). In other words, it's just like pointing out the faces in the puzzle. You don't have to change the puzzle or rearrange it, you only have to recognize that which you are already looking at. Meditation rearranges the puzzle; Dzogchen doesn't touch a thing. Thus the pointing-out instructions usually begin, "Without correcting or modifying your present awareness in any way, notice that . . ."

I cannot give the actual instructions, as those are the special province of the Dzogchen Master. But I can give you the Vedantan

Hindu version, since they are already in print, particularly in the writings of the illustrious Sri Ramana Maharshi. As I would word it:

The one thing we are always already aware of is . . . awareness itself. We already have basic awareness, in the form of the capacity to Witness whatever arises. As an old Zen Master used to say, "You hear the birds? You see the sun? Who is not enlightened?" None of us can even imagine a state where basic awareness is not, because we would still be aware of the imagining. Even in dreams we are aware. Moreover, these traditions maintain, there are not two different types of awareness, enlightened versus ignorant. There is only awareness. And this awareness, exactly and precisely as it is, without correction or modification at all, is itself Spirit, since there is nowhere Spirit is not.

The instructions, then, are to recognize awareness, recognize the Witness, recognize the Self, and abide as that. Any attempt to get awareness is totally beside the point. "But I still don't see Spirit!" "You are aware of your not seeing Spirit, and *that* awareness is itself Spirit!"

You can practice mindfulness, because there is forgetfulness; but you cannot practice awareness, because there is only awareness. In mindfulness, you pay attention to the present moment. You try to "be here now." But pure awareness is the present state of awareness *before* you try to do *anything* about it. Trying to "be here now" requires a future moment in which you will then be mindful; but pure awareness is *this* moment before you try anything. You are already aware; you are already enlightened. You might not be always already mindful, but you are always already enlightened.

The pointing-out instructions go on like this, sometimes for a few minutes, sometimes for a few hours, sometimes for a few days, until you "get" it, until you recognize your own True Face, the "face you had before your parents were born" (that is, timeless and eternal, prior to birth and death). And it is a recognition, not a cognition. It's like peering into the window of a department store, and seeing a vague figure staring back at you. You let the figure come into focus, and with a shock realize that it's your own reflection in the window. The entire world, according to these traditions, is nothing but the reflection of your own Self, reflected in the mirror of your own awareness. See? You are already looking right at it. . . .

Thus, according to these traditions, basic awareness is not hard to reach, it's impossible to avoid, and the so-called "paths" to the

Self are really obstacle courses. They prevent the recognition as long as they are engaged. There is *only* the Self, there is *only* God. As Ramana himself put it:

> There is neither creation nor destruction,
> Neither destiny nor free will;
> Neither path nor achievement;
> This is the final truth.

CW 5: Grace and Grit, 432–435

"Those who do in fact respond to the call of a greater tomorrow; those for whom integral culture has a deeply heartfelt ring; those in whom Spirit shines in such a way as to wish liberation for all sentient beings; those upon whom the light of the infinite is made to blaze in many hues; to whom the wind whispers tales of an all-embracing current running wildly through the Kosmos, a light that mysteriously casts no shadows in the hearts of those who see it; to all of those truly integral souls: carry your blistering vision forward, build soaring bridges where others dug moats, symphonically connect the previously unconnected, courageously pull together the ragged fragments that you find lying all around you, and we might yet live to see the day when alienation has lost its meaning, discord makes no sense, and the radiant Spirit of our own integral embrace shines freely throughout the Kosmos, announcing the home of our own awakened souls, the abode of a destiny you have always sought and finally, gloriously found."

Boomeritis, 424–425

5

Passionate Philosophy

In the following selections, Wilber as spiritual philosopher engages the most learned academics and enlightened sages by weaving humanity's intellectual and spiritual history into a grand integral tapestry. As a result of being inundated with technical terms from countless academic disciplines, Wilber has created a common language through which all subject areas can communicate with each other. Though this new integral vocabulary may not be familiar at first, it soon serves as a language of connectivity, bridging disciplines through a simple and skillful means of discourse. His philosophical writing is far from a dry exercise. Passion leaps off each page, joy paints vivid linguistic murals, compassion tenderly permeates each idea—even the critiques. At its best, passionate philosophy is not merely an intellectual transmission from one mind to another. Rather, it shakes the very core of your being.

Never does Wilber shy away from the humanity behind the thoughts—both the darkest shadows of our animal nature and the brilliant light of our divine potential. The world's collective knowledge—at all levels of depth—is included and expressed through the lens of vision-logic, which recognizes the holistic patterns and core links that fuel the integral vision. A philosophical adrenaline rush comes from discovering an utterly stunning unity within an ocean of diversity.

To have any meaning at all, philosophy must sizzle with passion, boil your brain, fry your eyeballs, or you're just not doing it right. And that applies to the other end of the spectrum of feelings as well. Real philosophy is as gentle as fog and as quiet as tears; it holds the world as if it were a delicate infant, raw and open and vulnerable. I sincerely hope that if I have brought anything to this field, it is a bit of passion. . . .

The one thing I do know, and that I would like to emphasize, is that any integral theory is just that—a mere theory. I am always surprised, or rather shocked, at the common perception that I am recommending an intellectual approach to spirituality, when that is the opposite of my view. Just because an author writes, say, a history of dancing, does not mean that the author is advocating that people stop dancing and merely read about it instead. I have written academic treatises that cover areas such as spirituality and its relation to a larger scheme of things, but my recommendation is always that people take up an actual spiritual practice, rather than merely read about it. An integral approach to dancing says, take up dancing itself, and sure, read a book about it, too. Do both, but in any event, don't merely read the book. That's like taking a vacation to Bermuda by sitting at home and looking through a book of maps. My books are maps, but please, go to Bermuda and see for yourself.

See for yourself if, in the depths of your own awareness, right here and now, you can find the entire Kosmos, because that is where it resides. Birds are singing—in your awareness. Ocean waves are crashing—in your awareness. Clouds are floating by—in the sky of your own awareness. What is this awareness of yours, that holds the entire universe in its embrace and knows the secrets even of God? In the still point of the turning world, in the secret center of the known universe, in the eyes of the very one reading this page, at the very source of thought itself, watch the entire Kosmos emerge, dancing wildly with a passion philosophy tries to capture, crowned with a glory and sealed with a wonder lovers seek to share, rushing through a radiant world of time that is but eternity's bid to be seen: what is this Self of yours?

An integral approach is merely an attempt to categorize, in conceptual terms, some of this glory as it manifests itself. But it is no more than that. Every one of my books has at least one sentence, usually buried, that says the following (this is the version found in *The Atman Project*): "There follows, then, the story of the Atman project. It is a sharing of what I have seen; it is a small offering of what I have remembered; it is also the Zen dust you should shake from your sandals; and it is finally a lie in the face of that Mystery which only alone is."

In other words, all of my books are lies. They are simply maps of a territory, shadows of a reality, gray symbols dragging their bellies across the dead page, suffocated signs full of muffled sound and faded glory, signifying absolutely nothing. And it is the nothing, the Mystery, the Emptiness alone that needs to be realized: not known but felt, not thought but breathed, not an object but an atmosphere, not a lesson but a life.

. . . Please use [maps] only as a reminder to take up dancing itself, to inquire into this Self of yours, this Self that holds this page and this Kosmos all in a single glance. And then express that glory in integral maps, and sing with passion of the sights you have seen, the sounds that the tender Heart has whispered only to you in the late hours of the quiet night, and come and join us and tell us what you have heard, in your own trip to Bermuda, in the vibrant Silence that you alone own, and the radiant Heart that we alone, together, can discover.

Foreword to *Ken Wilber: Thought as Passion* by Frank Visser, pp. xii–xv.

Men and women, as the Christian mystics are fond of saying, have (at least) three eyes of knowing: the eye of flesh, which apprehends physical events; the eye of mind, which apprehends images and desires and concepts and ideas; and the eye of contemplation, which apprehends spiritual experiences and states. And that, of course, is a simplified version of the spectrum of consciousness, reaching from body to mind to spirit.

cw 7: *The Eye of Spirit,* 447

So just as a knife cannot cut itself, the universe cannot totally see itself as an object without totally mutilating itself. The attempt to know the universe as an object of knowledge is thus profoundly and inextricably contradictory; and the more it seems to succeed, the more it actually fails, the more the universe becomes "false to itself." And yet oddly enough, this type of dualistic knowledge, wherein the universe is severed into subject vs. object (as well as truth vs. falsity, good vs. evil, etc.) is the very cornerstone of most Western philosophy, theology, and science. For Western philosophy is, by and large, Greek philosophy, and Greek philosophy is the philosophy of dualisms. Most of the great philosophical topics still debated today were created and molded by the philosophers of ancient Greece. These include the dualisms of truth vs. falsity, whose study is termed "logic"; that of good vs. evil, called "ethics"; and that of appearance vs. reality, named "epistemology." The Greeks also initiated the widescale study of "ontology," the examination of the ultimate nature or being of the universe, and their early inquiries centered around the dualisms of the one vs. the many, chaos vs. order, simplicity vs. complexity. Rutted firmly in these dualisms, Western thought throughout its history has continued to generate those of its own: instinct vs. intellect, wave vs. particle, positivism vs. idealism, matter vs. energy, thesis vs. antithesis, mind vs. body, behaviorism vs. vitalism, fate vs. free-will, space vs. time—the list is endless. Thus did Whitehead state that Western philosophy is an elaborate footnote to Plato.

This is indeed odd, for if dualistic knowledge is at root as contradictory as trying to make your finger touch its own tip or your foot step on itself, why wasn't it abandoned long ago, why did it exert such a pervasive influence throughout the course of European thought, why does it still dominate—in one subtle form or another— the major branches of Western intellection today? Unfortunately, to search the history of *mainstream* Western thought for a credible solution to the problem of dualism is only to come as close as possible to death from boredom.

CW 1: *The Spectrum of Consciousness*, 64–65

All in all, I think we can fairly conclude that each chakra represents both an appropriate center in the body and a particular stage in a type of spiritual growth. I say "type of spiritual growth" because there is much evidence in the orthodox traditions themselves (especially Tibetan Buddhism) that suggests that kundalini yoga is a valid but partial approach to even the energetics of higher consciousness, tending to ignore—with its exclusive emphasis on the ascending kundalini current—the equally important "descending" currents. Further, even the Hindu generally concedes that, except at its very summit, kundalini shakti is a phenomenon of the subtle body only. Hatha yoga addresses the gross body, and kundalini the subtle body, but it is jnana yoga that deals with the underlying reality of the causal body. Jnana yoga of Vedanta, Dzogchen and mahamudra of Vajrayana, chih-kuan and shikantaza of Zen—these simply investigate, through present awareness, any knot that arises in consciousness, and, finding it void of self-nature, are relieved of the burden of untying it.

Thus we return to the paradox with which we began this article—the chakras *do* appear to exist, and the chakras *are* knots. But the knots are illusory. Nothing binds us from the very start, but until we understand this, everything appears to. Nevertheless, kundalini theory, with its penetrating understanding of these shadowy knots themselves, offers sound, wise, and powerful advice on how to see through them, so that one may finally awaken, as if from a dream, to discover that the cosmos is one's body, and the sun one's solar self.

cw 1: "Are the Chakras Real?," 425–426

When the universe as a whole seeks to know itself, through the medium of the human mind, some aspects of that universe must remain unknown. With the awakening of the symbolic knowledge there *seems* to arise a split in the universe between the knower and the known, the thinker and the thought, *the subject and the object*; and our innermost consciousness, as knower and investigator of the external world, ultimately escapes its own grasp and remains as the Unknown, Unshown, and Ungraspable, much as your hand can grasp numerous objects but never itself, or your eye can see the world but not itself.

cw 1: *The Spectrum of Consciousness*, 63

The ultimate metaphysical secret, if we dare state it so simply, is that there are no boundaries in the universe. Boundaries are illusions, products not of reality but of the way we map and edit reality. And while it is fine to map out the territory, it is fatal to confuse the two.

cw 1: *No Boundary*, 462

At any rate, while I am encouraged by the glimmerings of a New Age, I conclude with a sober appraisal: we are nowhere near the Millennium. In fact, at this point in history, the most radical, pervasive, and earth-shaking transformation would occur simply if everybody truly evolved to a mature, rational, and responsible ego, capable of freely participating in the open exchange of mutual self-esteem. *There* is the "edge of history." There would be a *real* New Age. We are nowhere near the stage "beyond reason," simply because we are nowhere yet near universal reason itself.

CW 2: Up from Eden, 654–655

But look at all that the soul has passed through *in order* to be born! From the ultimate Oneness, the clear light of the omnipresent Dharmakaya, through the subtle Sambhogakaya, the divine and illuminative bliss, through the gross-reflecting mental realm of the Sidpa stage, and then into the gross body and pleromatic rebirth. Through all of that. And the individual *was* all of that. In the Bardo experience, she started out as God and ended up as typhon. And she can't remember a single thing that happened In Between. . . .

CW 2: The Atman Project, 264

In short, we cannot perceive our Self. And yet exactly here is the problem, the genesis of the Primary Dualism, for we *imagine* that we do see and know our Self, not realizing that whatever we see and know is a complex of perceived objects and thus could not be our Self—as Huang Po put it, "the perceived cannot perceive." . . .

But we do not realize this, although it is so obvious—or perhaps *because* it is so obvious. We cannot hear the hearer, smell the smeller, feel the feeler, touch the toucher, taste the taster—similarly, we cannot see the seer. But we *think* we can—just that is the problem, and just that is the genesis of the Primary Dualism.

This is what happens: the Seer, the THAT IN YOU WHICH KNOWS, in actuality is not separate from what it sees—it *is* what it sees, for the knower sees a thing by being that thing; as Saint Thomas Aquinas stated, "Knowledge comes about in so far as the object known is within the knower." This page, for instance, is identical to that in you which is reading it, or as William James expressed it, "The paper seen and the seeing of it are only two names for one indivisible fact." This is not to say that the page, the supposed object of our perception, doesn't exist in some sense (so that if I close my eyes the page actually vanishes off the face of the earth), only that *it does not exist as an object "out there."* Between Seer and page, subject and object: no gap, no distance, no space!

Because we suppose, however, that we can see the Seer, as when we say "I know who I am!" or "I am perfectly aware of myself!"—just because of this supposition that I now can see and know the Seer, we consequently and very naturally feel that this "seer" of which we are supposedly aware must reside "within" us, as Wittgenstein bluntly put it, "What is troubling us is the tendency to believe that the mind is a little man within." Thus it appears that this "seer," my "self," is separate from what it sees, and that is the Primary Dualism.

To put it another way, in imagining that we really do see the Seer, or know our Self as an object, we apparently (i.e., illusorily) turn our subjectivity into an object, called "self," which is a complex of (objective) ideas, feelings, identities, valuations, and so on. We mistake that complex of objects for Subjectivity, *we mistake what we can see for that which is doing the seeing*, not realizing that Subjectivity is never an object except in illusion, as when you see your eye you have cataracts. Our "self," our "ego," is not even a real subject. Because we can see and know it objectively, this "subject" is a pseudo-subject and this self is a pseudo-self, a pure case of mistaken identity. Identified with this pseudo-subject, all other objects seem separate from me—thus, the Primary Dualism. . . .

Put simply, that in you right now which knows, which sees, which reads this page—that is the Godhead, Mind, Brahman, and it cannot be seen or known as an object, just as an eye cannot see itself. Whatever you know about your "self" is an object; whatever you see, think, and feel about your "self"—that is a complex of perceived objects, the "ego." What is seen is the ego; what is doing the seeing is Mind. We have inadvertently identified with the former, with what can be seen, with the ego, or centaur, or persona, etc., and hence we are no longer identified with all phenomenal manifestation, we are separated from all that appears to be not-self.

cw 1: *The Spectrum of Consciousness*, 332–334

What one is attempting to "destroy" in contemplation *is not the mind but an exclusive identity of consciousness with the mind.*

cw 3: *A Sociable God*, 107

The "level" of Mind is in no way buried or hidden in the obscure depths of our psyche—on the contrary, the level of Mind is our present and ordinary state of consciousness, for, being infinite and absolutely all-inclusive, it is compatible with every imaginable level or state of consciousness. That is, the "no-level" of Mind cannot be a particular level set apart from other levels, for that would impose a spatial limitation on Mind. Mind is rather the all-inclusive dimensionless reality of which each level represents an illusory deviation. Now this must be emphasized—our present, everyday state of consciousness, whatever it may be, sad, happy, depressed, ecstatic, agitated, calm, worried or afraid—just that, just as it is, is the Level of Mind. Brahman is not a particular experience, level of consciousness or state of soul—rather it is precisely whatever level you happen to have now and realizing this confers upon one a profound center of peace that underlies and persists throughout the worst depressions, anxieties, and fears. Even though our scholarship in the field of pure mysticism, East and Western alike, has dramatically improved over the past few decades, there are those who continue to distort its "doctrines" in all manner of idiotic ways, claiming mystics are otherworldly, totally out of touch with everyday reality (whatever that means), self-centered, constantly immersed in trance, and so on. This tells us nothing about mystics but quite a bit about the ignorance of those who subscribe to such incredible views; and, furthermore, it completely overlooks the sayings of the great masters of every tradition that "your everyday and ordinary consciousness, that is the Tao."

To be sure, some mystics historically have led the secluded and self-absorbing life of a hermit, but this is a matter of personal style and not all to be confused with mysticism per se, any more than the life style of Rasputin is to be confused with Christianity per se. For, in fact, the highest ideal of the mystic is that expressed by the Bodhisattva, who in Mahayana Buddhism is one who sees the Godhead everywhere and everywhen, in every person, place, and thing, and thus does not have to retire into solitude and trance in order to find "god." The Bodhisattva's mystic vision is identical with whatever she happens to be doing at the moment, and whether that be dancing, working, crying, laughing, or intensely suffering, she knows that fundamentally "All shall be well, and all shall be well, and all manner of thing shall be well," for, as Hakuin put it, "This very earth is the Lotus Land of Purity; And this body is the body of Buddha."

Now precisely because Mind is everywhere and everywhen, because it is always already the case, there is no possibility or even meaning in "trying to find It" or in "trying to reach It," for that would imply a movement from a place where Mind is absent to a place where it is present—but there is no place where it is absent. Mind, being everywhere present, abides in no particular place where we can finally grab it. The no-level of Mind, therefore, we can never attain. But then, neither can we escape it.

cw 1: *The Spectrum of Consciousness*, 326–327

Philosophy cannot reach God—at most it can posit God morally (practically).

cw 3: *Eye to Eye*, 170

Q: Do you think the "final paradigm" is actually "final"? Do you think this realization, the realization of the sages, do you think that this is unchanging and forever invariant?

KW: No, not like that. Hegel actually went from thinking that "enlightenment" was an end state, a final product, to seeing it as an eternal process. The great Japanese meditation master, Dogen Zenji, had probably the greatest line ever on spiritual development. It manages to pack virtually everything you can say about spiritual development into four lines. Dogen said, "To study Buddhism"— but I'm going to take the liberty of changing the word "Buddhism" to "mysticism," because that is what it really refers to—"To study mysticism is to study the self. To study the self is to forget the self. To forget the self is to be one with all things. To be one with all things is to be enlightened by all things, and this traceless enlightenment continues forever."

In other words, enlightenment is a process, not an end state, not a product. It goes on forever. . . . "And this traceless enlightenment continues forever. . . . " That is the testimony, the confession of the world's great sages. And in that sense, and that sense only, you have the final paradigm, which continues forever as a process. . . . And it does not involve some sort of New Age hoopla and narcissism and me-ness and oh-boy. It involves "wu-shih" . . . nobody special. Nobody special . . . you see?

cw 4: "Paradigm Wars," 194–195

God ceases to be a mere symbol in your awareness but becomes the crowning level of your own compound individuality and structural adaptation, the integral of all possible societies, which you now recognize as your own true self.

CW 3: *A Sociable God*, 129–130

The mystical experience is indeed ineffable, or not capable of being entirely put into words; like any experience—a sunset, eating a piece of cake, listening to Bach's music—one has to have the actual experience to see what it's like. We don't conclude, however, that sunset, cake, and music therefore don't exist or aren't valid. Further, even though the mystical experience is largely ineffable, it *can* be communicated or transmitted, namely, by taking up spiritual practice under the guidance of a spiritual master or teacher (much as judo can be taught but not spoken; as Wittgenstein would have it, the mystical "can be shown but not said").

CW 4: "Two Humanistic Psychologies?," 227

Philosophically, we are going to have to face and acknowledge the fact that rational-mental statements about Spirit or Being always eventually degenerate in contradictions or paradoxes.

CW 3: *Eye to Eye*, 221

Every form of meditation is basically a way to transcend the ego, or die to the ego. In that sense, meditation mimics death—that is, death of the ego. If one progresses fairly well in *any* meditation system, one eventually comes to a point of having so exhaustively "witnessed" the mind and body that one actually rises above, or transcends, the mind and body, thus "dying" to them, to the ego, and awakening as subtle soul or even spirit. And this is actually experienced as a death. In Zen it is called the Great Death. It can be a fairly easy experience, a relatively peaceful transcendence of subject-object dualism, or— because it is a real death of sorts—it can also be terrifying. But subtly or dramatically, quickly or slowly, the sense of being a separate self dies, or is dissolved, and one finds a prior and higher identity in and as universal spirit.

CW 4: "Death, Rebirth, and Meditation," 352

The dichotomy between experience and construction is a false dichotomy. It is not that there is experience on the one hand and contextual molding on the other. *Every* experience *is* a context; every experience, even simple sensory experience, is always already situated, is always already a context, is always already a holon. When Derrida says that "nothing is ever simply present," this is true of every holon. As Whitehead would have it, every holon is already a prehensive unification of its entire actual universe: nothing is ever simply present (this is also very similar to the Eastern notion of karma, or the past enfolded in the present). Everything is always already *a* context *in* a context.

And thus, every holon—and therefore every experience—is always already situated, mediated, contextual. It is not that "original experiences" arrive to be reworked by mental concepts; the original experiences are not original, but a contextual prehensive mediation of boundless contexts. That mind *further* contextualizes sensory contexts is neither new nor avoidable.

Everything (every holon) is a mediated context, but contexts touch *immediately*. It does not require "mystical pure consciousness" to be in immediate contact with the data of experience. When any point in the mediated chain is known (or experienced), that knowing or prehending is an *immediate* event in itself, an immediate "touching." The touching is not a touching of something merely present but rather is itself pure Presence (or prehension). If there were *only* a mere mediation forever, then nothing would or could ever be known or experienced; there would be nothing to stop the sliding chain from spinning contextually forever (there is no point that it *could* enter consciousness).

But in any moment of prehension/experience (and in any domain—sensory, mental, spiritual), there is *immediate* apprehension of what is given at the moment, and *that* immediate apprehension is the datum (which William James correctly defined as the given pure experience), and *that* experiential prehension is *pure* in the sense that when contexts touch, they touch without further mediation (even if they are always already situated in and as mediated contexts).

At the moment of touch, there is no mediation; if there is mediation, there is no touching. To say everything is *merely* mediated is simply a fancy modern twist on pure skepticism, which is profoundly self-contradictory (it says, "I have an unshakeable foundation belief that foundations are not possible," which simply allows the skeptic to trash everybody else's beliefs while conveniently leaving his own unexamined).

At the moment of touch, in any domain, there is no mediation, only prehension. This is why knowledge (and experience) of any sort is possible in the first place. That there is a "first place" means that mediation *has stopped* at some point (the point of touching). This is why when experience occurs in any domain (sensory, mental, spiritual), it is simply given, it is simply the case, it simply shows up, even though the experienced and the experiencer are forever situated and contextual. I find myself in *immediate* experience of *mediated* worlds. (And that Immediacy, that pure Presence, that touching, is, as we will see, one way to view Spirit: *immediateness* is Spirit's prehension *of* the world—and what is prehended is Spirit *in* the world contextually.)

In short, experience is immediate prehension of whatever mediated contexts are given, and that is why all experience is *both* pure (immediate) and contextual (capable of being refined and recontextualized *indefinitely*). As we will see, this is why Habermas maintains that all validity claims have both an *immanent* (culture-bound) and a *transcendent* (pure) component, and it is the transcendent component that allows intersubjective communication and learning to occur in the first place.

CW 6: *Sex, Ecology, Spirituality*, 627–628

Satori is a "direct seeing into one's nature"—as perfectly direct as looking into the microscope to see the cell nucleus, with the important proviso in each case: only a trained eye need look.

CW 3: *A Sociable God*, 129

As for the Abyss itself, or pure Emptiness, it is indeed pure identity, and that is why I often refer to the "theosphere" as being translinguistic: as consciousness approaches unmanifest absorption, all contexts—all holons—are temporarily suspended or temporarily dissolved (there is then only pure Immediacy or pure Presence, the *same* pure Presence that apprehends mediated contexts when they are present); but even that "experience," contentless itself, awakens to find itself situated in a cultural context that will partially provide interpretations, but will not totally determine the experience, or else the experience could never surprise anybody, and it surprises everybody.

cw 6: *Sex, Ecology, Spirituality*, 632

The answer to the relation of the Absolute and the relative is therefore most definitely *not*: the Absolute created the world. It most definitely is *not*: the world is illusory and the Absolute alone is real. It is *not*: we perceive only the phenomenal reflection of a noumenal reality. It is *not*: fate and free will are two aspects of one and the same process. It is *not*: all things and events are different aspects of a single interwoven web-of-life. It is *not*: the body alone is real and the mind is a reflection of that only reality. It is *not*: mind and body are two different aspects of the total organism. It is *not*: mind emerges from hierarchical brain structure. In fact, it is not even: noumenon and phenomena are not-two and nondual.

Those are all merely *intellectual symbols* that purport to give the answer, but the real answer does not lie in sensibilia or intelligibilia, it lies in transcendelia, and that domain only discloses itself after the meditative exemplar is engaged, whereupon every single one of those intellectual answers is seen to be inadequate and off the mark; each generates nothing but more insolvable and insuperable difficulties, dilemmas, and contradictions. The answer is not more talk; the answer is satori, by whatever name we wish to use to convey valid contemplative awareness.

And, much more to the point, even if this answer could be stated in words—and in fact, the answer can be stated in words, because Zen masters talk about it all the time!—nonetheless, it would make no sense to anybody who had not also performed the injunction, just as mathematical symbols can be seen by anybody but understood only by those who have completed the training.

But open the eye of contemplation, and the answer is as obvious, as perfect, as unmistakable as the play of sunlight on a crystal clear pond, early on a cool spring morning.

You see, that was the answer.

cw 7: *The Eye of Spirit*, 501

What is important is not my particular version of an integral view, but rather that we all begin to enter into this extraordinary dialogue about the possibility of an integral approach in general, an approach that—we can say this in several different ways—integrates the hard-headed with the soft-hearted, the natural sciences with the noetic sciences, objective realities with subjective realities, the empirical with the transcendental.

And so let us hope that a decade from now somebody might spot a great mega-trend in consciousness studies—namely, the truly integral—and let it start right now with all of us who share this concern for holism, for embrace, for synthesizing, for integrating: let this outreach start with us, right here, right now.

Is a genuinely integral theory of consciousness even possible? Well, that would be my question to you all, and that would be my challenge. How big is our umbrella? How wide and how deep can we throw our net of good will? How many voices will we allow in this chorus of consciousness? How many faces of the Divine will smile on our endeavor? How many colors will we genuinely acknowledge in our rainbow coalition?

And when we pause from all this research, and put theory temporarily to rest, and when we relax into the primordial ground of our own intrinsic awareness, what will we find therein? When the joy of the robin sings on a clear morning dawn, where is our consciousness then? When the sunlight beams from the glory of a snow-capped mountain, where is consciousness then? In the place that time forgot, in this eternal moment without date or duration, in the secret cave of the heart where time touches eternity and space cries out for infinity, when the raindrop pulses on the temple roof, and announces the beauty of the Divine with every single beat, when the moonlight reflects in a simple dewdrop to remind us who and what we are, and when in the entire universe there is nothing but the sound of a lonely waterfall somewhere in the mists gently calling your name—where is consciousness then?

CW 8: *One Taste*, 376

Does the group allow free and rational inquiry into its teaching? Or does it discourage or even prevent critical analysis of its own tenets? Does it allow or encourage comparison and assessment of its methods and teachings with those of other paths, not as propaganda but as free inquiry?

Spiritual Choices, 248

You know the Zen koan, "What is the sound of one hand clapping?" Usually, of course, we need two hands to clap—and that is the structure of typical experience. We have a sense of ourselves as a subject in here, and the world as an object out there. We have these "two hands" of experience, the subject and the object. And typical experience is a smashing of these two hands together to make a commotion, a sound. The object out there smashes into me as a subject, and I have an experience—the two hands clap together and experience emerges.

And so the typical structure of experience is like a punch in the face. The ordinary self is the battered self—it is utterly battered by the universe "out there." The ordinary self is a series of bruises, of scars, the results of these two hands of experience smashing together. This bruising is called "duhkha," suffering. As Krishnamurti used to say, in that gap between the subject and the object lies the entire misery of humankind.

But with the nondual state, suddenly there are not two hands. Suddenly, the subject and the object are one hand. Suddenly, there is nothing outside of you to smash into you, bruise you, torment you. Suddenly, you do not *have* an experience, you *are* every experience that arises, and so you are instantly released into all space: you and the entire Kosmos are one hand, one experience, one display, one gesture of great perfection. There is nothing outside of you that you can want, or desire, or seek, or grasp—your soul expands to the corners of the universe and embraces all with infinite delight. You are utterly Full, utterly Saturated, so full and saturated that the boundaries to the Kosmos completely explode and leave you without date or duration, time or location, awash in an ocean of infinite care. You are released into the All, as the All—you are the self-seen radiant Kosmos, you are the universe of One Taste, and the taste is utterly infinite.

So what is the sound of that one hand clapping? What is the taste of that One Taste? When there is *nothing outside of you* that can hit you, hurt you, push you, pull you—what is the sound of that one hand clapping?

See the sunlight on the mountains? Feel the cool breeze? What is not utterly obvious? Who is not already enlightened? As a Zen Master put it, "When I heard the sound of the bell ringing, there was no I, and no bell, just the ringing." There is no twiceness, no twoness, in immediate experience! No inside and no outside, no subject and no object—just immediate awareness itself, the sound of one hand clapping.

So you are not in here, on this side of a transparent window, looking at the Kosmos out there. The transparent window has shattered, your bodymind drops, you are free of that confinement forever, you are no longer "behind your face" looking at the Kosmos—you simply are the Kosmos. You *are* all that. Which is precisely why you can swallow the Kosmos and span the centuries, and nothing moves at all. The sound of this one hand clapping is the sound the Big Bang made. It is the sound of supernovas exploding in space. It is the sound of the robin singing. It is the sound of a waterfall on a crystal-clear day. It is the sound of the entire manifest universe—and you are that sound.

CW 7: *A Brief History of Everything*, 259–261

The evidence for this Great Spectrum [of consciousness] is grounded at every point in *direct experience* that can be confirmed or rejected by any who adequately follow the interior experiments in consciousness. These experiments, generally known as meditation or contemplation, cannot be dismissed on the ground that they are "merely subjective" or "interior" apprehensions—after all, mathematics is "merely subjective" and "interior," but we don't dismiss that as unreal or illusory or meaningless. Just so, the contemplative sciences have amassed an extraordinary amount of phenomenological data— direct experiences—relating to the subtle and causal, or soul and spirit, levels. And if you want to know if this data is real, all you have to do is follow the experiment—contemplation—and see for yourself. Of those who adequately do so, the majority report a simple conclusion: you are directly introduced to your True Self, your Real Condition, your Original Face, and it is none other than Spirit itself.

CW 8: *One Taste*, 319

The totality of all manifestation at any time—the All—subsists in the low causal, as the sum total of the consequent and primordial nature of Spirit (in roughly Whitehead's sense), and this Totality is the *manifest* omega pull on each individual and finite thing: as such, it is ever-receding: each new moment has a new total horizon that can never be reached or fulfilled, because the moment of fulfillment itself creates a new whole of which the previous whole is now a part: cascading whole/parts all the way up, holons endlessly self-transcending and thus never finally self-fulfilled: rushing forward ceaselessly in time attempting to find the timeless.

And the *final* Omega, the *ultimate* and *unmanifest* Omega, the causal Formless, is the magnet *on the other side* of the horizon, which never itself enters the world of Form as a singularity or as a totality (or any other phenomenal event), and thus is never found at all in any version of manifestation, even though all manifestation will rest nowhere short of this infinite Emptiness.

Thus, from any angle, there is no ultimate Omega to be found in the world of Form. There is no Perfection in the manifest world. Were the world of Form to find Perfection and utter fulfillment, there would be nothing else for it to do and nowhere else for it to go: nothing further to want, to desire, to seek, to find: the entire world would cease its search, stop its drive, end its very movement: would become without motion, time, or space: would become the Formless. But the Formless is already there, on the other side of the horizon, which is to say, the Formless is already there as the deepest depth of this and every moment.

This Deepest Depth is the desire of all Form, which cannot itself be reached in the world of Form, but rather is the Emptiness of each and every Form: when all Forms are seen to be always already Formless, then dawns the Nondual empty Ground that is the Suchness and the Thusness of each and every display. The entire world of Form is always already Perfectly Empty, always already in the ever-present Condition of all conditions, always already the ultimate Omega that is not the goal of each and every thing but the Suchness of each and every thing: *just this*. The search is always already over, and Forms continue their eternal play as a gesture of the Divine, not seeking Spirit but expressing Spirit in their every move and motion.

cw 6: *Sex, Ecology, Spirituality*, 655

The conclusion seems obvious: when the eye of contemplation is abandoned, religion is left only with the eye of mind—where it is sliced to shreds by modern philosophy—and the eye of flesh—where it is crucified by modern science. If religion possesses something that is *uniquely* its own, it is contemplation. Moreover, it is the eye of contemplation, adequately employed, that follows all three strands of valid knowing. Thus religion's great, enduring, and unique strength is that, at its core, *it is a science of spiritual experience* (using "science" in the broad sense as direct experience, in any domain, that submits to the three strands of injunctions, data, and confirmation).

CW 8: *The Marriage of Sense and Soul*, 229

Consciousness as Such is released in Perfect Transcendence, which is not a transcendence from the world but a final transcendence as the World. Consciousness henceforth *operates*, not on the world, but only as the entire World Process, integrating and interpenetrating all levels, realms, and planes, high or low, sacred or profane.

CW 3: *Eye to Eye*, 242

And where the moons of Jupiter can be disclosed by the eye of flesh or its extensions (sensory data), and the Pythagorean theorem can be disclosed by the eye of mind and its inward apprehensions (mental data), the nature of Spirit can be disclosed only by the *eye of contemplation* and its directly disclosed referents: the direct experiences, apprehensions, and data of the spiritual domain.

CW 8: *The Marriage of Sense and Soul*, 230

As attention is progressively freed from the outer world of the external environment and the inner world of the bodymind, awareness starts to transcend the subject/object duality altogether. The illusory world of duality starts to appear as it is in reality—namely, as nothing but a manifestation of Spirit itself. The outer world starts to look divine, the inner world starts to look divine. That is, consciousness itself starts to become luminous, light-filled, numinous, and it seems to directly touch, even unite with, Divinity itself.

This is the path of the saints. Notice how saints, in both the East and West, are usually depicted with halos of light around their heads? That is often symbolic of the inner Light of the illumined and intuitive mind. At the psychic level you start to commune with Divinity or Spirit. But at the subtle, you find a union with Spirit, the *unio mystica*. Not just communion, union.

[In the causal, the] process is complete, the soul or pure Witness dissolves in its Source, and the *union* with God gives way to an identity with Godhead, or the unmanifest Ground of all beings. This is what the Sufis call the Supreme Identity. You have realized your fundamental identity with the Condition of all conditions and the Nature of all natures and the Being of all beings. Since Spirit is the suchness or condition of all things, it is perfectly compatible with all things. It is even nothing special. It is chop wood, carry water. For this reason, individuals who reach this stage are often depicted as very ordinary people, nothing special about them. This is the path of sages, of the wise men and women who are so wise you can't even spot it. They fit in, and go about their business. In the Ten Zen Ox Herding Pictures, which depict the stages on the path to enlightenment, the very last picture shows an ordinary person entering the marketplace. The caption says: They enter the marketplace with open hands. That's all it says.

cw 5: *Grace and Grit*, 228

Godhead as nondual Suchness (as opposed to unmanifest Source and Goal) is neither manifest nor unmanifest; it is as fully present in the lowest holon as in the highest holon, and in any manifest or unmanifest state, as the isness or suchness of any phenomenon.

cw 6: *Sex, Ecology, Spirituality*, 646–647

In your own being, the small self must die so that the big Self may resurrect.

This death and new Birth is described in several different terms by the traditions. In Christianity, of course, it finds its prototype in the figures of Adam and Jesus—Adam, whom the mystics call the "Old Man" or "Outer Man," is said to have opened the gates of Hell, while Jesus Christ, the "New Man" or "Inner Man," opens the gates of Paradise. Specifically, Jesus' own death and resurrection, according to the mystics, is the archetype of the death of the separate self and the resurrection of a new and eternal destiny from the stream of consciousness, namely, the divine or Christic Self and its Ascension. As Saint Augustine said, "God became man so that man may become God." This process of turning from "manhood" to "Godhood," or from the outer person to the inner person, or from the self to the Self, is known in Christianity as *metanoia*, which means both "repentance" and "transformation"—we repent of the self (or sin) and transform as the Self (or Christ), so that . . . "not I but Christ liveth in me." Similarly, Islam views this death-and-resurrection as both *tawbah*, which means "repentance," and *galb*, which means "transformation," both of which are summarized in al-Bistami's succinct phrase, "Forgetfulness of self is remembrance of God."

In both Hinduism and Buddhism, this death-and-resurrection is always described as the death of the individual soul (*jivatman*) and the reawakening of one's true nature, which metaphorically the Hindus describe as All-Being (*Brahman*) and the Buddhists as Pure Openness (*shunyata*). The actual moment of rebirth or breakthrough is known as enlightenment or liberation (*moksha* or *bodhi*). The *Lankavatara Sutra* describes this enlightenment experience as a "complete turning about in the deepest seat of consciousness." This "turning about" is simply the undoing of the habitual tendency to create a separate and substantial self where there is in fact only vast, open, clear awareness. This turning about or metanoia, Zen calls *satori* or *kensho*. "Ken" means true nature and "sho" means "directly seeing." Directly seeing one's true nature is becoming Buddha. As Meister Eckhart put it, "In this breaking through I find that God and I are both the same."

cw 5: *Grace and Grit*, 102–103

In the West, since Kant—and since the differentiations of modernity—religion (and metaphysics in general) has fallen on hard times. I maintain that it has done so precisely because it attempted to do with the eye of mind that which can be done only with the eye of contemplation. Because the mind could not actually deliver the metaphysical goods, and yet kept loudly claiming that it could, somebody was bound to blow the whistle and demand real evidence. Kant made the demand, and metaphysics collapsed—and rightly so, in its typical form.

Neither sensory empiricism, nor pure reason, nor practical reason, nor any combination thereof can see into the realm of Spirit. In the smoking ruins left by Kant, the only possible conclusion is that all future metaphysics and *authentic spirituality* must offer *direct experiential evidence*. And that means, in addition to sensory experience and its empiricism (scientific and pragmatic) and *mental experience* and its rationalism (pure and practical), there must be added *spiritual experience* and its mysticism (spiritual practice and its experiential data).

The possibility of the direct apprehension of sensory experience, mental experience, and spiritual experience radically defuses the Kantian objections and sets the knowledge quest firmly on the road of evidence, with each of its truth claims guided by the three strands of all valid knowledge (injunction, apprehension, confirmation; or exemplars, data, falsifiability) *applied at every level* (sensory, mental, spiritual—or across the entire spectrum of consciousness, however many levels we wish to invoke). Guided by the three strands, the truth claims of real science and real religion can indeed be redeemed. They carry cash value. And the cash is experiential evidence, sensory to mental to spiritual.

With this approach, religion regains its proper warrant, which is not sensory or mythic or mental but finally contemplative. The great and secret message of the experimental mystics the world over is that, with the eye of contemplation, Spirit can be seen. With the eye of contemplation, God can be seen. With the eye of contemplation, the great Within radiantly unfolds.

And in all cases, the eye with which you see God is the same eye with which God sees you: the eye of contemplation.

cw 8: *The Marriage of Sense and Soul*, 233

Arrayed against these naturalistic and empirical approaches are those that start with the immediacy of consciousness itself—let us call them the "interior" or the "introspection and interpretation" approaches. These approaches do not deny the importance of empirical or objectivist data, but they point out, as William James did, that the definition of the word "data" is "direct experience," and the only genuinely direct experience each of us has is his or her own immediate and interior experience. The primordial data, in other words, is that of consciousness, of intentionality, of immediate lived awareness, and all else, from the existence of electrons to the existence of neuronal pathways, are deductions away from immediate lived awareness. These secondary deductions may be very true and very important, but they are, and will always remain, secondary and derivative to the primary fact of immediate experience.

cw 7: *The Eye of Spirit*, 423–424

Genuine spirituality, we will see, is primarily a measure of depth and a disclosure of depth. There is *more* spirituality in reason's *denial* of

God than there is in myth's *affirmation* of God, precisely because there is *more depth*. (And the transrational, in turn, discloses yet more depth, yet more Spirit, than either myth or reason).

But the very *depth* of reason, its capacity for universal-pluralism, its insistence on universal tolerance, its grasp of global-planetary perspectivism, its insistence on universal benevolence and compassion: these are the manifestations of its genuine depth, its *genuine* spirituality. These capacities are not *revealed* to reason from *without* (by a mythic source); they issue from *within* its own structure, its own *inherent* depth (which is why it does not need recourse to a mythic god to implement its agenda of universal benevolence, why even an "atheist" acting from rational-universal compassion is more spiritual than a fundamentalist acting to convert the universe in the name of a mythic-membership god). That the Spirit of reason does not fly through the sky hurling thunderbolts and otherwise spend its time turning spinach into potatoes speaks more, not less, on its behalf.

cw 6: *Sex, Ecology, Spirituality,* 259

In this Theory of Everything, I have one major rule: *Everybody* is right. More specifically, everybody—including me—has some important pieces of truth, and all of those pieces need to be honored, cherished, and included in a more gracious, spacious, and compassionate embrace . . .

A Theory of Everything, 140

[The teachings of the world's greatest yogis, saints, and sages,] and their contemplative endeavors, were (and are) transrational through and through. That is, although all of the contemplative traditions aim at going within and beyond reason, they all *start* with reason, start with the notion that truth is to be established by *evidence*, that truth is the result of *experimental* methods, that truth is to be *tested* in the laboratory of personal *experience*, that these truths are open to all those who wish to *try the experiment* and thus disclose *for themselves* the truth or falsity of the spiritual claims—and that dogmas or given beliefs are precisely what hinder the emergence of deeper truths and wider visions.

Thus, each of these spiritual or transpersonal endeavors (which we will carefully examine) claims that there exist higher domains of awareness, embrace, love, identity, reality, self, and truth. But these claims are not dogmatic; they are not believed in merely because an authority proclaimed them, or because sociocentric tradition hands them down, or because salvation depends upon being a "true believer." Rather, the claims about these higher domains are a *conclusion* based on hundreds of years of experimental introspection and communal verification. False claims are *rejected* on the basis of *consensual evidence*, and further evidence is used to adjust and fine-tune the experimental conclusions.

These spiritual endeavors, in other words, are scientific in any meaningful sense of the word, and the systematic presentations of these endeavors follow precisely those of any *reconstructive science*.

cw 6: *Sex, Ecology, Spirituality*, 273

Some people take my system and make it into a be-all and end-all, as if Emptiness could ever be radically objectified in mental-linguistic forms. And so let me say, for the record, that that is not at all the way I view my own work. Not only do I hold *all* of it in provisional status, the so-called "highest" state is specifically "defined" as Formless, Mystery, Unknowing, Divine Ignorance, etc., radically beyond *any* particular objective phenomena, including any mental models, that might parade by in the face of formless Infinity. All such models have, at best, what the Hindus and Buddhists would call "relative truth" as opposed to "absolute truth," and much of my writing has been devoted to just that point. If certain individuals insist on misusing my work in this fashion, all I can do is decry it, and repeat again the words from the Preface to *The Atman Project*: the model that follows is of relative use but is "finally a lie in the face of that Mystery which only alone is."

cw 4: "Sociocultural Evolution," 332–333

One of the many amazing things about mystical experiences is that, however much culture does indeed mold these apprehensions, more often than not the apprehensions do not confirm a person in his or her cultural beliefs, but totally explode any cultural beliefs imaginable: the person is totally undone, like Paul on the road to Damascus, or totally surprised, or completely taken aback. Die-hard materialists can have these experiences as easily as purebred idealists, and both are completely stunned into awestruck silence: the depths of the Mystery are disclosing themselves, and a muted mind must only bend in reverential awe.

CW 6: *Sex, Ecology, Spirituality*, 661

The real purpose is to talk you into the contemplative awareness that is the mystical heart of each [wisdom] tradition but that is itself beyond all talk. The intent is to use thinking to tease us out of thinking, to dive to the very heart of the particular path, and to allow us to release ourselves into the openness and illumined nature of the very Divine itself. . . .

Because Spirit manifests itself only in and as the world of form—of apparently separate things and apparently different events, of seeming separation and isolation and alienation—it is in this diverse world that we must begin our search for the One beyond the Many, our Primordial Ground. Therefore, we need a vehicle, a *yana*, to take us to the formless shore beyond, even if the final realization is only that no vehicle was necessary or even possible. It is for this purpose that the world's great mystical paths have come into existence. They are not beliefs, not theories, not ideas, not theologies, and not doctrines. Rather, they are vehicles; they are experiential *practices*. They are experiments to *perform* (and thus see "through form"). They are something to *do* and then *be*, not something to merely think and then believe. Ultimately, there are no mystical doctrines or beliefs whatsoever; there are only mystical experiences and insights, all springing directly and immediately from the flow of one's own primordial experiencing in this very moment, illuminating all that is, like sunlight on the clearest of crystal autumn days.

CW 4: Foreword to *Coming Home: The Experience of Enlightenment
in Sacred Traditions* by Lex Hixon, 397–398

An experience that is not in time is not really an experience in the typical sense of the word, but rather the ground or opening in which all experiences arise (since experiences have a beginning and an end in time). This nondual realization is the immediateness of all experience and is not itself any particular experience. This, of course, could be said for any nondual realizer, from Buddha to Christ to Krishna to al-Hallaj, as their own teachings make quite clear. But it is not just the "highest goal" that Plotinus "experiences" or realizes and asks us to experimentally reproduce in the laboratory of our own awareness; it is every developmental stage leading to it, and then the "final" grasp of the Ground that is found *in each and every stage*, high or low: the hierarchy, having served its purpose as a ladder, having been long ago abandoned.

CW 6: *Sex, Ecology, Spirituality*, 659–660

Whether, in the end, you believe spiritual practice involves stages or not, authentic spirituality does involve *practice*. This is not to deny that for many people beliefs are important, faith is important, religious mythology is important. It is simply to add that, as the testimony of the world's great yogis, saints, and sages has made quite clear, authentic spirituality can also involve direct *experience* of a living Reality, disclosed immediately and intimately in the heart and consciousness of individuals, and fostered by diligent, sincere, prolonged spiritual practice. Even if you relate to spirituality as a peak experience, those peak experiences can often be specifically induced, or at least invited, by various forms of spiritual practice, such as active ritual, contemplative prayer, shamanic voyage, intensive meditation, and so forth. All of those open one to a direct experience of Spirit, and not merely beliefs or ideas about Spirit.

Therefore, don't just think differently, practice diligently.

CW 4: *Integral Psychology*, 568

Start with general doubt, says [Saint] Augustine, and doubt absolutely everything you can. You will find that you can doubt the reliability of logic (it might be wrong), you can even doubt the reality of sense impressions (they might be a hallucination). But even in the most intense doubt, you are aware of the doubt itself; in your *immediate awareness* there is *certainty*, even if it is only a certainty that you are doubting—and you can never shake that certainty. Any truth in the *exterior* world can be doubted, but always there is the *certainty* of interior *immediateness* or basic Wakefulness; and God, said Augustine, lies in and through that basic Wakefulness, whose certainty is never, and can never be, actually doubted.

Thus the existence of God, as the immediacy of self-presence (or basic Wakefulness), is an unshakable certainty. God is even the immediateness of the very presupposition, or actual ground, behind the doubt about God's existence. If you are aware of the thought "I don't believe in God," well, says Augustine, that is already God. Belief in God, and doubt in God, both presuppose God. . . .

God, for Augustine, is what you know *before* you know *anything* else, and upon which *everything* else depends, and something that can *never* actually be doubted.

God as the ground, not just of all being, but of our own immediate and primordial awareness—this is the call of Augustine. How similar to the Eastern traditions! . . . If you think you have not found or seen the primordial Self, the awareness of that lack *is itself* the supposedly lacking Self. These traditions are not saying that you have Buddha-nature but don't know it: you know it but won't admit it. . . .

Spirit, as basic Wakefulness, is not something that needs to be proven, but something that even the existence of doubt *always presupposes* as its own ground. And thus, Spirit (or consciousness or pure Ego or transcendental Self or basic openness) is not something hard to find but rather impossible to avoid. . . .

The path to ultimate Reality is not outside; it is inside. *Starting* with reason, one goes *within* reason, to the basic immediacy at its base, and that immediacy takes me *beyond* reason to the Ground of the Kosmos itself. So that finally, and ultimately, the Truth is not in me or inside me or egoically locked up in me, but is rather beyond me altogether: the ground of intimate presence opens up beyond me to the timeless and eternal Being of all beings. Going *within* me, I am finally *free* of me: and that is a timeless liberation from the fetters of being *only* me.

CW 6: *Sex, Ecology, Spirituality,* 367–369

When you practice meditation, one of the first things you realize is that your mind—and your life, for that matter—is dominated by largely subconscious verbal chatter. You are always talking to yourself. And so, as they start to meditate, many people are stunned by how much junk starts running through their awareness. They find that thoughts, images, fantasies, notions, ideas, concepts virtually dominate their awareness. They realize that these notions have had a much more profound influence on their lives than they ever thought.

In any case, initial meditation experiences are like being at the movies. You sit and watch all these fantasies and concepts parade by,

in front of your awareness. But the whole point is that you are finally becoming aware of them. You are looking at them impartially and
without judgement. You just watch them go by, the same as you
watch clouds float by in the sky. They come, they go. No praise, no
condemnation, no judgment—just "bare witnessing." If you judge
your thoughts, if you get caught up in them, then you can't transcend
them. You can't find higher or subtler dimensions of your own being.
So you sit in meditation, and you simply "witness" what is going on
in your mind. You let the monkey mind do what it wants, and you
simply watch.

And what happens is, because you impartially witness these
thoughts, fantasies, notions, and images, you start to become free of
their unconscious influence. You are looking at them, so you are not
using them to look at the world. Therefore you become, to a certain
extent, free of them. And you become free of the separate-self sense
that depended on them. In other words, you start to become free of
the ego. This is the initial spiritual dimension, where the conventional ego "dies" and higher structures of awareness are "resurrected." Your sense of identity naturally begins to expand and embrace
the cosmos, or all of nature. You rise above the isolated mind and
body, which might include finding a larger identity, such as with
nature or the cosmos—"cosmic consciousness," as R. M. Bucke
called it. It's a very concrete and unmistakable experience.

And, I don't have to tell you, this is an extraordinary relief! This
is the beginning of transcendence, of finding your way back home.
You realize that you are one with the fabric of the universe, eternally. Your fear of death begins to subside, and you actually begin to
feel, in a concrete and palpable way, the open and transparent nature
of your own being.

Feelings of gratitude and devotion arise in you—devotion to
Spirit, in the form of the Christ, or Buddha, or Krishna; or devotion
to your actual spiritual master; even devotion in general, and certainly devotion to all other sentient beings. The bodhisattva vow, in
whatever form, arises from the depths of your being, in a very powerful way. You realize you simply have to do whatever you can to
help all sentient beings, and for the reason, as Schopenhauer said,
that you realize that we all share the same nondual Self or Spirit or
Absolute. All of this starts to become obvious—as obvious as rain on
the roof. It is real and it is concrete.

cw 4: "Stages of Meditation," 357–358

Say you are walking downtown, looking in shop windows. You're looking at some of the merchandise, and all of a sudden you see a vague image dance in front of your eyes, the image of a person. Then all at once you realize that it is your own reflection in the shop window. You suddenly recognize yourself. You recognize your Self, your higher Self. You suddenly recognize who you are. And who you are is—a luminous spark of the Divine. But it has that shock of recognition—"Oh, that!"

It's a very concrete realization, and usually brings much laughter or much tears. The subtle Deity form or Light or Higher Self—those are all just archetypes of your own Being. You are encountering, via meditative development, and beginning a direct encounter with Spirit, with your own essence. So it shows up as light, as a being of light, as nada, as shabd, as clarity, numinosity, and so on. And sometimes it just shows up as a simple and clear awareness of *what is*—very simple, very clear. The point is that it is aware of all the dots on the wall. It is clearly aware of what is happening moment to moment, and therefore transcends the moment. It transcends this world, and starts to partake of the Divine. It has sacred outlook, however it might be expressed. That's the subtle—a face to face introduction to the Divine. You actually participate in Divinity, and in the awareness and wisdom of Divinity. It is a practice. It can be done. It has been done, many times.

cw 4: "Stages of Meditation," 359–360

If you continue simply witnessing—which helps you disidentify from lower and grosser forms, and become aware of the higher and subtler forms—even subtle objects or subtle dots themselves cease to arise. You enter a profound state of nonmanifestation, which is experienced like, say, an autumn night with a full moon. There is an eerie and beautiful numinosity to it all, but it's a "silent" or "black" numinosity. You can't really see anything except a kind of silvery fullness, filling all space. But because you're not actually seeing any particular object, it is also a type of Radical Emptiness. As Zen says, "stop the sound of that stream." This is variously known as shunyata, as the Cloud of Unknowing, Divine Ignorance, Radical Mystery, nirguna ("unqualifiable") Brahman, and so on. Brilliant formlessness, with no objects detracting from it.

It becomes obvious that you are absolutely one with this Fullness, which transcends all worlds and all planes and all time and all history. You are perfectly full, and therefore you are perfectly empty. "It is all things and it is no things," said the Christian mystic Boethius. Awe gives way to certainty. That's who you are, prior to all manifestation, prior to all worlds. In other words, it is seeing who or what you are timelessly, formlessly.

cw 4: "Stages of Meditation," 360–361

"Experience" is the wrong word altogether. This [nondual] realization is actually of the nonexperiential nature of Spirit. Experiences come and go. They all have a beginning in time, and an end in time. Even subtle experiences come and go. They are all wonderful, glorious, extraordinary. And they come, and they go.

But this nondual "state" is not itself another experience. It is simply the opening or clearing in which all experiences arise and fall. It is the bright autumn sky through which the clouds come and go—it is not itself another cloud, another experience, another object, another manifestation. This realization is actually of the utter fruitlessness of experience, the utter futility of trying to experience release or liberation. All experiences lose their taste entirely—these passing clouds.

You are not the one who experiences liberation; you are the clearing, the opening, the emptiness, in which any experience comes and goes, like reflections on the mirror. And you are the mirror, the mirror mind, and not any experienced reflection. But you are not apart from the reflections, standing back and watching. You *are* everything that is arising moment to moment. You can swallow the whole cosmos in one gulp, it is so small, and you can taste the entire sky without moving an inch.

This is why, in Zen, it is said that you cannot enter the Great Samadhi: it is actually the opening or clearing that is ever-present, and in which all experience—and all manifestation—arises moment to moment. It seems like you "enter" this state, except that once there, you realize there was never a time that this state wasn't fully present and fully recognized—"the gateless gate." And so you deeply understand that you never entered this state; nor did the Buddhas, past or future, ever enter this state.

In Dzogchen, this is the recognition of mind's true nature. All things, in all worlds, are self-liberated as they arise. All things are like sunlight on the water of a pond. It all shimmers. It is all empty. It is all light. It is all full, and it is all fulfilled. And the world goes on its ordinary way, and nobody notices at all.

CW 4: "Stages of Meditation," 362

In short, no direct experience can be fully captured in words. Sex can't be put into words; you've either had the experience or you haven't, and no amount of poetry will take its place. Sunsets, eating cake, listening to Bach, riding a bike, getting drunk and throwing up—believe me, none of those are captured in words.

And thus, so what if spiritual experiences can't be captured in words either? They are no more and no less handicapped in this regard than any other experience. If I say "dog" and you've had the experience, you know exactly what I mean. If a Zen master says "Emptiness," and you've had that experience, you will know exactly what is meant. If you haven't had the experience "dog" or the experience "Emptiness," merely adding more and more words will never, under any circumstances, convey it.

CW 6: *Sex, Ecology, Spirituality*, 279

There are several different ways that we can state . . . two important functions of religion. The first function—that of creating meaning for the self—is a type of *horizontal* movement; the second function—that of transcending the self—is a type of *vertical* movement (higher or deeper, depending on your metaphor). The first I have named *translation*; the second, *transformation*.

With translation, the self is simply given a new way to think or feel about reality. The self is given a new belief—perhaps holistic instead of atomistic, perhaps forgiveness instead of blame, perhaps relational instead of analytic. The self then learns to translate its world and its being in the terms of this new belief or new language or new paradigm, and this new and enchanting translation acts, at least temporarily, to alleviate or diminish the terror inherent in the heart of the separate self.

But with transformation, the very process of translation itself is challenged, witnessed, undermined, and eventually dismantled. With typical *translation*, the self (or subject) is given a new way to think about the world (or objects); but with radical *transformation*, the self itself is inquired into, looked into, grabbed by its throat and literally throttled to death.

Put it one last way: with horizontal translation—which is by far the most prevalent, widespread, and widely shared function of religion—the self is, at least temporarily, made happy in its grasping, made content in its enslavement, made complacent in the face of the screaming terror that is in fact its innermost condition. With translation, the self goes sleepy into the world, stumbles numbed and near-sighted into the nightmare of samsara, is given a map laced with morphine with which to face the world. And this, indeed, is the common condition of a religious humanity, precisely the condition that the radical or transformative spiritual realizers have come to challenge and to finally undo.

For authentic transformation is not a matter of belief but of the death of the believer; not a matter of translating the world but of transforming the world; not a matter of finding solace but of finding infinity on the other side of death. The self is not made content; the self is made toast.

cw8: *One Taste*, 304–305

Other worlds become *this world* with increasing development and evolution. . . .

Just so with the higher or transpersonal developments. Explain them to someone at the rational level, and all you get, at best, is that deer-caught-in-the-headlights blank stare (at worst, you get something like, "And did we forget to take our Prozac today?").

So the first thing I would like to emphasize is that the higher stages of transpersonal development are stages that are taken from those who have actually developed into those stages and who display palpable, discernible, and repeatable characteristics of that development. The stages themselves can be *rationally reconstructed* (explained in a rational manner after the fact), but they cannot be rationally experienced. They can be experienced only by a transrational contemplative development, whose stages unfold in the same manner as any other developmental stages, and whose experiences are every bit as real as any others.

But one must be adequate to the experience, or it remains an invisible other world. When the yogis and sages and contemplatives make a statement like, "The entire world is a manifestation of one Self," that is *not* a merely rational statement that we are to think about and see if it makes logical sense. It is rather a description, often poetic, of a direct apprehension or a direct experience, and we are to test this direct experience, not by mulling it over philosophically, but by taking up the experimental method of contemplative awareness, developing the requisite cognitive tools, and then directly looking for ourselves.

As Emerson put it, "What we are, that only can we see."

cw 6: *Sex, Ecology, Spirituality*, 275–276

The stunning message of the mystics is that in the very core of your being, you are God. Strictly speaking, God is neither within nor without—Spirit transcends all duality. But one discovers this by consistently looking *within*, until "within" becomes "beyond." The most famous version of this perennial truth occurs in the *Chandogya Upanishad*, where it says, "In this very being of yours, you do not perceive the True; but there in fact it is. In that which is the subtle essence of your own being, all that exists has its Self. An invisible and subtle essence is the Spirit of the whole universe. That is the True, that is the Self, and thou, thou art That."

Thou are That—*tat tvam asi*. Needless to say, the "thou" that is "That," the you that is God, is not your individual and isolated self or ego, this or that self, Mr. or Ms. So-and-so. In fact, the individual self or ego is precisely what blocks the realization of the Supreme Identity in the first place. Rather, the "you" in question is the deepest part of you—or, if you wish, the highest part of you—the subtle essence, as the Upanishad put it, that transcends your mortal ego and directly partakes of the Divine. In Judaism it is called the *ruach*, the divine and supraindividual spirit in each and every person, and not the *nefesh*, or the individual ego. In Christianity, it is the indwelling *pneuma* or spirit that is of one essence with God, and not the individual *psyche* or soul, which at best can worship God. As Coomaraswamy said, the distinction between a person's immortal-eternal spirit and a person's individual-mortal soul (meaning ego) is a fundamental tenet of the perennial philosophy. I think this is the only way to understand, for example, Christ's otherwise strange remarks that a person could not be a true Christian "unless he hateth his own soul." It is only by "hating" or "throwing out" or "transcending" your mortal soul that you discover your immortal spirit, one with All.

cw 5: *Grace and Grit*, 97–98

As for referring to the Real (Emptiness) as a continuously residing self (or True Self, or pure Consciousness, etc.): since Nagarjuna had already demonstrated that the Real is neither self nor no-self, but that in the *phenomenal* realm, there is no self without the states and no states without the self, then the metaphor of a True Self could in fact serve as a much better bridge:

Not that a phenomenal self gives way to no-self (for pure Emptiness is neither self nor no-self); and *not* that a phenomenal no-self gives way to pure Emptiness (there is no phenomenal no-self); but rather, a phenomenal self gives way to pure Emptiness (that strictly speaking is neither self nor no-self nor both nor neither).

And since in the *phenomenal* realm the self is necessary and useful (as Nagarjuna and Chandrakirti pointed out), then as a *bridging* metaphor, it was more adequate to speak of the phenomenal self (relatively real but ultimately illusory or phenomenal only) giving way to a True Self (that was no-phenomenal-self, and that strictly speaking was neither self nor no-self but pure Emptiness, free of all conceptual elaborations).

Thus Emptiness as True Self, Emptiness as pure Consciousness, Emptiness as Rigpa (pure knowing Presence), Emptiness as primordial Wisdom (*prajna, jnana, yeshe*), Emptiness as primordial Purity, even Emptiness as Absolute Subjectivity: all of these bridging notions began to spring up in the Mahayana and Vajrayana to supplement (or even replace) the notion of no-self, which, strictly speaking, was wrong both phenomenally and noumenally.

And indeed, starting with the *Nirvana Sutra*, the absolute was often metaphorically categorized as "Mahatman," the "Great Self" or "True Self," which was no-phenomenal-self: the selfless Self, so to speak (still metaphorical). And down to today (to give just a few examples), Zen master Shibayama would find that the ultimate state could best be metaphorically indicated as "Absolute Subjectivity." As he puts it, "The Master does not refer to the subjectivity that stands over against objectivity. It is 'Absolute Subjectivity,' which transcends both subjectivity and objectivity and freely creates and uses them. It is 'Fundamental Subjectivity,' which can never be objectified or conceptualized and is complete in itself, with the full significance of existence in itself" [*Zen Comments on the Mumonkan*, p. 92].

CW 6: *Sex, Ecology, Spirituality*, 729

Authentic spirituality, in short, must be based on direct spiritual experience, and this must be rigorously subjected to the three strands of valid knowledge: injunction, apprehension, and confirmation/rejection—or exemplar, data, and falsifiability. . . .

It is only when religion emphasizes its heart and soul and essence—namely, direct mystical experience and transcendental consciousness, which is disclosed not by the eye of flesh (give that to science) nor by the eye of mind (give that to philosophy) but rather by the eye of contemplation—that religion can both stand up to modernity and offer something for which modernity has desperate need: a genuine, verifiable, repeatable injunction to bring forth the spiritual domain.

CW 8: *The Marriage of Sense and Soul,* 227

Early morning, the orange sun is slowly rising, shining forth in empty luminous clarity. The mind and the sky are one, the sun is rising in the vast space of primordial awareness, and there is *just this*. Yasutani Roshi once said, speaking of satori, that it was the most precious realization in the world, because all the great philosophers had tried to understand ultimate reality but had failed to do so, yet with satori or awakening all of your deepest questions are finally answered: it's *just this*.

CW 8: *One Taste,* 383

Thus ultimately Emptiness takes no sides in a conceptual argument; Emptiness is not a view that can dislodge other views; it cannot be brought in to support one view as opposed to another: it is the Emptiness of all views, period.

CW 6: *Sex, Ecology, Spirituality,* 724

We cannot solve the absolute/relative problem using the eye of flesh or the eye of mind. This deepest of problems and mysteries directly yields its resolution only to the eye of contemplation. And, as both Kant and Nagarjuna forcefully demonstrated, if you try to state this solution in intellectual or rational terms, you will generate nothing but antinomies, paradox, contradiction.

CW 7: *The Eye of Spirit,* 498

Because above all, for Nagarjuna, absolute reality (Emptiness) is radically Nondual (*advaya*)—in itself it is *neither* self nor no-self, neither *atman* nor *anatman*, neither permanent nor momentary/flux. His dialectical analysis is designed to show that all such categories, being profoundly dualistic, make sense only in terms of each other and are thus nothing in themselves (the Emptiness of all views and all phenomena). This dialectical analysis applies to all things, all thoughts, all categories: they are all mutually dependent upon each other and thus are nothing in themselves. They therefore have a *relative* or phenomenal reality, but not *absolute* or *unconditioned* reality (which is Emptiness disclosed in nondual *prajna*, which is not a reality apart from the relative world of Form, but is itself the Emptiness or Suchness of all Forms).

CW 6: *Sex, Ecology, Spirituality*, 719

Big pictures and big maps help open the mind, and thus the heart, to an integral transformation.

A *Theory of Everything*, 135

Negation-and-affirmation (negate and preserve!) is found in all nondual contemplative schools. In Zen, to give only one example, it is said, "If all things return to the One, to what does the One return?" The answer: "The Many" (though the student has to demonstrate this understanding and not merely verbalize it; repeating the signifier without the developmental signified earns only a whack from the Master). So also the famous: "Before I studied Zen, mountains were mountains; when studying Zen, mountains were no longer mountains; when I finished studying Zen, mountains were once again mountains." The dividing line is the realization of Emptiness, or pure formless awareness (mountains were not mountains), in which all things then perfectly and freely arise as Emptiness just as they are (mountains were once again mountains, self-liberating). But one has first to realize the great death of Emptiness, or one remains merely lost in the mountains (shadows).

CW 6: *Sex, Ecology, Spirituality*, 658

Choose your big pictures with care.

CW 4: *Integral Psychology*, 435

When all is said and done, and argument and theory come to rest, and the separate self lays its weary head on the pillow of its own discontent, what then? When I relax into I-I, and the infinite spaciousness of primordial purity drenches me in Being; when I relax into I-I, and the eternal Emptiness of ever-present awareness saturates the self, fills it with a Fullness that cannot even be contained; then all the agitated anxieties of life return to their source in God and Goddess, and I-I alone shine in the world that I-I alone created. Where is suffering then?, and how do you even pronounce misery? There in the Heart, where the mathematics of torture and the physics of pain can find no purchase or way to disturb, then all things bright and beautiful come out to dance in the day's glorious sun, long forgotten by the contracting ways of the loveless and forlorn self, god of its own perception, engineer of its own agony.

It is, truly, a game; what dream walkers we all are! Nothing ever really happens here, nothing moves in time or space, it is all so painfully obvious that I avert my eyes from the blinding truth. But here we are, You and I, and it is You-and-I that is the form of Spirit in this and all the worlds. For in the entire Kosmos, there is only One Self; in the entire Kosmos, there is only One Spirit—and thus the Self that is reading this page is exactly the Self that wrote it.

Let us, then, You-and-I, recognize together who and what we are. And I will be with you until the ends of the world, and you will be with me, for there is only One Self, which is the miracle of Spirit. This is why we will be together forever, You-and-I, in the world of the Many-That-Are-One, and why we have never been separated. Just as Consciousness is singular, and the Self is One, and the Self neither comes nor goes, so You-and-I are that Self, forever and forever and endlessly forever.

Thank you deeply for coming on this journey with me, and guiding me at every point, and enlightening me through and through, and forgiving me all along, and being You-and-I.

cw 8: Introduction, 49–50

6

Always Already

Prior to form is formless Emptiness, and formless Emptiness is satu-
rated with form. This is the play of the Kosmos, that which is always
already simply Spirit. While myriad expressions of form unceasingly
arise and pass away each instant, beyond time and space is the eternal
now, the ever-present moment. This timeless eternity is always avail-
able to us, as if waiting to be recalled. It is through this sacred act of
remembrance that we may come to know that which was never born
and will never die.

In this chapter, Wilber elucidates how manifestation springs forth
from Absolute Spirit. He holds a mirror before us that we may begin
to recognize our own Original Face, our face before we were born.
Through momentary suspensions of our will, gaps in the implacable
churning of our ego, we can touch the eternal Absolute Spirit that pre-
cedes the manifest world, that which is known as One Taste. The fol-
lowing selections at once open such gaps and usher us through them
into the realization of One Taste that we already have, and always
have had.

This morning, only vast Emptiness.
I-I is only, alone with the Alone, all in All.
Fullness pushes me out of existence,
Radiance blinds me to the things of this world,
I see only infinite Freedom,
which means I see nothing at all.
There is a struggle to reanimate the soul,
to crank consciousness down and into the subtle,
to pull it down into ego and body,
and thus get out of bed at all.

But the Freedom is still there,
in this little twilight dawn,
and Release inhabits even
the smallest moves to make manifest
this glorious Estate.

CW 8: *One Taste*, 391

The desires of the flesh, the ideas of the mind, and the luminosities of the soul—all are perfect expressions of the radiant Spirit that alone inhabits the universe, sublime gestures of that Great Perfection that alone outshines the world. There is only One Taste in the entire Kosmos, and that taste is Divine, whether it appears in the flesh, in the mind, in the soul. Resting in that One Taste, transported beyond the mundane, the world arises in the purest Freedom and radiant Release, happy to infinity, lost in all eternity, and hopeless in the original face of the unrelenting mystery. From One Taste all things issue, to One Taste all things return—and in between, which is the story of this moment, there is only the dream, and sometimes the nightmare, from which we would do well to awaken.

CW 8: *One Taste*, 278

Do you recognize the Timeless One, even here and now, that is spontaneously aware of all of this? If so, please tell me, Who and What are you, when you are deeper than within? Clouds pass by, feelings pass by, thoughts pass by—but what in you does not pass by? Do you see That One? Can you say its Name?

Boomeritis, 121

Even the earth is floating in the vastness of space, the womb of the sky, the womb of all that is. Parts come together in the sky, fragments find their home in the vast expanse of all space, the great embracing spaciousness that you profoundly are.

Later I found out that the sky is neither male nor female, neither sun nor earth, but the great expanse that contains them both. But that I discovered only after a long and painful death. And would you like to know the secret to that?

Boomeritis, 178

The essence of mysticism is that in the deepest part of your own being, in the very center of your own pure awareness, you are fundamentally one with Spirit, one with Godhead, one with the All, in a timeless and eternal and unchanging fashion.

CW 5: *Grace and Grit*, 22

The soul's duty in this life is to remember. The Buddhist *smriti* and *sati-patthana*, the Hindu *smara*, the Sufi *zikr*, Plato's recollection, Christ's *anamnesis*: all of those terms are precisely translated as remembrance. "It is precisely a failure to remember," says Coomaraswamy, "that drags down from the heights the soul that has walked with God and had some vision of the truths, but cannot retain it." But there, of course, is the exact message of the *Thotrol* [the *Tibetan Book of the Dead*]. No wonder Neumann concluded that "Man's task in the world is to remember with his conscious mind what was knowledge before the advent of consciousness." Likewise, "The Saddik finds that which has been lost from birth and restores it to men."

And so, the soul that finally remembers all this, and sees it however vaguely, can only pause to wonder: How could I have forgotten? How could I have renounced that State which is the only Real? How could my soul have sunk to such that misery alone embraced it? But to see this now, to remember only God in all that passes and mark the grace of that very Self outside of which is nothing—how could the mark be ever missed? How could the mark be missed. . . .

At that final remembrance, the impact of only God in absolute Mystery and radical Unknowing dismantles once and for all the Atman project. There is no longer the Atman project, for there is only Atman, radical, radiant, all-pervading, perfectly ecstatic in its release, perfectly ordinary in its operation, perfectly obvious in its way. But Atman is Unseen. Atman is Unknown. Atman is Unspoken. Prior to all that arises, It is not other than all that arises, so it can be seen after all: Dogen Zenji—

> This slowly drifting cloud is pitiful!
> What dreamwalkers we all are!
> Awakened, the one great truth:
> Black rain on the temple roof.

For all the eons we have searched for this. For all the eons we have wanted this. But for all the eons there was only this: Black rain on the temple roof. . . .

And because there is always only Atman, the Atman project never occurred.

CW: The Atman Project, 268

If Mind or Tao or Godhead is the state that we are ardently searching, and yet outside Mind there is absolutely nowhere to go, it follows that we are already there! That we are already one with the Godhead, that what we are Now is Mind.

CW 1: The Spectrum of Consciousness, 328

And yet, what is it that gives me the overwhelming impression that I am aware of time, especially of time past, of my whole personal history, of all the things that were? For although I certainly understand that in my direct experience there is no past, only an endless present, I nevertheless am firmly convinced that I know something of the past. And no verbal sleight-of-hand can convince me otherwise, for there is something which speaks clearly and forcefully to me of things which happened minutes ago, days ago, even years ago. What is that? And how can it be denied?

The answer to the first question seems obvious: it is memory. For although I do not directly see the past, nor feel it, nor touch it, I can remember it. Memory alone assures me that there was a past, and, in fact, were it not for memory I would have no idea of time whatsoever. Further, I notice that other people seem to have a memory also, and they all substantially report the same type of past that I recall.

And so, I assume, *memory gives me a knowledge of the actual past*, even if I can't directly experience that past. But right here, claim the mystics, I have made a fatal mistake. The mystics agree that when I think of the past, all I really know is a certain memory—but, they add, *that memory is itself a present experience.* Alan Watts elaborates: "But what about memories? Surely by remembering I can also know what is past? Very well, remember something. Remember the incident of seeing a friend walking down the street. What are you aware of? You are not actually watching the veritable event of your friend walking down the street. You can't go up and shake hands with him, or get an answer to a question you forgot to ask him at the past time you are remembering. In other words, you are not looking at the actual past at all. You are looking at a present trace of the past. . . . From memories you infer that there have been past events. But you are not aware of any past events. You know the past only in the present and as part of the present."

Thus, I never know the actual past at all, I know only memories of the past, and those memories exist only as a present experience. Further, when what we call the "past" actually occurred, it was a present occurrence. At *no point, therefore, am I ever directly aware of an actual past*. In the same way, I never know the future, I know only anticipations or expectations—which nevertheless are themselves parts of present experience. Anticipation, like memory, is a present fact.

To see that the past as memory and the future as anticipation are both present facts is to see all time existing now.

cw 1: *No Boundary*, 493–494

Since all things are *already* Spirit, there is no way to *reach* Spirit. There is *only* Spirit in all directions, and so one simply rests in the spontaneous nature of the mind itself, effortlessly embracing all that arises as ornaments of your own primordial experience. The unmanifest and the manifest, or emptiness and form, unite in the pure nondual play of your own awareness—generally regarded as the ultimate state that is no state in particular.

cw 5: *Grace and Grit*, 290

Thus, whether we realize it or not, want it or not, care about it or not, understand it or not, we are It—always have been and always will be. . . .

Now because we are It, we can never attain It, get It, reach It, grab It, or find It, any more than we can run after our own feet. In a sense, then, all search for Mind is ultimately in vain. . . .

As a matter of fact, just because we are It, any search for It not only "is doomed to failure" but actually creates the impression that we lack It! By our very seeking, we apparently drive It away, just as if we misguidedly started looking for our head it would imply that we had lost it.

cw 1: *The Spectrum of Consciousness*, 329–330

Now if, while reading this, you decide to go "behind" the "self" to find what is really doing the looking, to find the Perceiver, the Seer, you will find only—this page! . . . But when this occurs (and it is occurring now), there won't be any you *as subject* nor any page *as object*, for both subject and object alike will have vanished into nondual Subjectivity, a state we inadequately try to express by saying that at this moment you are the page reading itself. For here, beyond all duality, *all objects are their own subjects*, subject and object being nothing but two different ways of approaching this reality called Mind.

This split, this gap between subject and object, this Primary Dualism, is the initiator of the spectrum of consciousness, and it continues to operate throughout all levels, forming that irreducible but illusory severance between thinker and thought, knower and known, feeler and feeling, I and me, psyche and soma, voluntary and involuntary, what is and what ought. In short, it marks off the persistent feeling of a separate "I," and each level of the spectrum is simply a variation of this primordially basic dualism, a variation marked by an ever-increasing restriction of the sense of identity, or pseudo-subjectivity, from the universe to organism to the ego to parts of the ego.

Now this *space*, this gap between subject and object, necessarily has a *time* component, for space and time are not separate Newtonian absolutes but rather a continuum. The time component of the Primary Dualism is none other than the *Secondary Dualism*, the dualism of life vs. death. We have been discussing the primary and secondary dualisms as if they were separate from one another, but this is merely an exegetical convenience, a device to make the complex story of the generation of the spectrum of consciousness a little easier to tell. In actuality, however, as soon as we live in space (the primary dualism), we live in time (the secondary dualism). . . .

Put bluntly, *the gap between you and this page is the same gap as that between you and the Now moment.* If you could live totally in the Now, you and this page (and all your other "objects") would be one, and conversely if you and this page were one, you would be living in the Now. The Primary Dualism and the Secondary Dualism are only two ways of describing this single space-time gap.

Naturally, then, since there is no way to find Mind through space by searching for It as an object "out there," there is no way to find Mind, through time by searching for It as a future occurrence. That is, just as there is no path to HERE, there is no path to NOW. In fact,

any Mind, God, or Brahman that we find in time would be a strictly temporal being, and not the Godhead at all. Most of us imagine
that we lack Mind at this time, but that we can find it some tomorrow if we work hard enough. But any Mind that we find tomorrow
will necessarily have a beginning in time, for it seems absent today
but present tomorrow. Strictly speaking, we cannot enter Eternity
since Eternity is ever-present, and any state we can *enter* is a purely
temporal state. We will find It Now, or we will find It not at all.

cw 1: The Spectrum of Consciousness, 335–337

When the individual truly sees that every move he makes is a move
away, a resistance, then the entire machination of resistance winds
down. When he sees this resistance in every move he makes, then,
quite spontaneously he surrenders resistance altogether. And the surrendering of this resistance is the opening of unity consciousness, the
actualization of no-boundary awareness. He awakens, as if from a
long and foggy dream, to find what he knew all along: he, as a separate self, does not exist. His real self, the All, was never born, will
never die. There is only Consciousness as Such in all directions,
absolute and all-pervading, radiant through and as all conditions, the
source and suchness of everything that arises moment to moment,
utterly prior to this world but not other than this world. All things
are just a ripple in this pond; all arising is a gesture of this one.

We have seen, then, that the special conditions of spiritual practice show the individual all of his resistances, while simultaneously
frustrating them at the very deepest levels. In short, the conditions
show us our wave-jumping, and then make it finally impossible. The
turning point comes when the person sees that *everything* he does is
nothing but wave-jumping, resisting, moving away from now in
search of wetter waves. Spiritual practice, whether a person realizes
it in these terms or not, hinges on this primal pivot.

cw 1: No Boundary, 573

Hence seeking after Mind inevitably backfires, and for reasons that
should now be obvious—for one, seeking implies searching or reaching out for an object, something "out there" that we can grasp, be it
a spiritual or material object, yet Mind is not an object. Whatever
you can think about, perceive, or grasp objectively is never, was

never, will never be that Absolute Subjectivity that is the Thinker, Perceiver, and Grasper. For another, seeking implies a present lack, yet right now we lack nothing, and it is only our anxious and misguided seeking that instills in us the apparent sense of lack, so that the more we seek the more acutely we feel this supposed lack, and because we will never never find It that way, after a while we become chronically panic-stricken, and so redouble our efforts, pulling tighter on the knot around our own throat. And for yet another, seeking is based on the implicit belief in some future attainment, a belief that if we do not have salvation today we can surely get it tomorrow, yet Mind knows no tomorrow, no time, no past nor future, so that in running after It in some imagined future we are only running away from It Now, for Mind exists nowhere but in *this* timeless Moment. As always, those who seek to save their souls will surely lose them.

The problem, then, is that the object of our search and the seeker of that object are actually one and the same, so that each of us has his head pursuing his own tail, as in the case of the beguiled snake Ouroborous, prototype of all vicious circles.

cw 1: *The Spectrum of Consciousness*, 331

Around the sea of Emptiness, a faint edge of bliss.
From the sea of Emptiness, a flicker of compassion.
Subtle illuminations fill the space of awareness,
As radiant forms coalesce in consciousness.
A world is taking shape,
A universe is being born.
I-I breathe out the subtlest patterns,
Which crystallize into the densest forms,
With physical colors, things, objects, processes,
That rush upon awareness in the darkness of its night,
To arise as glorious sun, radiant reminder of its source,
And slumbering earth, abode of the offspring of Spirit.

cw 8: *One Taste*, 419

It is extremely difficult to adequately discuss no-boundary awareness or nondual consciousness. This is because our language—the medium in which all verbal discussion must float—is a language of boundaries. As we have seen, words and symbols and thoughts themselves are actually nothing but boundaries, for whenever you think or use a word or name, you are already creating boundaries. Even to say "reality is no-boundary awareness" is still to create a distinction between boundaries and no-boundary! So we have to keep in mind the great difficulty involved with dualistic language. That "reality is no-boundary" is true enough, provided we remember that no-boundary awareness is a direct, immediate, and nonverbal awareness, and not a mere philosophical theory. It is for these reasons that the mystic-sages stress that reality lies beyond names and forms, words and thoughts, divisions and boundaries. Beyond all boundaries lies the real world of Suchness, the Void, the Dharmakaya, Tao, Braham, the Godhead. And in the world of suchness, there is neither good nor bad, saint nor sinner, birth nor death, for in the world of suchness there are no boundaries.

cw 1: *No Boundary*, 474–475

In the stillness of the night, the Goddess whispers. In the brightness of the day, dear God roars. Life pulses, mind imagines, emotions wave, thoughts wander. What are these but the endless movements of One Taste, forever at play with its own gestures, whispering quietly to all who would listen: is this not you yourself? When the thunder roars, do you not hear your Self? When the lightning cracks, do you not see your Self? When clouds float quietly across the sky, is this not your very own limitless Being, waving back at you?

cw 8: *One Taste*, 557–558

The real self *is* the real world, no separation, so sometimes the mystics will also say there is no self, no world. But that's all they mean, no separate self, no separate world. Eckhart called it fusion without confusion.

cw 5: *Grace and Grit*, 122

Clearly, in this present moment, if we would but examine it, there is no time. The present moment is a timeless moment, and a timeless moment is an eternal one—a moment which knows neither past nor future, before nor after, yesterday nor tomorrow. To enter deeply into this present moment is thus to plunge into eternity, to step through the looking glass and into the world of the Unborn and the Undying.

CW 1: No Boundary, 489

In the end we will find, I believe, the inherent joy in existence itself, a joy that stems from the great perfection of this and every moment, a wondrous whole in itself, a part of the whole of the next, a sliding series of wholes and parts that cascade to infinity and back, never lacking and never wanting because always fulfilled in the brilliance that is now. The integral vision, having served its purpose, is finally outshined by the radiance of a Spirit that is much too obvious to see and much too close to reach, and the integral search finally succeeds by letting go of the search itself, there to dissolve in a radical Freedom and consummate Fullness that was always already the case, so that one abandons a theory of everything in order simply to be Everything, one with the All in this endless awareness that holds the Kosmos kindly in its hand. And then the true Mystery yields itself, the face of Spirit secretly smiles, the Sun rises in your very own heart and the Earth becomes your very own body, galaxies rush through your veins while the stars light up the neurons of your night, and never again will you search for a mere theory of that which is actually your own Original Face.

A Theory of Everything, 141

When all things are nothing but God, there are then no things, and no God, but only *this*.

No objects, no subjects, only this. No entering this state, no leaving it; it is absolutely and eternally and always already the case: the simple feeling of being, the basic and simple immediacy of any and all states, prior to the four quadrants, prior to the split between inside and outside, prior to seer and seen, prior to the rise of worlds, ever-present as pure Presence, the simple feeling of being: empty awareness as the opening or clearing in which all worlds arise, ceaselessly: I-I is the box the universe comes in.

Abiding as I-I, the world arises as before, but now there is no one to witness it. I-I is not "in here" looking "out there": there is no in here, no out there, only this. It is the radical end to all egocentrism, all geocentrism, all biocentrism, all sociocentrism, all theocentrism, because it is the radical end of all centrisms, period. It is the final *decentering* of all manifest realms, in all domains, at all times, in all places. As Dzogchen Buddhism would put it, because all phenomena are primordially empty, all phenomena, just as they are, are self-liberated as they arise.

In that pure empty awareness, I-I am the rise and fall of all worlds, ceaselessly, endlessly. I-I swallow the Kosmos and span the centuries, untouched by time or turmoil, embracing each with primordial purity, fierce compassion. It has never started, this nightmare of evolution, and therefore it will never end.

It is as it is, self-liberated at the moment of its very arising. And it is only *this*.

The All is I-I. I-I is Emptiness. Emptiness is freely manifesting. Freely manifesting is self-liberating.

Zen, of course, would put it all much more simply, and point directly to just *this*.

> Still pond
> A frog jumps in
> Plop!

> CW 6: *Sex, Ecology, Spirituality*, 318

Much work, of course, remains to be done. But the foundation is there, it has been won through for us; the basics are in existence. These roads are open to us: roads present but untraveled; paths cut clear but not chosen.

Can we not embrace these roots? Can we not see Spirit as the Life of Evolution and the Love of Kosmos itself? Does not the Good of Spirit, its Eros, release both Nature and Mind from the torments we have inflicted on them in vain attempts to make them each the source of infinite value? Does not the Goodness of Spirit, its Agape, embrace both Mind and Nature in a loving caress that heals the self-inflicted wounds? Does not the refluxing movement of God and the effluxing movement of the Goddess embrace the entire Circle of Ascent and Descent? Can we not round out the original insights and see that Spirit always manifests in all four quadrants equally? Is not Spirit here and now in all its radiant glory, eternally present as every I and every We and every It? Will not our more adequate interpretations of Spirit facilitate Spirit's rescue of us?

As Plotinus knew: Let the world be quiet. Let the heavens and the earth and the seas be still. Let the world be waiting. Let the self-contraction relax into the empty ground of its own awareness, and let it there quietly die. See how Spirit pours through each and every opening in the turmoil, and bestows new splendor on the setting Sun and its glorious Earth and all its radiant inhabitants. See the Kosmos dance in Emptiness; see the play of light in all creatures great and small; see finite worlds sing and rejoice in the play of the very Divine, floating on a Glory that renders each transparent, flooded by a Joy that refuses time or terror, that undoes the madness of the loveless self and buries it in splendor.

Indeed, indeed: let the self-contraction relax into the empty ground of its own awareness, and let it there quietly die. See the Kosmos arise in its place, dancing madly and divine, self-luminous and self-liberating, intoxicated by a Light that never dawns nor ceases. See the worlds arise and fall, never caught in time or turmoil, transparent images shimmering in the radiant Abyss. Watch the mountain walk on water, drink the Pacific in a single gulp, blink and a billion universes rise and fall, breathe out and create a Kosmos, breathe in and watch it dissolve.

Let the ecstasy overflow and outshine the loveless self, driven mad with the torments of its self-embracing ways, hugging mightily samsara's spokes of endless agony, and sing instead triumphantly with Saint Catherine, "My being is God, not by simple participation, but by a true transformation of my Being. My *me* is God!" And let the joy sing with Dame Julian, "See! I am God! See! I am in all things! See! I do all things!" And let the joy shout with Hakuin, "This very body is the Body of Buddha! and this very land the Pure Land!"

And this Earth becomes a blessed being, and every I becomes a God, and every We becomes God's sincerest worship, and every It becomes God's most gracious temple.

And comes to rest that Godless search, tormented and tormenting. The knot in the Heart of the Kosmos relaxes to allow its only God, and overflows the Spirit ravished and enraptured by the lost and found Beloved. And gone the Godless destiny of death and desperation, and gone the madness of a life committed to uncare, and gone the tears and terror of the brutal days and endless nights where time alone would rule.

And I-I rise to taste the dawn, and find that love alone will shine today. And the Shining says: to love it all, and love it madly, and always endlessly, and ever fiercely, to love without choice and thus enter the All, to love it mindlessly and thus be the All, embracing the only and radiant Divine: now as Emptiness, now as Form, together and forever, the Godless search undone, and love alone will shine today.

cw 6: *Sex, Ecology, Spirituality*, 549–550

Always already suffering death Now, we are always already living eternally. The search is always already over.

cw 1: *The Spectrum of Consciousness*, 373

Like Moses, the soul can see from afar, but never actually enter, the Promised Land. As Teresa would say, after the butterfly (soul) emerged from the death of the chrysalis (ego), so now the little butterfly must die. When the soul itself grows quiet, and rests from its own weariness; when the witness releases its final hold, and dissolves into its ever-present ground; when the last layer of the Self is peeled into the purest emptiness; when the final form of the self-contraction unfolds in the infinity of all space; then Spirit itself, as ever-present awareness, stands free of its own accord, never really lost, and therefore never really found. With a shock of the utterly obvious, the world continues to arise, just as it always has.

In the deepest within, the most infinite beyond. In ever-present awareness, your soul expands to embrace the entire Kosmos, so that Spirit alone remains, as the simple world of what is. The rain no longer falls on you, but within you; the sun shines from inside your heart and radiates out into the world, blessing it with grace; supernovas swirl in your consciousness, the thunder is the sound of your own exhilarated heart; the oceans and rivers are nothing but your blood pulsing to the rhythm of your soul. Infinitely ascended worlds of light dance in the interior of your brain; infinitely descended worlds of night cascade around your feet; the clouds crawl across the sky of your own unfettered mind, while the wind blows through the empty space where your self once used to be. The sound of the rain falling on the roof is the only self you can find, here in the obvious world of crystalline one taste, where inner and outer are silly fictions and self and other are obscene lies, and ever-present simplicity is the sound of one hand clapping madly for all eternity. In the greatest depth, the simplest what is, and the journey ends, as it always does, exactly where it began.

CW 4: *Integral Psychology*, 540

Not in Emptiness, but as Emptiness, I am released from the fate of a never-ending addition of parts, and I stand free as the Source and Suchness of the glorious display. I taste the sky and swallow whole the Kosmos, and nothing is added to me; I disappear in a million forms and nothing is subtracted; I rise as the sun to greet my own day, and nothing moves at all.

CW 6: *Sex, Ecology, Spirituality*, 532

It seems that we are part and parcel of a single and all-encompassing evolutionary current that is itself Spirit-in-action, the mode and manner of Spirit's creation. The same currents that run through our human blood run through swirling galaxies and colossal solar systems, crash through the great oceans and course throughout the cosmos, move the mightiest of mountains as well as our own moral aspirations—one and the same current moves throughout the All, and drives the entire Kosmos in its every lasting gesture, an extraordinary morphogenetic field that exerts a pull and pressure which refuses to surrender until you remember who and what you are, and that you were carried to this realization by that single current of an all-pervading Love, and here "there came fulfillment in a flash of light, and vigor failed the lofty fantasy, but now my will and my desires were moved like a wheel revolving evenly, by the Love that moves the sun and other stars."

CW 4: *Integral Psychology*, 585

Absolute Spirit is the fundamental reality. But in order to create the world, the Absolute manifests itself, or goes out of itself—in a sense, the Absolute forgets itself and empties itself into creation (although never really ceasing to be itself). Thus the world is created as a "falling away" from Spirit, as a "self-alienation" of Spirit, although the Fall is never anything but a play of Spirit itself.

CW 8: *The Marriage of Sense and Soul*, 173

When I directly view, say, a great Van Gogh, I am reminded of what all superior art has in common: the capacity to simply take your breath away. To literally, actually, make you inwardly gasp, at least for that second or two when the art first hits you, or more accurately, first enters your being: you swoon a little bit, you are slightly stunned, you are open to perceptions that you had not seen before. Sometimes, of course, it is much quieter than that: the work seeps into your pores gently and yet you are changed somehow, maybe just a little, maybe a lot; but you are changed.

No wonder that for the East and West alike, until just recent times, art was often associated with profound spiritual transformation. And I don't mean merely "religious" or "iconographic" art.

Some of the great modern philosophers, Schelling to Schiller to Schopenhauer, have all pinpointed a major reason for great art's power to transcend. When we look at any beautiful object (natural or artistic), we suspend all other activity, and we are simply aware, we only want to contemplate the object. While we are in this contemplative state, we do not want anything from the object; we just want to contemplate it; we want it to never end. We don't want to eat it, or own it, or run from it, or alter it: we only want to look, we want to contemplate, we never want it to end.

In that contemplative awareness, our own egoic grasping in time comes momentarily to rest. We relax into our basic awareness. We rest with the world as it is, not as we wish it to be. We are face to face with the calm, the eye in the center of the storm. We are not agitating to change things; we contemplate the object as it is. Great art has this power, this power to grab your attention and suspend it: we stare, sometimes awestruck, sometimes silent, but we cease the restless movement that otherwise characterizes our every waking moment.

It doesn't matter what the actual *content* of the art is; not for this. Great art grabs you, against your will, and then suspends your will. You are ushered into a quiet clearing, free of desire, free of grasping, free of ego, free of the self-contraction. And through that opening or clearing in your own awareness may come flashing higher truths, subtler revelations, profound connections. For a moment you might even touch eternity; who can say otherwise, when time itself is suspended in the clearing that great art creates in your awareness?

You just want to contemplate; you want it never to end; you forget past and future; you forget self and same. The noble Emerson: "These roses under my window make no reference to former roses or to better ones; they are for what they are; they exist with God today. There is no time for them. There is simply the rose; it is perfect in every moment of its existence. But man postpones or remembers; he does not live in the present, but with reverted eye laments the past, or heedless of the riches that surround him, stands on tiptoe to foresee the future. He cannot be happy and strong until he too lives with nature in the present, above time."

Great art suspends the reverted eye, the lamented past, the anticipated future: we enter with it into the timeless present; we are with God today, perfect in our manner and mode, open to the riches and the glories of a realm that time forgot, but that great art reminds us of: not by its content, but by what it does in us: suspends the desire to be elsewhere. And thus it undoes the agitated grasping in the heart of the suffering self, and releases us—maybe for a second, maybe for a minute, maybe for all eternity—releases us from the coil of ourselves.

That is exactly the state that great art pulls us into, no matter what the actual content of the art itself—bugs or Buddhas, landscapes or abstractions, it doesn't matter in the least. In this particular regard—from this particular context—great art is judged by its capacity to take your breath away, take your self away, take time away, all at once.

And whatever we mean by the word "spirit"—let us just say, with Tillich, that it involves for each of us our ultimate concern—it is in that simple awestruck moment, when great art enters you and changes you, that spirit shines in this world just a little more brightly than it did the moment before.

Take it one step further: What if we could somehow manage to see *everything* in the entire universe as being exquisitely beautiful, like the finest piece of great art? What if we right now saw every single thing and event, without exception, as an object of extraordinary beauty?

Why, we would be momentarily frozen in the face of that vision; all of our grasping and avoiding would come quickly to rest; we would be released from the self-contraction and ushered into the choiceless contemplation of all that is. Just as a beautiful object or artwork momentarily suspends our will, so the contemplation of the universe as an object of beauty would open us to the choiceless awareness of that universe, not as it should be or might be or could be, but simply as it is.

Could it then be possible, just possible, that when the beauty of all things without exception is perceived, we are actually standing directly in the eye of Spirit, for which the entire Kosmos is an object of Beauty, just as it is, precisely because the entire Kosmos is in fact the radiant Art of Spirit itself?

In this extraordinary vision, the entire Kosmos is the Artwork of your own highest Self in all its shining creativity, which is exactly why every object in the universe is in truth an object of radiant Beauty when perceived with the eye of Spirit.

And conversely: if you could right here, right now, actually see every single thing and event in the entire universe as an object of sheer Beauty, then you would of necessity be undone as ego and stand instead as Spirit. You would want nothing from the Kosmos at that moment except to contemplate its unending Beauty and Perfection. You would not want to run from the universe, or grasp it, or alter it at all: in that contemplative moment you will neither fear nor hope, nor move at all. You will want nothing whatsoever, except to Witness it all, contemplate it unendingly, you want it never to end. You are radically free of will, free from grasping, free from all mean motion and commotion. You are a center of pure and clear awareness, saturated in its Being by the utter Beauty of everything it contemplates.

Not a single particle of dust is excluded from this Beauty; no object whatsoever, no matter how "ugly" or "frightening" or "painful"— not a single thing is excluded from this contemplative embrace, for each and every thing is radically, equally, unendingly the brilliant radiance of Spirit. When you behold the primordial Beauty of every single thing in the universe, then you behold the glory of the Kosmos in the eye of Spirit, the I of Spirit, the radical I-I of the entire universe. You are full to infinity, radiant with the light of a thousand suns, and all is perfect just as it is, always and eternally, as you contemplate this, your greatest Artwork, the entire Kosmos, this thing of Beauty, this object of unending joy and bliss radiant in the Heart of all that arises.

Think of the most beautiful person you have ever seen. Think of the exact moment you looked into his or her eyes, and for a fleeting second you were paralyzed: you couldn't take your eyes off that vision. You stared, frozen in time, caught in that beauty. Now imagine that *identical* beauty radiating from every single thing in the entire universe: every rack, every plant, every animal, every cloud, every person, every object, every mountain, every stream—even the garbage dumps and broken dreams—every single one of them, radiating that beauty. You are quietly frozen by the gentle beauty of everything that arises around you. You are released from grasping, released from time, released from avoidance, released altogether into the eye of Spirit, where you contemplate the unending beauty of the Art that is the entire World.

That all-pervading Beauty is not an exercise in creative imagination. It is the actual structure of the universe. That all-pervading Beauty is in truth the very nature of the Kosmos right now. It is not something you have to imagine, because it is the actual structure of perception in all domains. If you remain in the eye of Spirit, every object is an object of radiant Beauty. If the doors of perception are cleansed, the entire Kosmos is your lost and found Beloved, the Original Face of primordial Beauty, forever, and forever, and endlessly forever. And in the face of that stunning Beauty, you will completely swoon into your own death, never to be seen or heard from again, except on those tender nights when the wind gently blows through the hills and the mountains, quietly calling your name.

CW 7: *The Eye of Spirit,* 540–544

TREYA KILLAM WILBER: Is enlightenment actually experienced as a real death, or is that just a common metaphor?

KEN WILBER: Actual ego-death, yes. It's no metaphor. The accounts of this experience, which may be very dramatic but can also be fairly simple and nondramatic, make it clear that all of a sudden you simply wake up and discover that, among other things, your real being is everything you are now looking at, that you are literally one with all manifestation, one with the universe, however corny that might sound, and that you did not actually become one with God and All, you have eternally been that oneness but didn't realize it.

Along with that feeling, or the discovery of the all-pervading Self, goes the very concrete feeling that your small self simply died, actually died. Zen calls satori "the Great Death." Eckhart was just as blunt: "The soul," he said, "must put itself to death." Coomaraswamy explains: "It is only by making stepping stones of our dead selves, until we realize at last that there is literally nothing with which we can identify our Self, that we can become what we are." Or Eckhart again, "The kingdom of God is for none but the thoroughly dead."

CW 5: *Grace and Grit,* 103

What causes suffering is the grasping and desiring of the separate self, and what ends it is the meditative path that transcends self and desire. The point is that suffering is inherent in the knot or contraction known as self, and the only way to end suffering is to end the self. It's not that after enlightenment, or after spiritual practice in general, you no longer feel pain or anguish or fear or hurt. You do. It's simply that they no longer threaten your existence, and so they cease to be problematic. You are no longer identified with them, dramatizing them, energizing them, threatened by them. On the one hand, there is no longer any fragmented self to threaten, and on the other, the big Self can't be threatened since, being the All, there is nothing outside of it that could harm it. A profound relaxing and uncoiling occurs in the heart.

cw 5: *Grace and Grit*, 103–104

When bodymind drops, when I am nowhere to be found, there is such an infinite Emptiness, a radical Fullness, endlessly laced with luminosity. I-I open as the Kosmos, here where no object corrupts primordial Purity, here where concepts are too embarrassed to speak, here where duality hides its face in shame, and suffering cannot even remember its name. Nothing ever happens here, in the fullness of infinity, singing self-existing bliss, alive with self-liberating gestures, always happy to be home. Infinite gratitude meets utter simplicity in the openness of this moment, for there is *just this*, forever and forever and hopelessly forever.

cw 8: *One Taste*, 477

Suddenly, without any warning, at any time or place, with no apparent cause, it can happen.

cw 1: *No Boundary*, 433

Not a single experience is closer to or further from One Taste. You cannot engineer a way to get closer to God, for there is only God—the radical secret of the Nondual schools.

At the same time, all of this occurs within some very strong ethical frameworks, and you are not simply allowed to play Dharma Bums and call that being Nondual. In most of the traditions, in fact, you have to master the first three stages of transpersonal development (psychic, subtle, and causal) before you will even be allowed to talk about the fourth or Nondual state. "Crazy wisdom" occurs in a very strict ethical atmosphere.

But the important point is that in the Nondual traditions, you take a vow, a very sacred vow, which is the foundation of all of your training, and the vow is that *you will not disappear into cessation*—you will *not* hide out in nirvana, you will not evaporate in nirodh, you will not abandon the world by tucking yourself into nirvikalpa.

Rather, you promise to ride the surf of samsara until all beings caught in that surf can see that it is just a manifestation of Emptiness. Your vow is to pass through cessation and into Nonduality as quickly as possible, so you can help all beings recognize the Unborn in the very midst of their born existence.

So these Nondual traditions do not necessarily abandon emotions, or thoughts, or desires, or inclinations. The task is simply to see the Emptiness of all Form, not to actually get rid of all Form. And so Forms continue to arise, and you learn to surf. The Enlightenment is indeed primordial, but this Enlightenment continues forever, and it forever changes its Form because new Forms always arise, and you are one with those.

So the call of the Nondual traditions is: Abide as Emptiness, embrace all Form. The liberation is in the Emptiness, never in the Form, but Emptiness embraces all forms as a mirror all its objects. So the Forms continue to arise, and, as the sound of one hand clapping, you are all those Forms. You are the display. You and the universe are One Taste. Your Original Face is the purest Emptiness, and therefore every time you look in the mirror, you see only the entire Kosmos.

CW 7: *A Brief History of Everything*, 268–269

With the awakening of constant consciousness, you become something of a divine schizophrenic, in the popular sense of "split-minded," because you have access to *both* the Witness and the ego. You are actually "whole-minded," but it sounds like it's split, because you are aware of the constant Witness or Spirit in you, and you are also perfectly aware of the movie of life, the ego and all its ups and downs. So you still feel pain and suffering and sorrow, but they can no longer convince you of their importance—you are no longer the victim of life, but its Witness.

In fact, because you are no longer afraid of your feelings, you can engage them with much greater intensity. The movie of life becomes more vivid and vibrant, precisely because you are no longer grasping or avoiding it, and thus no longer trying to dull or dilute it. You no longer turn the volume down. You might even cry harder, laugh louder, jump higher. Choiceless awareness doesn't mean you cease to feel; it means you feel fully, feel deeply, feel to infinity itself, and laugh and cry and love until it hurts. Life jumps right off the screen, and you are one with all of it, because you don't recoil.

cw 8: *One Taste*, 344–345

Ah, but we humans don't just want Spirit, we want agitation as well. We don't just want the simple Feeling of Being, we want to feel . . . *something*. Something *special*. We want to feel rich, or we want to feel famous, or we want to feel important; we want to stand out, make a mark, be a somebody. And so we divide up the simple Feeling of Being—we qualify it, categorize it, name it, separate it. We do not want to impartially *witness* the world as I-I and then *be* the world in the Feeling of One Taste. And so, instead of being the world, we want to be somebody. We want, that is, to suffer the lacerations of finite limitation, and this we do, horribly, when we become a some-body. Abandoning the simple Feeling of Being—where I-I am the world—we identify with a little body in a pitifully small space, and we want this little body to rise up over all other bodies and triumph: we will be somebody, by god.

But if I remain in the simple Feeling of Being, what does it matter if a friend gets a new house and I do not? Her joy is my joy, in the simple Feeling of One Taste. What does it matter if a colleague receives accolades and I do not? His happiness is my happiness, in the simple Feeling of One Taste. When there is but one Self looking out through all eyes, do I not rejoice in good fortune wherever it occurs, since it is the good fortune of my own deepest Self? And when suffering occurs anywhere in the universe, do I not also suffer, since it is the suffering of my own deepest Self? When one young child cries from hunger, do I not suffer? When one young husband delights in seeing his wife come home, do I not rejoice?

Traherne got it exactly: "The streets were mine, the temple was mine, the people were mine. The skies were mine, and so were the sun and moon and stars, and all the world was mine, and I the only

Spectator [Witness] and enjoyer of it. I knew no churlish proprieties, nor bounds, nor divisions; but all proprieties and divisions were mine; all treasures and the possessors of them. So that with much ado I was corrupted and made to learn the dirty devices of the world, which I now unlearn. . . ."

In the simple Feeling of Being, where I-I am the world, jealousy and envy can find no purchase; all happiness is my happiness, all sadness is my sadness—and therefore, paradoxically, suffering ceases. Tears do not cease, nor do smiles—just the insane notion that I am somebody in the face of my own display. To cease being somebody—when "bodymind drops"—when I-I rests in Emptiness and embraces the entire world of Form: all of this is given in the simple Feeling of Being, the simple Feeling of One Taste. I simply feel Existence, pure Presence, nondual Isness, simple Suchness, present Thusness. I simply feel Being, I do not feel being this or being that—I am free of being this or being that, which are merely forms of suffering. But as I rest in the simple, present, effortless sensation of existence, all is given unto me.

You *already* possess the simple Feeling of Being. And so, again, please tell me: Who is not *already* enlightened?

CW 8: *One Taste*, 559–560

7

Being-in-the-World

It is not enough to ascend into the heights of Heaven if you are not to the same degree engaged with the manifestations of this world. Likewise, an embrace of this world becomes even more spiritual insofar as it discovers Pure Space in the folds of earthly life. In this chapter, Wilber's writings highlight how the Divine manifests in and through the everyday world of our lives and our communities.

Wilber issues a clarion call to liberate all perspectives into an integral chorus of inclusion-in-diversity. He invites everyone to be Spirit in this world, to be in compassionate relationship with all beings and their perspectives, and to be able to take on viewpoints that differ from or contradict one's own. All individuals are embedded in communities of understanding, which create various horizons of meaning. The interplay of these horizons of meaning is what gives the global village such a dynamic potential and why an integral understanding of Being-in-the-World is so essential.

The process of cultivating mutual understanding between beings is at the very heart of Wilber's ethic of the Other, which he calls the basic moral imperative: *to promote the greatest depth of consciousness for the greatest span of beings. That is, we need to honor the rich diversity of beings and their respective capacities to perceive, experience, and have awareness of their worlds. In this way Wilber recognizes the Divine spark of all beings from ants to angels.*

For Wilber, Being-in-the-World includes the deep realization that such things as our bodies, our relationships, and great art, can all be passageways into the lightness of the Divine's clear and vast radiance. Being-in-the-World means that nothing is left out, everything can serve our own transformation and opening. Here the profane and the sacred, the mundane and the spiritual, join to complete God.

So THE WHOLE POINT, I think, is that we want to find ourselves in sympathetic attunement with all aspects of the Kosmos. We want to find ourselves at home in the Kosmos. We want to touch the truth in [all domains]. We begin to do so by noticing that each speaks to us with a different voice. If we listen carefully, we can hear each of these voices whispering gently their truths, and finally joining in a harmonious chorus that quietly calls us home. We can fully resonate with those liberating truths, if we know how to recognize and honor them.

From attunement to atonement to at-onement: we find ourselves in the overpowering embrace of a Kosmic sympathy on the very verge of Kosmic consciousness itself . . . if we listen very carefully.

cw 7: *A Brief History of Everything*, 147

It is often said that in today's modern and postmodern world, the forces of darkness are upon us. But I think not; in the Dark and the Deep there are truths that can always heal. It is not the forces of darkness but of shallowness that everywhere threaten the true, and the good, and the beautiful, and that ironically announce themselves as deep and profound. It is an exuberant and fearless shallowness that everywhere is the modern danger, the modern threat, and that everywhere nonetheless calls to us as savior.

We might have lost the Light and the Height; but more frightening, we have lost the Mystery and the Deep, the Emptiness and the Abyss, and lost it in a world dedicated to surfaces and shadows, exteriors and shells, whose prophets lovingly exhort us to dive into the shallow end of the pool head first.

"History," said Emerson, "is an impertinence and an injury if it be anything more than a cheerful apologue or parable of my being and becoming." What follows, then, is a cheerful parable of your being and your becoming, an apologue of that Emptiness which forever issues forth, unfolding and enfolding, evolving and involving, creating worlds and dissolving them, with each and every breath you take. This is a chronicle of what you have done, a tale of what you have seen, a measure of what we all might yet become.

cw 6: *Sex, Ecology, Spirituality*, 7

But there is a strange and horrible thing about one's daemon [the Greek word that in classical mythology refers to "a god within"]: When honored and acted upon, it is indeed one's guiding spirit; those who bear a god within bring genius to their work. When, however, one's daemon is heard but unheeded, it is said that the daemon becomes a demon, or evil spirit—divine energy and talent degenerates into self-destructive activity. The Christian mystics, for example, say that the flames of Hell are but God's love denied, angels reduced to demons.

CW 5: *Grace and Grit*, 71

What does a "space" or "clearing" mean in this regard? Originating with Heidegger, but taking on numerous other (yet related) meanings, the idea is essentially this: reality is not a pregiven monological entity lying around for all to see; rather, various social practices and cultural contexts create an opening or clearing in which various types of subjects and objects can appear. For example, as I would put it, the magic worldspace creates a clearing in which animistic objects can appear; the mythic worldspace creates a space in which a caring God can appear; the rational worldspace creates a clearing in which worldcentric compassion can appear; the psychic worldspace creates a space in which the World Soul can appear; the causal worldspace creates a clearing in which the Abyss can be recognized. None of those are simply lying around out there and hitting the eyeballs of everybody. There is no single "pregiven world" (*the* essential insight of postmodernism).

CW 6: *Sex, Ecology, Spirituality*, 775

By understanding [the variety of] different truths, and acknowledging them, we can more sympathetically include them in an integral embrace. We can more expansively attune ourselves to the Kosmos. The final result might even be an attunement with the All, might even be Kosmic consciousness itself. Why not? But I think first we need to understand these various truths, so they can begin to speak to us, in us, through us—and we can begin to hear their voices and honor them, and thus invite all of them together into a rainbow coalition, an integral embrace.

These truths are behind much of the great postmodern rebellion. They are the key to the interior and transcendental dimensions; they speak eloquently in tongues of hidden gods and angels; they point to the heart of holons in general, and invite us into that interior world; they are antidote to the flat and faded world that passes for today.

We might even say that [the] four types of truth [the interiors and exteriors of individuals and collectives] are the four faces of Spirit as it shines in the manifest world.

cw 7: *A Brief History of Everything*, 128

A true humanistic psychology is built upon processes of intersubjective understanding and mutual recognition, about which quantum physics has not a single thing to say. Surely we do not want to base our new humanism on a power-driven monologue with rocks.

cw 6: *Sex, Ecology, Spirituality*, 742

To understand the whole, it is necessary to understand the parts. To understand the parts, it is necessary to understand the whole. Such is the circle of understanding.

We move from part to whole and back again, and in that dance of comprehension, in that amazing circle of understanding, we come alive to meaning, to value, and to vision: the very circle of understanding guides our way, weaving together the pieces, healing the fractures, mending the torn and tortured fragments, lighting the way ahead—this extraordinary movement from part to whole and back again, with healing the hallmark of each and every step, and grace the tender reward. . . .

I believe the integral vision will come upon you slowly but surely, carefully but fiercely, deliberately but radiantly, so that you and I will find ourselves sharing in the same circle of understanding, abiding in the same eye of Spirit, dancing in the freedom of the whole, expressed in all its parts.

cw 7: *The Eye of Spirit*, 419–420

The entire Kosmos exists as a network of rights and responsibilities correlative with degrees of depth and consciousness. Nothing is ever merely instrumental to anything, and everything ultimately, finally, has perfectly equal Ground-value as a perfect manifestation of primordial Purity, radiant Emptiness.

cw 6: *Sex, Ecology, Spirituality*, 766

So my supposedly "individual thought" is actually a phenomenon that intrinsically has (at least) . . . four aspects to it—intentional, behavioral, cultural, and social. And around the holistic circle we go: the social system will have a strong influence on the cultural world-view, which will set limits to the individual thoughts that I can have, which will register in the brain physiology. And we can go around that circle in any direction. They are all interwoven. They are all mutually determining. They all cause, and are caused by, the others, in concentric spheres of contexts within contexts indefinitely.

cw 7: *The Eye of Spirit*, 429

Reality is not composed of things or processes; it is not composed of atoms or quarks; it is not composed of wholes nor does it have any parts. Rather, it is composed of whole/parts, or holons.

This is true of atoms, cells, symbols, ideas. They can be understood neither as things nor processes, neither as wholes nor parts, but only as simultaneous whole/parts, so that standard "atomistic" and "wholistic" attempts are both off the mark. There is nothing that isn't a holon (upwardly and downwardly forever).

Before an atom is an atom, it is a holon. Before a cell is a cell, it is a holon. Before an idea is an idea, it is a holon. All of them are wholes that exist in other wholes, and thus they are all whole/parts, or holons, first and foremost (long before any "particular character-istics" are singled out by us).

Likewise, reality might indeed be composed of processes and not things, but all processes are only processes within other processes—that is, they are first and foremost holons. Trying to decide whether the fundamental units of reality are things or processes is utterly beside the point, because either way, they are all holons, and center-ing on one or the other misses the central issue. Clearly some things exist, and some processes exist, but they are each and all holons.

Therefore we can examine what *holons* have in common, and this releases us from the utterly futile attempt to find common processes or common entities on all levels and domains of existence, because that will never work; it leads always to reductionism, not true synthesis.

For example, to say that the universe is composed primarily of quarks is already to privilege a particular domain. Likewise, at the other end of the spectrum, to say that the universe is really composed primarily of our symbols, since these are all we really know—that, too, is to privilege a particular domain. But to say that the universe is composed of holons neither privileges a domain nor implies special fundamentalness for any level. Literature, for example, is *not* composed of subatomic particles; but both literature and subatomic particles are composed of holons.

cw 6: *Sex, Ecology, Spirituality*, 41–42

A holon's agency *enacts* a worldspace (brings forth a domain of distinctions), and does so relatively autonomously, with the added understanding that a holon's agency is partly a result of its historical "structural couplings" with the appropriate milieu. Agency as agency-in-communion thus enacts a worldspace codetermined by subject and object. . . .

[A] worldspace is not simply pregiven and then merely *represented* via a *correspondence* of agency with its allegedly separable communions (other agencies). Rather, the coherency of its agency (autonomy), structurally coupled with other communing agencies, enacts a worldspace mutually codetermined.

cw 6: *Sex, Ecology, Spirituality*, 569

The prime directive asks us to honor and appreciate the necessary, vital, and unique contribution provided by each and every wave of consciousness unfolding, and thus act to *protect and promote the health of the entire spiral*, and not any one privileged domain. At the same time, it invites us to offer, as a gentle suggestion, a conception of a more complete spectrum of consciousness, a full spiral of development, so that individuals or cultures (including ours) that are not aware of some of the deeper or higher dimensions of human possibilities may choose to act on those extraordinary resources, which in turn might help to defuse some of the recalcitrant problems that have not yielded to less integral approaches.

A Theory of Everything, 102–103

The agency of each holon establishes an opening or clearing in which similar-depthed holons can manifest to each other, for each other: agency-in-communion (all the way down).

cw 6: *Sex, Ecology, Spirituality*, 570

I am often asked, why even attempt an integration of the various worldviews? Isn't it enough to simply celebrate the rich diversity of various views and not try to integrate them? Well, recognizing diversity is certainly a noble endeavor, and I heartily support that pluralism. But if we remain merely at the stage of celebrating diversity, we ultimately are promoting fragmentation, alienation, separation and despair. You go your way, I go my way, we both fly apart—which is often what has happened under the reign of the pluralistic relativists, who have left us a postmodern Tower of Babel on too many fronts. It is not enough to recognize the many ways in which we are all different; we need to go further and start recognizing the many ways that we are also similar. Otherwise we simply contribute to heapism, not wholism. Building on the rich diversity offered by pluralistic relativism, we need to take the next step and weave those many strands into a holonic spiral of unifying connections, an interwoven Kosmos of mutual intermeshing. We need, in short, to move from pluralistic relativism to universal integralism—we need to keep trying to find the One-in-the-Many that is the form of the Kosmos itself.

A Theory of Everything, 112

Finding God through sex? And why not? The only thing that is astonishing in that equation is that it ever should have seemed odd to begin with. For many of the world's great wisdom traditions, particularly in their mature phases, sexuality was deeply viewed as an exquisite expression of spirituality—and a path to further spiritual realization. After all, in the ecstatic embrace of sexual love, we are taken far beyond ourselves, released from the cramp of the separate self, delivered at least temporarily into timeless, spaceless, blissful union with the wondrous beloved: and what better definition of spiritual release is there than that? We all taste God, taste Goddess, taste pure Spirit in those moments of sexual rapture, and wise men and women have always used that rapture to reveal Spirit's innermost secrets.

Foreword to *Finding God Through Sex* by David Deida, ix

I do believe . . . that *some* things about the transrational domains can be hinted at with a skillful but controlled use of reason, just as a painter can, with a skillful but controlled use of a 2-D canvas, convey the feeling of a 3-D perspective. This is what I attempt to do with my sketches of the higher or transrational levels of development . . .

CW 4: "Sociocultural Evolution," 338

Gaia's main problems are not industrialization, ozone depletion, over-population, or resource depletion. Gaia's main problem is *the lack of mutual understanding and mutual agreement in the noosphere* about how to proceed with those problems. We cannot rein in industry if we cannot reach mutual understanding and mutual agreement based on a worldcentric moral perspective concerning the global commons. And we reach that *worldcentric* moral perspective through a difficult and laborious process of interior growth and transcendence.

CW 7: A Brief History of Everything, 337

The fabric of the future will necessarily incorporate the rich diversity of female voices, and it will do so in a more gracious, graceful, and generous fashion than does today's world, if livable future we are to have at all.

One the one hand, of course, men and women share a vast array of common and universal experiences: we are all born, we all die, and in between we laugh and love and loathe and cherish; we play, and work, and fight, and fear. We breathe the same air, are sustained by the same Earth, have our heads in the same sky, and wonder all about it. . . . [W]e are, finally, a common humanity interrelated with global commons and all of Gaia's inhabitants.

But within those profound commonalties, there are wonderful differences: between cultures, between individuals, and between the sexes. And we seem to be at an extraordinary and auspicious moment in human evolution, where many of these rich differences, previously undervalued or even devalued altogether, are now being unleashed.

CW 4: Foreword to The Fabric of the Future: Women Visionaries Illuminate
the Path to Tomorrow, 392–393

Both the Left- and Right-Hand (interior and exterior) dimensions start from immediate apprehension or immediate experience, and that immediate experience, as William James explained, is properly called a datum, whether it occurs "internally" or "externally." Even if the data themselves are mediated by other factors (culture, mental sets, instruments, etc.), nonetheless at the moment of awareness, the immediacy of the experience is the pure datum in that occasion. Whether I am perceiving a tree "out there" or a desire for food "in here," they are both, at the moment of awareness, conveyed to me in pure immediacy (even though that immediacy may have mediating factors).

The Right-Hand path simply sticks to sensory immediacy, and ties its theorizing to the aspects of holons that can be detected with the external senses or their extensions: its data are sensory, which always means external senses (it doesn't even trust interior senses, since those are "private" and supposedly "not shareable"). Monological and empiric-analytic modes use an enormous amount of interior, conceptual, *a priori* cognitions, but eventually this approach ties all of them to the immediacy of externally perceived exteriors. And, as I said, that can be done, and is an important (if limited) mode of knowledge.

The Left-Hand path starts with the same immediacy of given experience, or immediate apprehension (it is the same immediacy as the external or Right-Hand dimension, because in the moment of direct apprehension, there is neither subject nor object, neither Left nor Right, as James explained). But unlike the Right-Hand path, which sticks to the objective/exteriors of holons as the basic immediacy gives way to subject and object, the Left-Hand path investigates the interior/subjective dimension of that basic immediacy as it gives way to subject and object.

And that is where and why interpretation enters the Left-Hand scene (and not so much the Right, where the blank stare at surfaces is most valued). Although in my own interior, I know depth directly by acquaintance (the immediate experience on any level is known directly, whether that be sensory impulses or archetypal light), nonetheless if you and I are going to share these experiences, we must communicate our depth to each other. And whereas the external surfaces are "out there" for all to see, the interior apprehensions can only be shared by communicative exchange which requires that we each interpret what the other is communicating. And that is why interpretation (hermeneutics) is inescapable for the Left-Hand paths.

The Right-Hand path of course uses interpretation in its own theorizing—it interprets the data—but the data are all ultimately data that do not respond communicatively or interiorly (the data are just the exterior surfaces, whether that be rocks, brain chemistry, or suicide rates: they don't complicate the scene by talking back: no nasty dialogues here).

Thus, what really irks the Right-Hand path about the Left Hand is not that its data aren't immediate (because they are; it is the same immediacy that is also the starting point for the Right-Hand path), but rather the necessity for introspection, interiority, and interpretation, all of which are rejected as not publicly shareable, which is of course nonsense: what the Right-Hand path itself accepts as data is determined only communicatively.

In short, both the Right- and Left-Hand paths start with the same immediacy of given experience, but the Right Hand sticks to "external surfaces" that, as objects of investigation, do not have to respond communicatively (it is monological), whereas the Left-Hand goes a step further and investigates those holons that do respond communicatively (dialogically, hermeneutically, interpretively). The one sticks to surfaces, the other investigates the depths. And since surfaces can be seen, the one asks, "What does it do?"; but since depth does not sit on the surface, the other must ask "What does it mean?" ("What is under the surface?").

cw 6: *Sex, Ecology, Spirituality*, 624–625

Integral studies appear to be the only truly global studies now in existence, studies that span the entire spectrum of human growth and aspiration. The coming decade, I have no doubt, will witness the emergence of integral studies as a truly comprehensive field of human endeavor. And although I do not think that the world is entering anything resembling a "new age" or "transpersonal transformation," I do believe that integral studies will always be that one beacon to men and women who see Spirit in the world and the world in Spirit.

cw 4: "Paths Beyond Ego in the Coming Decade," 420–421

Love for a specific person is radiant when it arises in Emptiness. It is still love, it is still intensely personal, it is still very specific; but it is a wave that arises from an ocean of infinity. It is as if a great sea of love brings forth a wave, and that wave carries the force and thrill of the entire sea in its every breaking crest. The sensation is like watching an early morning sunrise in the desert: a vast open clear blue spaciousness, within which there arises, on the horizon, an intense

red-yellow fire. You are the infinite sky of Love, in which a particular fire-ball of personal love arises.

One thing is certain: infinite love and personal love are not mutually exclusive—the latter is just an individual wave of an infinite
ocean. When I lie awake, next to her, early in the morning, doing
meditation, nothing really changes in the contemplation except this:
there is a whole-body bliss, paradoxically faint but intense, that edges
my awareness. It is sexual energy reconnected to its source in the subtle regions of the bodymind. I will often touch her lightly as I meditate; it definitely completes an energy circuit, and she can feel it, too.

But that is what men and women (as well as "butch/femme" pair-
ings across sexual orientations) can do for each other, and that is the
core claim of Tantra as well: in a very concrete, visceral way, the
union of male and female is the union of Eros and Agape, Ascending
and Descending, Emptiness and Form, Wisdom and Compassion.
Not theoretically but concretely, in the actual distribution of prana
or energy currents in the body itself. And this is why, in the very
highest Tantric teachings (anuttaratantrayoga), the mere visualization of sexual congress with the divine consort is not enough for final
enlightenment. Rather, for ultimate enlightenment, one must take an
actual partner—real sex—in order to complete the circuits conducive
to recognizing the already-enlightened mind.

cw 8: *One Taste,* 461

Various phenomena follow patterns that do not themselves show up
as phenomena (much as the rules of a card game do not appear on
any of the cards). The *subjective space* in which experienced phenomena arise is itself constructed and follows patterns that do not
ordinarily show up in naive (or even bracketed) experience; and further, the subjective space itself develops only via *intersubjective* patterns of dialogical and interpretive cognitions, *none of which show
up in a simple phenomenology of immediate lived experience.*

cw 6: *Sex, Ecology, Spirituality,* 583

The general idea of integral practice is clear enough: *Exercise body,
mind, soul, and spirit in self, culture, and nature* . . . Pick a basic
practice from each category, or from as many categories as pragmat-
ically possible, and practice them concurrently. The more categories

engaged, the more effective they all become (because they are all intimately related as aspects of your own being). Practice them diligently, and coordinate your integral efforts to unfold the various potentials of the bodymind—until the bodymind itself unfolds in Emptiness, and the entire journey is a misty memory from a trip that never even occurred.

cw 4: *Integral Psychology*, 546

I would like to propose the thesis that the Basic Moral Intuition (BMI)—present at all stages of human growth—is "Protect and promote the greatest depth for the greatest span." This BMI represents (*is a direct result of*) the manifestation of Spirit in the four quadrants (or simply the Big Three)—the depth in I expanded to include others (we) in a corresponding objective state of affairs (it). That is all individuals intuit Spirit, and since Spirit *manifests as* the Big Three, then the basic spiritual intuition is felt in all three domains, and thus the basic spiritual intuition ("Honor and actualize Spirit") shows up as "Promote the greatest depth for the greatest span," or so I maintain.*

cw 6: *Sex, Ecology, Spirituality*, 640–641

But if you desire to see into your own depths and interpret them more adequately, then you will have to *talk* to somebody who has seen those depths before and helped others interpret them more adequately. In this intersubjective dialogue with a therapeutic helper, you will hold hands and walk the path of more adequate interpretations, you will enter a circle of intersubjective depth, and the more clearly you can interpret and articulate this depth, the less baffling you will become to yourself, the clearer you will become to yourself, the more transparent you will be.

And eventually, as we'll see, you might even become transparent to the Divine, liberated in your own infinite depth. But in any event, none of this, at any level, will open to you if you insist on hugging only the surfaces.

cw 7: *A Brief History of Everything*, 137

---

* For a summary of the four quadrants, see the introduction to *The Eye of Spirit*, cw 7, 429–450.

You cannot have a global spirituality, a bodhisattvic spirituality, a post-postconventional spirituality, an authentically transpersonal spirituality, unless the perspectives of all sentient beings are taken into account and fully honored. Unless, that is, you integrate the deep capacities of reason and vision-logic, and then proceed from there.

Anybody can say they are being "spiritual"—and they are, because everybody has some type and level of concern. Let us therefore see their actual conception, in thought and action, and see how many perspectives it is in fact concerned with, and how many perspectives it actually takes into account, and how many perspectives it attempts to integrate, and thus let us see how deep and how wide runs that bodhisattva vow to refuse rest until all perspectives whatsoever are liberated into their own primordial nature.

cw 7: *The Eye of Spirit*, 624

The mystic's claim is that mystical . . . validity claims are anchored in extralinguistic realities that, however much they are molded by cultural factors, are not merely the product of shifting cultural and provincial-only fashions (the referents of the transcendental signifiers exist in a worldspace that is disclosed to those with the appropriate developmental signifieds, even if these are always already culturally situated. Thus, cultural context does not prevent natural science from making and redeeming universal claims, nor likewise does it prevent mystical science from making and redeeming not-merely-culture-bound claims).

cw 6: *Sex, Ecology, Spirituality*, 647

Transcendence restores humor. Spirit brings smiling. Suddenly, laughter returns. Too many representatives of too many movements—even very good movements, such as feminism, ecology, and spiritual studies—seem to lack humor altogether. In other words, they lack lightness, they lack a distance from themselves, a distance from the ego and its grim game of forcing others to conform to its contours. There is self-transcending humor, or there is the game of egoic power. But we have chosen egoic power and politically correct thought police; grim Victorian reformers pretending to be defending civil rights; messianic new-paradigm thinkers who are going to save the planet and heal the world. No wonder Mencken wrote that

"Every third American devotes himself to improving and lifting up his fellow citizens, usually by force; this messianic delusion is our national disease." Perhaps we should all trade two pounds of ego for one ounce of laughter.

CW 8: *One Taste*, 582

It is always already undone, you see, and always already over. In the simple feeling of Being, worlds are born and die—they live and dance and sing a while and melt back into oblivion, and nothing ever really happens here, in the simple world of One Taste. A thousand forms will come and go, a million worlds will rise and fall, a billion souls will love and laugh and languish fast and die, and One Taste alone will embrace them all. And I-I will be there, as I-I always have been, to Witness the rise and miraculous fall of my infinite easy Worlds, happening now and forever, now and forever, now and always forever it seems.

And then again, I might just stay here, and watch the sunset one more time, through the misty rain that is now falling, quietly all around.

CW 8: *One Taste*, 623

For the real intent of my writing is not to say, You must think in this way. The real intent is: here are some of the many important facets of this extraordinary Kosmos; have you thought about including them in your own worldview? My work is an attempt to make room in the Kosmos for all of the dimensions, levels, domains, waves, memes, modes, individuals, cultures, and so on ad infinitum. I have one major rule: *everybody* is right. More specifically, everybody—including me—has some important pieces of truth, and all of those pieces need to be honored, cherished, and included in a more gracious, spacious, and compassionate embrace. To Freudians I say, Have you looked at Buddhism? To Buddhists I say, Have you studied Freud? To liberals I say, Have you thought about how important some conservative ideas are? To conservatives I say, Can you perhaps include a more liberal perspective? And so on, and so on, and so on. . . . At no point have I ever said: Freud is wrong, Buddha is wrong, liberals are wrong, conservatives are wrong. I have only suggested that they are true but partial. My critical writings have never attacked the central beliefs of any discipline, only the claims that the particular discipline has the only truth—and on those grounds I have often been harsh. But every approach, I honestly believe, is essentially true but partial, true but partial, true but partial.

And on my own tombstone, I dearly hope that someday they will write: He was true but partial. . . .

cw 8: Introduction, 49

Tantra, in the general sense, presents the ultimate Nondual reality as the sexual embrace of God and the Goddess, of Shiva and Shakti, of Emptiness and Form. Neither Ascent nor Descent is final, ultimate, or privileged, but rather, like the primordial yin and yang, they generate each other, depend upon each other, cannot exist without the other, and find their own true being by dying into the other, only to awaken together, joined in bliss, as the entire Kosmos, finding that eternity is wildly in love with the productions of time, the nondual Heart radiating as all creation, and blessing all creation, and singing this embrace for all eternity—an embrace that we are all asked to repeat in our own awareness, moment to moment, endlessly, miraculously, as the immediate presence of One Taste. This is the Nondual vision, this union of Reflux and Efflux, God and the Goddess, Emptiness and Form, Wisdom and Compassion, Eros and Agape, Ascent and Descent—perfectly and blissfully united in One Taste, the radical sound of one hand clapping.

cw 7: *A Brief History of Everything*, 284

We artificially split our awareness into compartments such as subject vs. object, life vs. death, mind vs. body, inside vs. outside, reason vs. instinct—a divorce settlement that sets experience cutting into experience and life fighting with life. The result of such violence, although known by many other names, is simply unhappiness. Life becomes suffering, full of battles. But all of the *battles* in our experience—our conflicts, anxieties, sufferings, and despairs—are created by the *boundaries* we misguidedly throw around our experience.

cw 1: *No Boundary*, 429

"The typical New Age notion is that you want good things to happen to you, so think good thoughts; and because you create your own reality, those thoughts will come true. Conversely, if you are sick, it's because you have been bad. The mystical notion, on the other hand, is that your deepest Self transcends *both* good and bad, so by accepting *absolutely everything* that happens to you—by equally embracing both good and bad *with equanimity*—you can transcend the ego altogether. The idea is *not* to have one thing that is good smash into another thing called my ego, but to gently rise above both."

Boomeritis, 336

What is so remarkable about mutual understanding is not that I can take a simple word like "dog" and point to a real dog and say, "I mean that." What is so remarkable is that *you* know what *I* mean by that! Forget the simple empirical pointing! Instead, look at this intersubjective understanding. It is utterly amazing. It means you and I can inhabit each other's interior to some degree. You and I can *share* our *depth*. When we point to *truth*, and we are situated in *truthfulness*, we can reach *mutual understanding*. This is a miracle. If Spirit exists, you can begin to look for it here.

CW 7: *A Brief History of Everything*, 156

"You can be God, or you can be an ego pretending to be God. It's your choice."

Boomeritis, 376

And so the whispering voice from every corner of the Kosmos says: let truth and truthfulness and goodness and beauty shine as the seals of a radiant Spirit that would never, and could never, abandon us.

CW 7: *A Brief History of Everything*, 161

The Above has been denied; the Below has been ignored—and we are asked to remain—in the middle—paralyzed. Waiting, perhaps, to see what a rat would do in the same circumstances or, at a bit deeper level, looking for inspiration in the dregs of the *id*.

CW 1: *The Spectrum of Consciousness*, 39

The finite self is going to die—magic will not save it, mythic gods will not save it, rational science will not save it—and facing that cutting fact is part of becoming authentic. This was one of Heidegger's constant points. Coming to terms with one's mortality and one's finitude—this is part of finding one's own authentic being-in-the-world (authentic agency-in-communion).

The existentialists have beautifully analyzed this authentic self, the actual centauric self—its characteristics, its mode of being, its stance in the world—and most important, they have analyzed the common lies and bad faith that sabotage this authenticity. We lie about our mortality and finitude by constructing immortality symbols—vain attempts to beat time and exist everlastingly in some mythic heaven, some rational project, some great artwork, through which we project our incapacity to face death. We lie about the responsibility for our own choices, preferring to see ourselves as passive victims of some outside force. We lie about the richness of the present by projecting ourselves backward in guilt and forward in anxiety. We lie about our fundamental responsibility by hiding in the herd mentality, getting lost in the Other. In place of the authentic or actual self, we live as the inauthentic self, the false self, fashioning its projects of deception to hide itself from the shocking truth of existence.

CW 7: *A Brief History of Everything*, 228

In this moment and this moment and this, an individual *is* Buddha, is Atman, is the Dharmakaya—*but*, in this moment and this moment and this, he ends up as John Doe, as a separate self, as an isolated body apparently bounded by other isolated bodies. At the beginning of *this* and every moment, each individual *is* God as the Clear Light; but by the *end* of this same moment—in a flash, in the twinkling of an eye—he winds up as an isolated ego.

CW 2: *The Atman Project*, 267

To see our resistance to unity consciousness is to be able, for the first time, to deal with it and finally to drop it—thus removing the secret obstacle to our own liberation.

CW 1: *No Boundary*, 566

There is *intersubjectivity woven into the very fabric of the Kosmos at all levels.* This is not just the Spirit in "me," not just the Spirit in "it," not just the Spirit in "them"—but the Spirit in "us," in all of *us.*

cw 7: *A Brief History of Everything,* 156

Kosmic consciousness is not the obliteration of individuality but its consummate fulfillment, at which point we can speak of Self or no-self, it matters not which: your Self is the Self of the entire Kosmos, timeless and therefore eternal, spaceless and therefore infinite, moved only by a radiant Love that defies date or duration.

cw 3: Introduction, 14–15

All lesser stages, no matter how occasionally ecstatic or visionary, are still beset with the primal mood of ego, which is sickness unto death. Even the saint, according to the sages, has yet to finally surrender his or her soul, or separate-self sense, and this prevents the saint from attaining absolute identity with and as Godhead.

cw 3: *A Sociable God,* 66

When Spirit is de-mythologized, it can be approached *as* Spirit, in its Absolute Suchness (*tathata*), and not as a cosmic Parent.

cw 3: *A Sociable God,* 87

For no reason that can be stated in words, a subtle ripple is generated in [the] infinite [ocean of Consciousness as Such, timeless, spaceless, infinite, and eternal]. This ripple could not in itself detract from infinity, for the infinite can embrace any and all entities. But this subtle ripple, awakening to itself, *forgets* the infinite sea of which it is just a gesture. The ripple therefore feels set apart from infinity, isolated, separate.

This ripple, very rarefied, is . . . the very beginning, however slight, of the wave of selfhood. At this point, however, it is still very subtle, still "close" to the infinite, still blissful.

But somehow not really satisfied, not profoundly at peace. For in order to find that utter peace, the ripple would have to return to the ocean, dissolve back into radiant infinity, forget itself and remember the absolute. But to do so, the ripple would have to die—it would have to accept the death of its separate-self sense. And it is terrified of this.

Since all it wants is the infinite, but since it is terrified of accepting the necessary death, it goes about seeking infinity in ways that prevent it. Since the ripple *wants* release and is *afraid* of it at the same time, it arranges a *compromise* and a *substitute*. Instead of finding actual Godhead, the ripple pretends itself to be god, cosmocentric, heroic, all-sufficient, immortal. . . .

Driven by this Atman-project—the attempt to get infinity in ways that prevent it and force substitute gratifications—the ripple creates ever tighter and ever more restricted modes of consciousness. . . .

[Yet behind] the ignorant drama of the separate self, there nonetheless lies Atman. All of the tragic drama of the self's desire and mortality was the just the play of the Divine, a cosmic sport, a gesture of Self-forgetting so that the shock of Self-realization would be the more delightful. The ripple *did* forget the Self, to be sure—but it was a ripple *of* the Self, and remained so throughout the play.

cw 3: *Eye to Eye*, 268–269

On the one hand, spirit is the *highest* of all possible domains; it is the Summit of all realms, the Being beyond all beings. It is the domain that is a subset of no other domain, and thus preserves its radically transcendental nature. On the other hand, since spirit is all-pervading and all-inclusive, since it is the set of all possible sets, the Condition of all conditions and the Nature of all natures, it is not properly thought of as a realm set apart from other realms, but as the Ground or Being of *all* realms, the pure *That* of which all manifestation is but a play or modification. And thus spirit preserves (paradoxically) its radically immanent nature.

cw 4: *Quantum Questions*, 260–261

That which witnesses, and that which is witnessed, are only one and the same. The entire World Process then arises, moment to moment, as one's own Being, outside which, and prior to which, nothing exists. That Being is totally beyond and prior to anything that arises, and yet no part of that Being is other to what arises.

cw 3: *Eye to Eye*, 241

And there, hidden in the secret cave of the Heart, where God and the Goddess finally unite, where Emptiness embraces all Form as the lost and found Beloved, where Eternity joyously sings the praises of noble Time, where Shiva uncontrollably swoons for luminescent Shakti, where Ascending and Descending erotically embrace in the sound of one hand clapping—there forever in the universe of One Taste, the Kosmos recognizes its own true nature, self-seen in a tacit recognition that leaves not even a single soul to tell the amazing tale.

And remember? There in the Heart, where the couple finally unite, the entire game is undone, this nightmare of evolution, and you are exactly where you were prior to the beginning of the whole show. With a sudden shock of the utterly obvious, you recognize your own Original Face, the face you had prior to the Big Bang, the face of utter Emptiness that smiles as all creation and sings as the entire Kosmos—and it is all undone in that primal glance, and all that is left is the smile, and the reflection of the moon on a quiet pond, late on a crystal clear night.

CW 7: *A Brief History of Everything*, 363

The observer in you, the Witness in you, transcends the isolated *person* in you and opens instead—from within or from behind, as Emerson said—onto a vast expanse of awareness no longer obsessed with the individual bodymind, no longer a respecter or abuser of persons, no longer fascinated by the passing joys and set-apart sorrows of the lonely self, but standing still in silence as an opening or clearing through which light shines, not from the world but into it—"a light shines *through us* upon things." *That which* observes or witnesses the self, the person, is precisely to that degree *free* of the self, the person, and *through that opening* comes pouring the light and power of a Self, a Soul, that, as Emerson puts it, "would make our knees bend." . . .

And those persons *through whom* the soul shines, *through whom* the "soul has its way," are not therefore weak characters, timid personalities, meek presences among us. They are personal plus, not personal minus. Precisely because they are no longer exclusively identified with the individual personality, and yet because they still preserve the personality, then *through that* personality flows the force and fire of the soul. They may be soft and often remain in silence, but it is a thunderous silence that veritably drowns out the egos chattering loudly all around them. Or they may be animated and very outgoing, but their dynamism is magnetic, and people are drawn somehow to the presence, fascinated. Make no mistake: these are strong characters, these souls, sometimes wildly exaggerated characters, sometimes world-historical, precisely because their personalities are plugged into a universal source that rumbles through their veins and rudely rattles those around them.

CW 6: *Sex, Ecology, Spirituality*, 289–290

In the Eastern traditions, one of the main functions of this soul art is to serve as a support for contemplation. In the extraordinary tradition of Tibetan *thangka* painting, for example, the buddhas and bodhisattvas that are depicted are not symbolic or metaphoric or allegorical, but rather direct representations of one's own subtle-level potentials. By visualizing these subtle forms in meditation, one opens oneself to those corresponding potentials in one's own being.

The point is that soul art, of any variety, is not metaphoric or allegorical; *it is a direct depiction of the direct experience of the subtle level*. It is not a painting of sensory objects seen with the eye of flesh, and it is not a painting of conceptual objects seen with the eye of mind; it is a painting of subtle objects seen with the eye of contemplation.

That means that artist and critic and viewer alike must be alive to that higher domain in order to participate in this art. As Brancusi reminded us, "Look at my works until you see them. Those who are closer to God have seen them." As Kandinsky put it, the aim is to "proclaim the reign of Spirit . . . to proclaim light from light, the flowing light of the Godhead," all seen, not with the eye of flesh or the eye of mind, but with the eye of contemplation, and then rendered into artistic material form as a reminder of, and a call to, that extraordinary vision.

As the eye of contemplation deepens, and consciousness evolves from the subtle to the causal (and nondual), subtle forms give way to the formless (e.g., *nirvikalpa*, *ayin*, *nirodh*) and eventually to the nondual (*sahaja*), which I will together treat as the domain of pure Spirit. The art of this domain takes no particular referent at all, because it is bound to no realm whatsoever. It might therefore *take its referent from any or all levels*—from the sensorimotor/body level (such as in a Zen landscape) to the subtle and causal levels (such as in Tibetan *thangkas*). What characterizes this art is not its content, but the utter absence of the self-contraction in the artist who paints it, an absence that, in the greatest of this art, can at least temporarily evoke a similar freedom in the viewer (which was Schopenhauer's profound insight about the power of great art: it brings transcendence). . . .

Art, then, is one of the important dimensions of every level in the Great Holarchy of Being. Art is the Beauty of Spirit as it expresses itself on each and every level of its own manifestation. Art is in the eye of the beholder, in the I of the beholder: Art is the I of Spirit.

CW 8: *The Marriage of Sense and Soul*, 250–251

The secret of all genuinely spiritual works of art is that they issue from nondual or unity consciousness, no matter what "objects" they portray. . . . The artwork, no matter what the object, becomes transparent to the Divine, and is a direct expression of Spirit.

The viewer momentarily *becomes* the art and is for that moment released from the alienation that is ego. Great spiritual art dissolves ego into nondual consciousness, and is to that extent experienced as an epiphany; a revelation, release or liberation from the tyranny of the separate-self sense. To the extent that a work can usher one into the nondual, then it is spiritual or universal, no matter whether it depicts bugs or Buddhas.

CW 4: "In the Eye of the Artist," Foreword to *Sacred Mirrors: The Visionary Art of Alex Grey*, 379

The Self is not this, not that, precisely because it is the pure Witness of this or that, and thus in all cases transcends any this and any that. The Self cannot even be said to be "One," for that is just another quality, another object that is perceived or witnessed. The Self is not "Spirit"; rather, it is that which, right now, is witnessing that concept. The Self is not the "Witness"—that is just another word or concept, and the Self is that which is witnessing that concept. The Self is not Emptiness, the Self is not a pure Self—and so on. . . .

[Sri] Ramana [Maharshi] often refers to the Self by the name "I-I," since the Self is the simple Witness of even the ordinary "I." We are all, says Ramana, perfectly aware of the I-I, for we are all aware of our capacity to witness in the present moment. But we *mistake* the pure I-I or pure Seer with some sort of object *that can be seen* and is thus precisely *not* the Seer or the true Self, but is merely some sort of memory or image or identity or self-concept, all of which are objects, none of which is the Witness of objects. We identify the I-I with this or that I, and thus identified with a mere finite and temporal object, we suffer the slings and arrows of all finite objects, whereas the Self remains ever as it is, timeless, eternal, unborn, unwavering, undying, ever and always present.

cw 6: *Sex, Ecology, Spirituality*, 314–315

When an artist is alive to the spiritual domains, he or she can depict and convey those domains in artistic rendering, which wrestles Spirit into matter and attempts to speak through that medium. When great artists do so, the artwork then reminds us of our own higher possibilities, our own deepest nature, our own most profound ground, which we all are invited to rediscover. The purpose of truly transcendent art is to express something you are not yet, but that you can become. . . .

It calls us beyond ourselves, it takes us beyond ourselves, to a transpersonal land where Spirit is real, where God is alive, where Buddha smiles and the Tao sings, where our own original face shines with a glory that time forgot and space cannot recall. We are confronted with the best that we can be, the deepest we can feel, the highest we can see, and so we go away . . . a little better than we were a minute before.

cw 4: Foreword to *The Mission of Art* by Alex Grey, 394–395

Different meditation practices engineer different states and different experiences, but pure Presence itself is unwavering, and thus the highest approach in Dzogchen is "Buddhahood without meditation": not the creation but the *direct recognition* of an already perfectly present and freely given primordial Purity, of the pure Emptiness of this and every state, embracing equally all forms: embracing a self, embracing a no-self, embracing whatever arises.

But in no case is primordial Emptiness a particular state versus another state, or a particular concept versus another concept, or a particular view versus a different view: it is the pure Presence in which any and all forms arise. It certainly is not "no-self" as opposed to "self." It is rather the opening or clearing in which, right now, all manifestation arises in your awareness, remains a bit, and fades: the unwavering clearing itself never enters the stream of time, but cognizes each and all with perfect Presence, primordial Purity, fierce Compassion, unflinching Embrace.

This unwavering Presence is not entered. There is no stepping into it or falling out of it. The Buddhas never entered this state, nor do ordinary people lack it (the Buddhas never entered it because nobody ever fell out of it). It is absolutely *not an experience*—not an experience of momentary states, not an experience of self, not an experience of no-self, not an experience of relaxing, not an experience of surrendering: it is the Empty opening or clearing in which *all* of those experiences come and go, an opening or clearing that, were it not always already perfectly Present, no experiences could arise in the first place.

This pure Presence is not a change of state, not an altered state, not a different state, not a state of peace or calm or bliss (or anger or fear or envy). It is the simple, pure, immediate, present awareness in which all of those states come and go, the opening or clearing in which they arise, remain, pass; arise, remain, pass. . . .

And yet there is something that does not arise or remain or pass— the simple opening, the immediateness of awareness, the simple feeling of Being, of which all particular states and particular experiences are simply ripples, wrinkles, gestures, folds: the clouds that come and go in the sky . . . and you are the sky. You are not behind your eyes staring out at the clouds that pass; you are the sky in which, and through which, the clouds float, endlessly, ceaselessly, spontaneously, freely, with no obstruction, no barriers, no contractions, no glitches: no moving parts in one's true nature, nothing to break down. In spring it rains; in winter it snows. Remarkable, this empty clearing.

You do not *become* this opening or clearing; you do not become the sky. You are not always the sky, nor are you already the sky: you are *always already* the sky: it is always already spontaneously accomplished: and that is why the clouds can come and go in the first place. The sunlight freely plays on the water. Remarkable! Birds are already singing in the woods. Amazing! The ocean already washes on the shore, freely wetting the pebbles and shells. What is not accomplished? Hear that distant bell ringing? Who is not enlightened?

And yet, and yet: how best to refer to this always already Emptiness? What words could a fish use to refer to water? How could you point out water to a fish? Drenched in it, never apart from it, upheld by it—what are we to do? Splash water in its face? What if its original face *is* water?

cw 6: *Sex, Ecology, Spirituality*, 730–731

Art is the perception and depiction of the Sublime, the Transcendent, the Beautiful, the Spiritual. Art is a window to God, an opening to the Goddess, a portal through which you and I, with the help of the artist, may discover depths and heights of our soul undreamt of by the vulgar world. Art is the eye of Spirit, through which the Sublime can reach down to us, and we up to It, and be transfigured and transformed in the process. Art, at its best, is the representation of your very own soul, a reminder of who and what you truly are, and therefore can become.

cw 4: Foreword to *Drinking Lightning* by Philip Rubinov-Jacobson, 404

Ramana Maharshi used to say, "You thank God for the good things that happen to you, but don't thank Him for the bad things as well, and that is where you go wrong." (That, incidentally, is also exactly where the new age movement goes wrong.) The point being that God is not a mythic Parent punishing or rewarding egoic tendencies, but the impartial Reality and Suchness of *all* manifestation. As even Isaiah, in a rare moment, realized: "I make the light to fall on the good and the bad alike; I, the Lord, do all these things." As long as we are caught in the dualities of good versus bad, pleasure versus pain, health versus illness, life versus death, then we are locked out of that nondual and supreme identity with *all* of manifestation, with the entire universe of "one taste." Ramana maintained that only in befriending our suffering, our illness, our pain, could we truly find a larger and more encompassing identity with the All, with the Self, who is not the victim of life but its impartial Witness and Source. And especially, Ramana said, befriend death, the ultimate teacher.

cw 5: *Grace and Grit*, 373

I have it on good authority that Spirit does not belong to any particular church, but resides in the deepest part of your very own heart every time you love.

Foreword to *Finding God Through Sex* by David Deida, p. x

And who knows, we might, you and I just might, in the upper reaches of the spectrum of consciousness itself, directly intuit the mind of some eternal Spirit—a Spirit that shines forth in every I and every we and every it, a Spirit that sings as the rain and dances as the wind, a Spirit of which every conversation is the sincerest worship, a Spirit that speaks with your tongue and looks out from your eyes, that touches with these hands and cries out with this voice—and a Spirit that has always whispered lovingly in our ears: Never forget the Good, and never forget the True, and never forget the Beautiful.

cw 7: *The Eye of Spirit*, 450

The Self doesn't live forever in time, it lives in the timeless present prior to time, prior to history, change, succession. The Self is present as Pure Presence, not as everlasting duration, a rather horrible notion.

cw 5: *Grace and Grit*, 103

And so: given the measure of your own authentic realization, you were actually thinking about *gently whispering* into the ear of that near-deaf world? No, my friend, you must shout. Shout from the heart of what you have seen, shout however you can.

But not indiscriminately. Let us proceed carefully with this transformative shout. Let small pockets of radically transformative spirituality, authentic spirituality, focus their efforts, and transform their students. And let these pockets slowly, carefully, responsibly, humbly, begin to spread their influence, embracing an *absolute tolerance* for all views, but attempting nonetheless to advocate a true and authentic and integral spirituality—by example, by radiance, by obvious release, by unmistakable liberation. Let those pockets of transformation gently persuade the world and its reluctant selves, and challenge their legitimacy, and challenge their limiting translations, and offer an awakening in the face of the numbness that haunts the world at large.

Let it start right here, right now, with us—with you and with me—and with our commitment to breathe into infinity until infinity alone is the only statement that the world will recognize. Let a radical realization shine from our faces, and roar from our hearts, and thunder from our brains—this simple fact, this obvious fact: that you, in the very immediateness of your present awareness, are in fact the entire world, in all its frost and fever, in all its glories and its grace, in all its triumphs and its tears. You do not see the sun, you are the sun; you do not hear the rain, you are the rain; you do not feel the earth, you are the earth. And in that simple, clear, unmistakable regard, translation has ceased in all domains, and you have transformed into the very Heart of the Kosmos Itself—and there, right there, very simply, very quietly, it is all undone.

Wonder and remorse will then be alien to you, and self and others will be alien to you, and outside and inside will have no meaning at all. And in that obvious shock of recognition—where my Master is my Self, and that Self is the Kosmos at large, and the Kosmos is my Soul—you will walk very gently into the fog of this world, and transform it entirely by doing nothing at all.

And then, and then, and only then—you will finally, clearly, carefully and with compassion, write on the tombstone of a self that never even existed: There is only Spirit.

CW 8: *One Taste*, 312–313

8

One without a Second

*Written in Wilber's early twenties, the following essay confronts a
paradox that has remained central to his thinking: Spirit is both
completely transcendent (beyond everything) and completely immanent (inherent in everything).*

*Over the years Wilber has offered numerous metaphors to help us
approach this paradox, such as a spiral, a nest, an ocean with waves,
or a ladder. When he uses a ladder to represent the evolution of consciousness, the ladder's highest rung symbolizes Spirit as transcen-
dently apart from and above all other forms of manifestation.*

*The paradox is that Spirit totally and evenly infuses every rung
of the ladder. In this way, Spirit exists equally in thumbtack and
computer, serpent and Adam, "dirt and deity." Carrying the ladder
metaphor further, Spirit—as the all-pervading ground of Being—
even includes the space between the ladder's rungs! This essential
paradox of Spirit is the focus of "One without a Second." The higher one climbs on Spirit's ladder, the more likely one is to fall off and
discover the all-pervading embrace of Spirit.*

IN THE *Chandogya Upanishad*, Brahman—the absolute reality, the
ultimate state of consciousness—is described in glaringly simple
and straightforward terms: the Absolute is "One without a second."
That inspired Upanishadic text does not describe the ultimate as the
creator, controller, ruler, or lord of a second; neither does it speak of
One opposed to a second, nor One outside a second, nor over, above,
or beyond a second—but One without a second. The Absolute, in
other words, is that which has nothing outside It, nothing apart from
It, nothing other to It, a fact expressed in Isaiah as "I am the Lord,

and there is none else." All of which means that there is really nothing outside Brahman, nothing outside the Absolute. In the words of an old Zen Master:

> All the Buddhas and all sentient beings are nothing but the One Mind, beside which nothing exists. Above, below, and around you, all is spontaneously existing, for there is nowhere which is outside the Buddha-Mind.

Of course, if there were anything outside the Absolute, that would immediately impose a limitation on It, for the Absolute would then be one outside a second instead of One without a second. And so it is in this sense that Brahman, the Buddha-Mind, the Godhead is called absolutely all-encompassing, all-inclusive, and all-pervading. When the Upanishads say "All the world is Brahman," and "This, too, is Brahman"; when the *Lankavatara Sutra* proclaims that "The world is nothing but Mind," and "All is Mind"; when the *Awakening of Faith* states that "All things are only of the One Mind"; when the Taoist texts insist that "There is nothing outside the Tao; you cannot deviate from It"— well, they mean just that. To quote the apocryphal Acts of Peter:

> Thou are perceived of the spirit only, thou art unto me father, thou my mother, thou my brother, thou my friend, thou my bondsman, thou my steward: thou art All and All is in thee: and thou art, and there is nought else that is save thee only.

This being true because, as Christ said in the Gospel of Saint Thomas:

> I am the Light that is above them all, I am the All, the All came forth from Me and the All attained to Me. Cleave a piece of wood, I am there; Lift up the stone and you will find Me there.

Now the statement that all the world is really Brahman usually fires up in overly imaginative minds such fancies as uniform, all-pervading, featureless but divine goo; the instantaneous and total evaporation of all diversity and multiplicity, leaving behind an immaculate but amorphous All-knowing, All-merciful, celestial Vacuum. We flounder in such mental frenzies only because we expect the statement "All is Brahman" to be a logical proposition, containing some type of mental information about the universe, and taken thus, we can only picture its meaning to be the reduction of all multiplicity to uniform, homogeneous, and unchanging mush.

But "All is Brahman" should not be mistaken as a philosophical conclusion, a logical theory, or a merely verbal explanation of reality. For the sages of every time and place have unanimously maintained that the Absolute is actually ineffable, unspeakable, utterly beyond words, symbols, and logic. And not because it is too mysterious or too sublime or too complex for words, but rather because it is too simple, too obvious, too close to be caught in the net of symbols and signs. Because there is nothing outside It, there is no way to define or classify It. As Johannes Scotus (Erigena) remarked, "God does not know Himself, what He is, because He is not a *what*; in a certain respect He is incomprehensible to Himself and to every intellect." Or, as Shankara, the Master of Vedanta Hinduism, explains:

> Now there is no class to which Brahman belongs, no common genus. It cannot therefore be denoted by words which signify a category of things. Nor can it be denoted by quality, for it is without qualities; nor yet by activity because it is without activity—"at rest, without parts or activity," according to the Scriptures. Neither can it be denoted by relationship, for it is "without a second" and is not the object of anything but its own self. Therefore it cannot be defined by word or idea; as the Scripture says, it is the One "before whom words recoil."

This, indeed, is also the point of Wittgenstein's philosophy; namely, we cannot make any valid statements about Reality as a whole because there is no place outside it where we can take up a stance so as to describe it. In other words, "we could only say things about the world as a whole if we could get outside the world, if, that is to say, it ceased to be for us the whole world. . . . (But) for us, it cannot have a boundary, since it has nothing outside it." And having no boundary, no limits—being one without a second—it cannot be defined or classified. You can define and classify, for example, a "fish" because there are things that are not fish, such as rocks, trees, and alligators; and drawing a mental line between what is fish and what is not fish, you are able to define and classify it. But you cannot define or say "what" Brahman is, for there is nothing It is not—being one without a second, there is nothing outside It and so nowhere to draw the classifying line.

Hence, the Absolute, the real world as it is, is also called pure Emptiness, since all definitions and propositions and statements about reality are void and meaningless. Even such statements as "Reality is the Limitless" won't quite do, for the "limitless" excludes that which is "limited." Rather, the Absolute is finally Void of all conceptual elaborations, and so even the word "void," if taken to be a logical idea, is to be denied validity. In the words of Nagarjuna:

> It cannot be called void or not void,
> Or both or neither;
> But in order to point it out,
> It is called "the Void."

Since all propositions about reality are void and invalid, the same of course holds true for the statement "All is Brahman," if this statement is taken as a logical proposition. If, for instance, Brahman were taken as a concrete and categorical fact *among other facts*, then "All is Brahman" would be sheerest nonsense: as any logician will tell us, to predicate something of everything is to predicate it of nothing. But Brahman is not so much a fact among other facts, but the Fact of all facts. "All is Brahman" is not a merely logical proposition; it is more of an experiential or contemplative revelation, and while the logic of the statement is admittedly quite flawed, the experience itself is not. And the experience All-is-Brahman makes it quite clear that there is not one thing outside the Absolute, even though when translated into words, we are left with nonsense. But, as Wittgenstein would say, although It cannot be said, It can be *shown*.

Now the insight that there is nothing outside of Brahman implies also that there is nothing *opposed* to It; that is to say, the Absolute is that which has no opposite. Thus It is also called the Nondual, the Not-two, the No-opposite. To quote the third Patriarch of Zen:

> All forms of dualism
> Are ignorantly contrived by the mind itself.
> They are like visions and flowers in the air:
> Why bother to take hold of them?
> When dualism does no more obtain,
> Even Oneness itself remains not as such.
> The True Mind is not divided—

> When a direct identification is asked for,
> We can only say, "Not-Two!"

But, as Seng-ts'an points out, "Not-two" does not mean just One. For pure Oneness is most dualistic, excluding as it does its opposite of Manyness. The single One opposes the plural Many, while the Nondual embraces them both. "One without a second" means "One without an opposite," not One opposed to Many. Thus, as we have already hinted, we mustn't picture the Absolute as excluding diversity, as being an undifferentiated monistic mush, for Brahman embraces both unity and multiplicity.

Now the import of what has been said thus far is that since there is really nothing outside the Nondual, there is no point in either space or time where the Absolute is not. And it isn't that a *part* of the Absolute is present in every thing—as in pantheism—for that is to introduce a boundary within the infinite, assigning to each thing a different piece of the infinite pie. Rather, the *entire* Absolute is completely and wholly present at every point of space and time, for the simple reason that you can't have a different infinite at each point. The Absolute, as Saint Bonaventure put it, is "A sphere, whose center is everywhere and whose circumference nowhere," so that, in the words of Plotinus, "while it is nowhere, nowhere is it not."

Yet notice that the Absolute can be entirely present at every point of space only if It is itself spaceless. Just as, to use Eckhart's example, your eyes can see things which are colored red only because your eyes themselves are without red color or "red-less," so also the Absolute can embrace all space because It is itself without space or "space-less."

Thus, the infinite is not a point, or a space—even a very Big Space or a dimension among other points, spaces, and dimensions; but is rather point-less, spaceless, dimensionless—not one among many but one without a second. In just this fashion, the *whole* of the infinite can be present at all points of space, for being itself spaceless, it does not contend with space and so is free to utterly embrace it, just as water, being shape-less and form-less, can fill containers of all shapes and forms. And since the infinite is present in its entirety at every point of space, *all* of the infinite is fully present right HERE. In fact, to the eye of the infinite, no such place as *there* exists (since, put crudely, if you go to some other place over *there*, you will still only find the very same infinite as *here*, for there isn't a different one at each place).

And so also with time. The Absolute can be present in its entirety at every point of time only if It is itself timeless. And that which is timeless is eternal, for, as Wittgenstein rightly pointed out, Eternity is "not infinite temporal duration but timelessness." That is to say, Eternity is not everlasting time but a moment without time. Hence, being timeless, *all* of Eternity is wholly and completely present at every point of time—and thus, all of Eternity is already present right NOW. To the eye of Eternity, there is no *then*, either past or future.

Point without dimension or extension, Moment without date or duration—such is the Absolute. And while It is nowhere, nowhere is It not. That, simply, is the meaning of omnipresence—the Absolute is simultaneously present everywhere and everywhen in its entirety. "Who sees not God everywhere sees him truly nowhere."

With all of the foregoing, it won't be hard to understand that all metaphysical traditions have universally claimed that the Absolute is literally Unattainable. For if it were possible for a person to *attain* the Absolute, this would imply moving from a point where the Absolute is not to a point where It is—yet there is no point where It is not. In other words, it's impossible to attain It because it's impossible to escape It in the first place. And so it is important to realize that since the Absolute is already one with everything everywhere, we can in no way manufacture or attain to our union with It. No matter what we do or don't do, try to do or try not to do, we can never attain It. In the words of Shankara:

> As Brahman constitutes a person's Self, it is not something to
> be attained by that person. And even if Brahman were alto-
> gether different from a person's Self, still it would not be
> something to be attained; for as it is omnipresent it is part of
> its nature that it is ever present to everyone.

Or read carefully the following from the great Zen Master Huang Po:

> That there is nothing which can be attained is not idle talk;
> it is the truth. You have always been one with the Buddha,
> so do not pretend you can attain to this oneness by various
> practices. If, at this very moment, you could convince your-
> selves of its unattainability, being certain indeed that nothing
> at all can ever be attained, you would already be Bodhi-
> minded. Hard is the meaning of this saying! It is to teach

you to refrain from seeking Buddhahood, since any search is doomed to failure.

Or, just to push the point home, consider the words of Sri Ramana Maharshi:

> There is no reaching the Self. If Self were to be reached, it would mean that the Self is not here and now but that it has yet to be obtained. What is got afresh will also be lost. So it will be impermanent. What is not permanent is not worth striving for. So I say the Self is not reached. You *are* the Self; you are already That.

Thus the Absolute, the Buddha-Mind, the real Self cannot be attained. For to attain union with the Absolute implies bringing together two things, and yet in all reality there is only One without a second. The attempt to bring the soul and God together merely perpetuates the illusion that the two are separate. As the above quotes make clear, the Self is already present, and we're already It.

Now it is sometimes said that whereas we are indeed already one with the Absolute, most of us nevertheless do not realize that this is so; that whereas union with God cannot be attained, *knowledge of that union can be attained*; that whereas we cannot manufacture the Supreme Identity, we can realize it. And that realization, that attainment of the knowledge of our Supreme Identity, is everywhere said to be the very Ultimate State of Consciousness, enlightenment, satori, *moksha*, *wu*, release, liberation.

Now there is certainly some degree of truth in the statement that we are all Buddhas but don't know it, and that we must therefore attain this knowledge for complete liberation. But on closer inspection this is not entirely satisfactory. For by the truth of nonduality, to know God is to be God: the two are not at all separate. So there is not one thing called God and another thing called knowledge of God. Rather, it is that knowledge is but one of the names of God. And if we cannot attain God, neither can we attain knowledge of God—since the two are actually one and the same. Put it another way: since the Ultimate State of Consciousness *is* Brahman, and since Brahman cannot be attained, neither can the Ultimate State of Consciousness.

If this conclusion seems odd, then go ahead and suppose, on the contrary, that the Ultimate State of Consciousness could be attained, or reached, or entered. What would that imply? Only that that state of consciousness which you *entered* would necessarily have a beginning in time; that that state of consciousness is therefore not timeless and eternal; and that, in short, that state of consciousness is precisely not the Ultimate State of Consciousness. The Ultimate State of Consciousness cannot be entered because it is timeless, without beginning or end, and conversely, any state of consciousness you can enter is not the Ultimate State of Consciousness.

Hsuan-tse heard of a meditation master named Chih-huang, and when he went to visit him, Chih-huang was meditating.

"What are you doing there?" inquired Hsuan-tse.

"I am entering into a samadhi, a highest state of consciousness."

"You speak of *entering*, but how do you enter into a *samadhi*—with a thoughtful mind or with a thoughtless mind? If you say with a thoughtless mind, all nonsentient beings such as plants or bricks could attain *samadhi*. If you say with a thoughtful mind, all sentient beings could attain it."

"Well," replied Chih-huang, "I am not conscious of either being thoughtful or being thoughtless."

Hsuan-tse's verdict was swift-coming. "If you are conscious of neither, you are actually in *samadhi* all the time; why do you even talk at all of entering into or coming out of it? If, however, there is any entering or coming out, it is not the Great *Samadhi*."

So what does it mean that you can't enter the Ultimate State of Consciousness? What does it mean that never, under any circumstances, at any time, through any effort, can you enter the Ultimate State of Consciousness? Only that the Ultimate State of Consciousness is already fully and completely present. And that means the Ultimate State of Consciousness is in no way different from your ordinary state of consciousness or from any other state of consciousness you might have at this or any moment. "Your ordinary mind, just that is the Tao," says Nansen. Whatever state you have now, regardless of what you think of it and regardless of its nature, is absolutely It. You therefore cannot enter It because you have always been in It from the very beginning.

Of course, this should have been obvious all along. Since the Ultimate State of Consciousness is Brahman, and since Brahman is absolutely all-inclusive, the Ultimate State of Consciousness is equally all-inclusive. That is to say, the Ultimate State of Consciousness is not a state among other states but a state inclusive of all states. This means most emphatically that the Ultimate State of Consciousness is not an altered state of consciousness, for—being one without a second—there is no alternative to It. The Ultimate State of Consciousness is perfectly compatible with every state of consciousness and altered state of consciousness, and there is no state of consciousness apart from or outside of It. As René Guénon explains it, "The state of *Yogi* is not then analogous with any particular state whatsoever, but embraces all possible states as the principle embraces all its consequences."

All of this points inescapably to the fact that you not only are already one with the Absolute, you already know you are. As Huang Po said, "The Buddha-Nature and your perception of it are one." And since, as we have seen, the Buddha Nature is always present, then so is your perception of It. If you maintain that you are Buddha but don't know it, you necessarily introduce a very subtle dualism between the Buddha Nature and your perception of It, imagining that the one is while the other is yet to come, and such is not possible. Truly, as we cannot manufacture the Absolute, we cannot manufacture knowledge of the Absolute. Both are already present.

> Rekison Roshi was asked by a monk, "What is this 'apprehending of a sound and being delivered'?" Rekison took up some fire-tongs, struck the firewood, and asked, "You hear it?" "I hear it," replied the monk. "Who is not delivered?" asked Rekison.

That the Ultimate State of Consciousness is not a state apart or in any way different from the Present State of Consciousness is the point so many people seem to miss. Hence, they misguidedly seek to engineer for themselves a "higher" state of consciousness, radically different from their present state of awareness, wherein it is imagined that the Supreme Identity can be realized. Some imagine that this particular and exclusive "higher" state of consciousness is connected with specific brain-wave patterns, such as predominant amounts of high amplitude alpha waves. Others maintain that an individual's neurological system must undergo several changes, evolving as it were to a point where this "higher" state of consciousness can finally emerge. Some even believe that physiological stress has to be removed through meditative techniques and *then* the "higher" state of consciousness will result. But all this chatter totally overlooks the inescapable fact that *any* state of consciousness that can be entered, or that emerges after various practices, must have a beginning in time, and thus is not and could never be the timeless and eternal Ultimate State of Consciousness.

Moreover, to imagine that certain steps can be taken in order to realize the Ultimate State of Consciousness and attain liberation is actually to make the Ultimate State an *effect*. That is to say, to believe certain stages or various steps or particular practices can lead to liberation is inescapably to make liberation the *result* of these steps, the *consequence* of these stages, the *effect* of these causes. Yet long ago Shankara saw the utter absurdity of such a notion:

> If Brahman were represented as supplementary to certain actions, and release were assumed to be the effect of those actions, it would be temporal, and would have to be considered merely as something holding a preeminent position among the described temporal fruits of actions with their various degrees.
>
> But as Release is shown to be of the nature of the eternally free Self, it cannot be charged with the imperfection of temporality. Those, on the other hand, who consider Release to be the effect of something maintain that it depends on the action of mind, speech, or body. So, likewise, those who consider it to be a mere modification. Noneternality of Release is the certain consequence of these two opinions; for we observe in common life that things which are modifications, such as sour milk and the like, and things which are effects, such as jars, etc., are non-eternal.

And what of the opinion that we all have Buddha Nature but as yet just don't know it? And that through some sort of action, such as meditation, we can attain to this knowledge? Shankara is decisive:

> It might be said that Release might be a quality of the Self which is merely hidden and becomes manifest on the Self being purified by some action; just as the quality of clearness becomes manifest in a mirror when the mirror is cleaned by means of the action of rubbing. This objection is invalid, we reply, because the Self cannot be the abode of any action. For an action cannot exist without modifying that in which it abides. But if the Self were modified by an action its noneternality would result therefrom; an altogether unacceptable result.

In short, since the Ultimate State of Consciousness is your Present State of Consciousness, there is obviously no way to cause, produce effect, or manufacture that which is already the case—and even if you could, the result would be noneternal. But when we imagine that the Ultimate State of Consciousness is different from the state of consciousness we have now, we then foolheartedly seek ways to usher in this supposedly different and miraculous state of "higher" consciousness totally ignorant of the fact that even if we get this "higher" state of consciousness it is not the Ultimate State because it is the result of certain steps and therefore has a beginning in time. And yet, think we, some knowledge of the Absolute awaits us in this particular higher state of consciousness. But as Eckhart so forcefully explained, if we imagine God can be found in a *particular* state of consciousness, then when that state slips from us, that god slips with it.

"Contrary to widespread belief," writes Alan Watts, "the knowledge and contemplation of the infinite is not a state of trance, for because of the truth that there is no opposition between the infinite and the finite, knowledge of the infinite may be compatible with all possible states of mind, feeling, and sensation. [This] knowledge is an inclusive, not an exclusive, state of consciousness."

In fact, it's only because we keep insisting that the Ultimate State of Consciousness be different from the Present State of Consciousness that makes it so hard to admit to ourselves that we already know our Buddha Nature. We imagine, for instance, that nirvana is different from samsara, that enlightenment is different from ignorance, that Brahman is different from maya (illusion). Yet Nagarjuna clearly states: "There is no difference whatsoever between nirvana and samsara; there is no difference whatsoever between samsara and nirvana. There is not the slightest bit of difference between these two." And Hsuan-chueh begins his celebrated *Song of Realizing the Tao*:

> See you not that easygoing Man of Tao, who has
>   abandoned learning and does not strive?
> He neither avoids false thoughts nor seeks the true,
> For ignorance is in reality the Buddha nature,
> And this illusory, changeful body is the body of Truth.

And pure Vedanta has never understood maya or illusion to be different from Brahman, but rather as something Brahman is doing. And yet we seek to escape samsara as if it weren't nirvana; we try to overcome ignorance as if it weren't enlightenment; we strive to wipe out maya as if it weren't Brahman. Fénelon, Archbishop of Cambrai, has the only acceptable comment on this state of affairs: "There is no more dangerous illusion than the fancies by which people try to avoid illusion."

Hence, all seeking, spiritual or otherwise, is ultimately irrelevant; and viewing the Ultimate State of Consciousness as a particular altered state of consciousness is absolutely unacceptable. I am not at all denying that some very miraculous altered states of consciousness can certainly be attained—they can be attained for the simple reason that they are partial and exclusive and hence can be developed and perfected. But what has that to do with the all-inclusive Ultimate State of Consciousness? You can surely train yourself to enter alpha states; you can develop your ability with a mantra; you can learn to halt all thoughts from rising—but only because these are exclusive and partial states of consciousness apart from other states, and for that very reason can selectively be given more attention and effort than the others. But you cannot train yourself to enter that state of consciousness which you have never left and which includes all possible states of consciousness. There is just no place outside the Ultimate State of Consciousness where you can take up a position to train yourself in It. Listen to Huang Po once again:

> Bodhi (knowledge of the Buddha-Nature) is no state. The Buddha did not attain to it. Sentient beings do not lack it. It cannot be reached with the body nor sought with the mind. All sentient beings are already of one form with Bodhi.
>
> If you know positively that all sentient beings are already one with Bodhi, you will cease thinking of Bodhi as something to be attained. You may recently have heard others talking about this "attaining of the Bodhi-Mind," but this may be called an intellectual way of driving the Buddha away. By following this method, you only APPEAR to achieve Buddhahood; if you were to spend aeon upon aeon in that way, you would only achieve the Sambhogakaya (blissful states) and Nirmanakaya (transformed states). What connection would all that have with your original and real Buddha-Nature?

Upon hearing this, many of us nevertheless feel that "Yes, I do understand that somehow I must already be one with the Absolute, but I still just don't know it!" But that is manifestly not true. The very fact that you are now seeking Buddha shows that you already know you are Buddha. "Console thyself," wrote Pascal, "thou wouldst not seek Me if thou hadst not found Me." And Saint Bernard expressed the very same sentiment, "No one is able to seek Thee, save because he has first found." Or, as Blyth put it, "In order to be enlightened, we must first be enlightened."

Of course, individuals might indeed feel that they don't really know It, despite all the best assurances of the Masters. And the reason It might not seem evident to them is the somewhat peculiar nature of this ever-present Bodhi-knowledge; namely, it is nondual. A person doesn't seem to know It only because he is so used to seeing things dualistically, where he as subject holds out and looks at an object, either mental or physical, and feels that, yes, he sees that object very clearly, with "he" and "that object" being two different things altogether. He, as subject, then naturally assumes that he can also see Brahman in the same way, as an object out there to look at and grasp. It thus seems that he, the grasper, should be able to get Brahman, the grasped. But Brahman won't split into getter and got. In all of reality there is only One without a second, and yet out of habit the person tries to make It two, to split It so as to finally grab It and exclaim, "Aha! I've got It!" He tries to make it an experience to be grasped among other experiences. But Brahman is not a particular experience, being one without a second, and so he is left grasping at ghosts and clutching at smoke.

And so it is that we all inevitably end up feeling that we just can't see It, no matter how hard we try. *But the fact that we always can't see It is perfect proof that we always know It.* In the words of the *Kena Upanishad*:

> If you think that you know Brahman well, what you know of Its nature is in reality but little; for this reason Brahman should still be more attentively considered by you. . . . Whoever among us understands the following words: "I do not know It, and yet I know It," verily that man knows it. He who thinks that Brahman is not comprehended, by him Brahman is comprehended; but he who thinks that Brahman is comprehended knows It not. Brahman is unknown to those who know It and is known to those who do not know It at all.

That is, the very state of not-knowing Brahman is the Ultimate State of Consciousness, *and that is exactly how you feel right now.* Says a Zen poem:

> When you seek to know It, you cannot see It.
> You cannot take hold of It,
> But neither can you lose It.
> In not being able to get It, you get It.
> When you are silent, It speaks.
> When you speak, It is silent.
> The great gate is wide open to bestow alms,
> And no crowd is blocking the way.

Since you are Brahman, you obviously can't *see* Brahman, just as, for instance, an eye cannot see itself and an ear cannot hear itself. The *Brihadaranyaka Upanishad* says, "Thou couldst not see the seer of sight, thou couldst not hear the hearer of hearing, nor perceive the perceiver of perception, nor know the knower of knowledge." And the *Zenrin* puts it simply, "Like a sword that cuts, but cannot cut itself; Like an eye that sees, but cannot see itself." In fact, if your eye tries to see itself, it sees absolutely nothing. Likewise, the Void is what you right now don't see when you try to look for Brahman. That Void is exactly what you have always been looking for and have always never found nor seen. And *that* very not-seeing is It. And since you always don't see It, you always know It. Because any individual, explains Saint Dionysus, "by the very fact of not seeing and not knowing God, truly understands him who is beyond sight and knowledge; knowing this, too, that he is in all things that are felt and known."

As you rest in your present awareness, you might perceive some sensation in the body, or you might be aware of thoughts passing by in front of the mind's eye, or you might be seeing the clouds float by. But there is one thing you cannot see: you cannot see the Seer. You see thoughts, things, clouds, mountains, but never the Seer, never the Self, never the pure Witness. Precisely because it sees thoughts, it is not itself a thought; precisely because it sees things, it is not itself a thing—it is radically free of all such objects, all such sights, all such ripples in the stream.

So what is this Witness in you that is aware of you? Who is aware of your thoughts, your feelings, your self, right now? What is that pure awareness? Of course, you cannot see this Seer! Anything you see is just more objects: you see thoughts float by, clouds float by, sensations float by. But the Seer itself is not an object, and thus can never be seen.

And so, for just a moment, simply be the Seer. Simply rest as the Seer, rest as the Witness, rest as that which sees but cannot be seen. As you rest in that emptiness, that absence, that clearing, that open-ing, you will begin to sense a vast freedom, a vast release from things seen, a vast release from the pain of being an object. You will rest as Emptiness, as the ancient Unseen, as the primordial Unborn, floating in the great Liberation.

When you rest as Emptiness, you are in touch with your Original Face, the face you had prior to the Big Bang. This great Emptiness is the primordial background that has always already been your True Self, a Self never lost and therefore never found. This Emptiness is the great background in which the entire universe arises moment to moment. And this great background is—by any other name—God.

That which is aware of you right now, is God. That which is your own innermost awareness, right now, is God. That which sees but is never seen, is God. That Witness in you right now, ever present as pure Presence, is God. That vast Freedom, that great Emptiness, that primordial Purity, your own present state of awareness, right now, is God. And thus, most fundamentally and forever, it is God who speaks with your tongue, and listens with your ears, and sees with your eyes, this God who is closer to you than you are to yourself, this God who has never abandoned you and never could, this God who is every breath you take, the very beat of your tender heart, who beholds the entire majesty before your eyes, yet is never, never seen.

Still don't see It? How right you already are. For each and every one of us, "by the very fact of not seeing and not knowing God, truly understands him who is beyond sight and knowledge; knowing this, too, that he is in all things that are felt and known."

cw 3: *Eye to Eye*, 419–432

9

The Brilliant Clarity
of Ever-Present Awareness

*In this closing expression, Wilber articulates the ultimate spiritual
summation, tracing sacred steps from the root of the Great Search to
the faintest intuitive glimmers of Spirit to the enlightened creativity
of awakening. Relax, now, in the simple feeling of Being, and allow
yourself a taste of this final and most treasured narrative . . .*

> Where are we to locate Spirit? What are we actually
> allowed to acknowledge as Sacred? Where exactly is the
> Ground of Being? Where is this ultimate Divine?

THE GREAT SEARCH

THE REALIZATION of the Nondual traditions is uncompromising:
there is only Spirit, there is only God, there is only Emptiness in
all its radiant wonder. All the good and all the evil, the very best and
the very worst, the upright and the degenerate—each and all are radically perfect manifestations of Spirit precisely as they are. There is
nothing but God, nothing but the Goddess, nothing but Spirit in all
directions, and not a grain of sand, not a speck of dust, is more or less
Spirit than any other.

This realization undoes the Great Search that is the heart of the separate-self sense. The separate-self is, at bottom, simply a sensation of
seeking. When you feel yourself right now, you will basically feel a tiny
interior tension or contraction—a sensation of grasping, desiring,

wishing, wanting, avoiding, resisting—it is a sensation of effort, a sensation of seeking.

In its highest form, this sensation of seeking takes on the form of the Great Search for Spirit. We wish to get from our unenlightened state (of sin or delusion or duality) to an enlightened or more spiritual state. We wish to get from where Spirit is not, to where Spirit is.

But there is no place where Spirit is not. Every single location in the entire Kosmos is equally and fully Spirit. Seeking of any sort, movement of any sort, attainment of any sort: all profoundly useless. The Great Search simply reinforces the mistaken assumption that there is some place that Spirit is not, and that I need to get from a space that is lacking to a space that is full. But there is no space lacking, and there is no space more full. There is only Spirit.

The Great Search for Spirit is simply that impulse, the final impulse, which prevents the present realization of Spirit, and it does so for a simple reason: the Great Search presumes the loss of God. The Great Search reinforces the mistaken belief that God is not present, and thus totally obscures the reality of God's ever-present Presence. The Great Search, which pretends to love God, is in fact the very mechanism of pushing God away; the mechanism of promising to find tomorrow that which exists only in the timeless now; the mechanism of watching the future so fervently that the present always passes it by—very quickly—and God's smiling face with it.

The Great Search is the loveless contraction hidden in the heart of the separate-self sense, a contraction that drives the intense yearning for a tomorrow in which salvation will finally arrive, but during which time, thank God, I can continue to be myself. The greater the Great Search, the more I can deny God. The greater the Great Search, the more I can feel my own sensation of seeking, which defines the contours of my self. The Great Search is the great enemy of what is.

Should we then simply cease the Great Search? Definitely, if we could. But the effort to stop the Great Search is itself more of the Great Search. The very first step presumes and reinforces the seeking sensation. There is actually nothing the self-contraction can do to stop the Great Search, because the self-contraction and the Great Search are two names for the same thing.

If Spirit cannot be found as a future product of the Great Search, then there is only one alternative: Spirit must be fully, totally, completely present right now—AND you must be fully, totally, completely aware of it right now. It will not do to say that Spirit is present but I don't realize it. That would require the Great Search; that would demand that I seek a tomorrow in which I could realize that Spirit is fully present, but such seeking misses the present in the very first step. To keep seeking would be to keep missing. No, the realization itself, the awareness itself: this, too, must somehow be fully and completely present right now. If it is not, then all we have left is the Great Search, doomed to presume that which it wishes to overcome.

There must be something about our *present* awareness that contains the entire truth. Somehow, no matter what your state, you are immersed fully in everything you need for perfect enlightenment. You are somehow looking right at the answer. One hundred percent of Spirit is in your perception right now. Not 20 percent, not 50 percent, not 99 percent, but literally 100 percent of Spirit is in your awareness right now—and the trick, as it were, is to recognize this ever-present state of affairs, and not to engineer a future state in which Spirit will announce itself.

And this simple recognition of an *already present* Spirit is the task, as it were, of the great Nondual traditions.

To Meet the Kosmos

Many people have stern objections to "mysticism" or "transcendentalism" of any sort, because they think it somehow denies this world, or hates this earth, or despises the body and the senses and its vital life, and so on. While that may be true of certain dissociated (or merely Ascending) approaches, it is certainly not the core understanding of the great Nondual mystics, from Plotinus and Eckhart in the West to Nagarjuna and Lady Tsogyal in the East.

Rather, these sages universally maintain that absolute reality and the relative world are "not-two" (which is the meaning of "nondual"), much as a mirror and its reflections are not separate, or an ocean is one with its many waves. So the "other world" of Spirit and "this world" of separate phenomena are deeply and profoundly "not-two," and this nonduality is a direct and immediate realization which occurs in certain meditative states—in other words, seen with the eye of contemplation—although it then becomes a very simple, very ordinary perception, whether you are meditating or not. Every single thing you perceive is the radiance of Spirit itself, so much so that Spirit is not seen apart from that thing: the robin sings, and just that is it, nothing else. This becomes your constant realization, through all changes of state, very naturally, just so. And this releases you from the basic insanity of hiding from the Real.

But why is it, then, that we ordinarily don't have that perception?

All the great Nondual wisdom traditions have given a fairly similar answer to that question. We don't see that Spirit is fully and completely present right here, right now, because our awareness is clouded with some form of *avoidance*. We do not want to be choicelessly aware of the present; rather, we want to run away from it, or run after it, or we want to change it, alter it, hate it, love it, loathe it, or in some way agitate to get ourselves into, or out of, it. We will do anything except come to rest in the pure Presence of the present. We will not rest with pure Presence; we want to be elsewhere, quickly. The Great Search is the game, in its endless forms.

In nondual meditation or contemplation, the agitation of the separate-self sense profoundly relaxes, and the self uncoils in the vast expanse of all space. At that point, it becomes obvious that you are not "in here" looking at the world "out there," because that duality has simply collapsed into pure Presence and spontaneous luminosity.

This realization may take many forms. A simple one is something like this: You might be looking at a mountain, and you have relaxed into the effortlessness of your own present awareness, and then suddenly the mountain is all, you are nothing. Your separate-self sense is suddenly and totally gone, and there is simply everything that is arising moment to moment. You are perfectly aware, perfectly conscious, everything seems completely normal, except you are nowhere to be found. You are not on this side of your face looking at the mountain out there; you simply are the mountain, you are the sky, you are the clouds, you are everything that is arising moment to moment, very simply, very clearly, just so.

We know all the fancy names for this state, from unity consciousness to sahaj samadhi. But it really is the simplest and most obvious state you will ever realize. Moreover, once you glimpse that state—what the Buddhists call One Taste (because you and the entire universe are one taste or one experience)—it becomes obvious that you are not entering this state, but rather, it is a state that, in some profound and mysterious way, has been your primordial condition from time immemorial. You have, in fact, never left this state for a second.

This is why Zen calls it the Gateless Gate: on this side of that real-ization, it looks like you have to do something to enter that state—it looks like you need to pass through a gate. But when you do so, and you turn around and look back, there is no gate whatsoever, and never has been. You have never left this state in the first place, so obviously you can't enter it. The gateless gate! "Every form is Emptiness just as it is," means that all things, including you and me, are always already on the other side of the gateless gate.

But if that is so, then why even do spiritual practice? Isn't that just another form of the Great Search? Yes, actually, spiritual practice is a form of the Great Search, and as such, it is destined to fail. But that is exactly the point. You and I are already convinced that there are things that we need to do in order to realize Spirit. We feel that there are places that Spirit is not (namely, in me), and we are going to cor-rect this state of affairs. Thus, we are already committed to the Great Search, and so nondual meditation makes use of that fact and engages us in the Great Search in a particular and somewhat sneaky fashion (which Zen calls "selling water by the river").

William Blake said that "a fool who persists in his folly will become wise." So nondual meditation simply speeds up the folly. If you really think you lack Spirit, then try this folly: try to become Spirit, try to discover Spirit, try to contact Spirit, try to reach Spirit: meditate and meditate and meditate in order to get Spirit!

But of course, you see, you cannot really do this. You cannot reach Spirit any more than you can reach your feet. You always already are Spirit, you are not going to reach it in any sort of temporal thrash-ing around. But if this is not obvious, then try it. Nondual medita-tion is a serious effort to do the impossible, until you become utter-ly exhausted of the Great Search, sit down completely worn out, and notice your feet.

It's not that these nondual traditions deny higher states; they don't. They have many, many practices that help individuals reach specific states of postformal consciousness. These include states of transcen-dental bliss, love, and compassion; of heightened cognition and ex-trasensory perception; of Deity consciousness and contemplative prayer. But they maintain that those altered states—which have a be-ginning and an end in time—ultimately have nothing to do with the timeless. The real aim is the stateless, not a perpetual fascination with changes of state. And that stateless condition is the true nature of this and every conceivable state of consciousness, so any state you have will do just fine. Change of state is not the ultimate point; recognizing the Changeless is the point, recognizing primordial Emptiness is the point, recognizing unqualifiable Godhead is the point, recognizing pure Spirit is the point, and if you are breathing and vaguely awake, that state of consciousness will do just fine.

Nonetheless, traditionally, in order to demonstrate your sincerity, you must complete a good number of preliminary practices, including a mastery of various states of meditative consciousness, summating in a stable post-postconventional adaptation, all of which is well and good. But none of those states of consciousness are held to be final or ultimate or privileged. And changing states is not the goal at all. Rather, it is precisely by entering and leaving these various meditative states that you begin to understand that *none* of them constitute enlightenment. All of them have a beginning in time, and thus none of them are the timeless. The point is to realize that change of state is *not* the point, and that realization can occur in *any* state of consciousness whatsoever.

EVER-PRESENT AWARENESS

This primordial recognition of One Taste—not the creation but the recognition of the fact that you and the Kosmos are One Spirit, One Taste, One Gesture—is the great gift of the Nondual traditions. And in simplified form, this recognition goes like this:

(What follows are various "pointing-out" instructions, direct pointers to mind's essential nature or intrinsic Spirit. Traditionally this involves a great deal of intentional repetition. If you read this material in the normal manner, you might find the repetitions tedious and perhaps irritating. If you would like the rest of this particular section to work for you, please read it in a slow and leisurely manner, letting the words and the repetitions sink in. You can also use these sections as material for meditation, using no more than one or two paragraphs—or even one or two sentences—for each session.)

We begin with the realization that the pure Self or transpersonal Witness is an *ever-present* consciousness, even when we doubt its existence. You are right now aware of, say, this book, the room, a window, the sky, the clouds. . . . You can sit back and simply notice that you are aware of all those objects floating by. Clouds float through the sky, thoughts float through the mind, and when you notice them,

you are effortlessly aware of them. There is a simple, effortless, spontaneous witnessing of whatever happens to be present.

In that simple witnessing awareness, you might notice: I am aware
of my body, and therefore I am not just my body. I am aware of my
mind, and therefore I am not just my mind. I am aware of my self,
and therefore I am not just that self. Rather, I seem somehow to be
the Witness of my body, my mind, my self.

This is truly fascinating. I can see my thoughts, so I am not those
thoughts. I am aware of bodily sensations, so I am not those sensations. I am aware of my emotions, so I am not merely those emotions. I am somehow the Witness of all of that!

But what is this Witness itself? Who or What is it that witnesses
all of these objects, that watches the clouds float by, and thoughts
float by, and objects float by? Who or What is this true Seer, this pure
Witness, which is at the very core of what I am?

That simple witnessing awareness, the traditions maintain, is
Spirit itself, is the enlightened mind itself, is Buddha-nature itself, is
God itself, *in its entirety*.

Thus, according to the traditions, getting in touch with Spirit or
God or the enlightened mind is not something difficult to achieve. It is
your own simple witnessing awareness in exactly this moment. If you
see this book, you already have that awareness—all of it—right now.

A very famous text from Dzogchen or Maha-Ati Buddhism (one
of the very greatest of the Nondual traditions) puts it like this: "At
times it happens that some meditators say that it is difficult to recognize the nature of the mind"—in Dzogchen, "the nature of the
mind" means primordial Purity or radical Emptiness—it means nondual Spirit by whatever name. The point is that this "nature of the
mind" is *ever-present witnessing awareness*, and some meditators,
the text says, find this hard to believe. They imagine it is difficult or
even impossible to recognize this ever-present awareness, and that
they have to work very hard and meditate very long in order to attain
this enlightened mind—whereas it is simply their own ever-present
witnessing awareness, fully functioning right now.

The text continues: "Some male or female practitioners believe it
to be impossible to recognize the nature of mind. They become
depressed with tears streaming down their cheeks. There is no reason at all to become sad. It is not at all impossible to recognize. Rest
directly in that which thinks that it is impossible to recognize the
nature of the mind, and that is exactly it."

As for this ever-present witnessing awareness being hard to contact: "There are some meditators who don't let their mind rest in itself [simple present awareness], as they should. Instead they let it watch outwardly or search inwardly. You will neither see nor find [Spirit] by watching outwardly or searching inwardly. There is no reason whatsoever to watch outwardly or search inwardly. Let go directly into this mind that is watching outwardly or searching inwardly, and that is exactly it."

We are aware of this room; just that is it, just that awareness is ever-present Spirit. We are aware of the clouds floating by in the sky; just that is it, just that awareness is ever-present Spirit. We are aware of thoughts floating by in the mind; just that is it, just that awareness is ever-present Spirit. We are aware of pain, turmoil, terror, fear; just that is it.

In other words, the ultimate reality is not something seen, but rather the ever-present Seer. Things that are seen come and go, are happy or sad, pleasant or painful—but the Seer is none of those things, and it does not come and go. The Witness does not waver, does not wobble, does not enter that stream of time. The Witness is not an object, not a thing seen, but the ever-present Seer of all things, the simple Witness that is the I of Spirit, the center of the cyclone, the opening that is God, the clearing that is pure Emptiness.

There is never a time that you do not have access to this Witnessing awareness. At every single moment, there is a spontaneous awareness of whatever happens to be present—and that simple, spontaneous, effortless awareness is ever-present Spirit itself. Even if you think you don't see it, that very awareness is it. And thus, the ultimate state of consciousness—intrinsic Spirit itself—*is not hard to reach but impossible to avoid.*

And just that is the great and guarded secret of the Nondual schools.

It does not matter what objects or contents are present; whatever arises is fine. People sometimes have a hard time understanding Spirit because they try to see it as an object of awareness or an object of comprehension. But the ultimate reality is not anything seen, it is the Seer. Spirit is not an object; it is radical, ever-present Subject, and thus it is not something that is going to jump out in front of you like a rock, an image, an idea, a light, a feeling, an insight, a luminous cloud, an intense vision, or a sensation of great bliss. Those are all nice, but they are all objects, which is what Spirit is not.

Thus, as you rest in the Witness, you won't see anything in particular. The true Seer is nothing that can be seen, so you simply begin by disidentifying with any and all objects:

I am aware of sensations in my body; those are objects, I am not those. I am aware of thoughts in my mind; those are objects, I am not those. I am aware of my self in this moment, but that is just another object, and I am not that.

Sights float by in nature, thoughts float by in the mind, feelings float by in the body, and I am none of those. I am not an object. I am the pure Witness of all those objects. I am Consciousness as such.

And so, as you rest in the pure Witness, you won't see anything in particular—whatever you see is fine. Rather, as you rest in the radical subject or Witness, as you stop identifying with objects, you will simply begin to notice a sense of vast Freedom. This Freedom is not something you will see; it is something you are. When you are the Witness of thoughts, you are not bound by thoughts. When you are the Witness of feelings, you are not bound by feelings. In place of your contracted self there is simply a vast sense of Openness and Release. As an object, you are bound; as the Witness, you are Free.

We will not see this Freedom, we will rest in it. A vast ocean of infinite ease.

And so we rest in this state of the pure and simple Witness, the true Seer, which is vast Emptiness and pure Freedom, and we allow whatever is seen to arise as it wishes. Spirit is in the Free and Empty Seer, not in the limited, bound, mortal, and finite objects that parade by in the world of time. And so we rest in this vast Emptiness and Freedom, in which all things arise.

We do not reach or contact this pure Witnessing awareness. It is not possible to contact that which we have never lost. Rather, we rest in this easy, clear, ever-present awareness by simply noticing what is *already* happening. We already see the sky. We already hear the birds singing. We already feel the cool breeze. The simple Witness is already present, already functioning, already the case. That is why we do not contact or bring this Witness into being, but simply notice that it is always already present, as the simple and spontaneous awareness of whatever is happening in this moment.

We also notice that this simple, ever-present Witness is completely effortless. It takes no effort whatsoever to hear sounds, to see sights, to feel the cool breeze: it is already happening, and we easily rest in that effortless witnessing. We do not follow those objects, nor avoid them. Precisely because Spirit is the ever-present Seer, and not any limited thing that is seen, we can allow all seen things to come and go exactly as they please. "The perfect person employs the mind as a mirror," says Chuang Tzu. "It neither grasps nor rejects; it receives, but does not keep." The mirror effortlessly receives its reflections, just as you effortlessly see the sky right now, and just as the Witness effortlessly allows all objects whatsoever to arise. All things come and go in the effortless mirror-mind that is the simple Witness.

When I rest as the pure and simple Witness, I notice that I am not caught in the world of time. The Witness exists only in the timeless present. Yet again, this is not a state that is difficult to achieve but impossible to avoid. The Witness sees only the timeless present because only the timeless present is actually real. When I think of the past, those past thoughts exist right now, in this present. When I think of the future, those future thoughts exist right now, in this present. Past and future thoughts both arise right now, in simple ever-present awareness.

And when the past actually occurred, it occurred right now. When the future actually occurs, it will occur right now. There is only right now, there is only this ever-present present: that is all I ever directly know. Thus, the timeless present is not hard to contact but impossible to avoid, and this becomes obvious when I rest as the pure and simple Witness, and watch the past and future float by in simple ever-present awareness.

That is why when we rest as the ever-present Witness, we are not in time. Resting in simple witnessing awareness, I notice that time floats by in front of me, or through me, like clouds float through the sky. And that is exactly why I can be aware of time; in my simple Presentness, in my I AMness as pure and simple Witness of the Kosmos, I am timeless.

Thus, as I right now rest in this simple, ever-present Witness, I am face to face with Spirit. I am with God today, and always, in this simple, ever-present, witnessing state. Eckhart said that "God is closer to me than I am to myself," because both God and I are one in the ever-present Witness, which is the nature of intrinsic Spirit itself, which is exactly what I am in the state of my I AMness. I am not this, I am not that; I rest as pure open Spirit. When I am not an object, I am God. (And every I in the entire Kosmos can say that truthfully.)

I am not entering this state of the ever-present Witness, which is

Spirit itself. I cannot *enter* this state, precisely because it is ever-present. I cannot *start* Witnessing; I can only notice that this simple Witnessing is *already* occurring. This state never has a beginning in time precisely because it is indeed ever-present. You can neither run from it nor toward it; you *are* it, always. This is exactly why Buddhas have *never* entered this state, and sentient beings have *never* left it.

When I rest in the simple, clear, ever-present Witness, I am resting in the great Unborn, I am resting in intrinsic Spirit, I am resting in primordial Emptiness, I am resting in infinite Freedom. I cannot be seen, I have no qualities at all. I am not this, I am not that. I am not an object. I am neither light nor dark; neither large nor small; neither here nor there; I have no color, no location, no space and no time; I am an utter Emptiness, another word for infinite Freedom, unbounded to infinity. I am the opening or clearing in which the entire manifest world arises right now, but I do not arise in it—it arises in me, in this vast Emptiness and Freedom that I am.

Things that are seen are pleasant or painful, happy or sad, joyous or fearful, healthy or sick—but the Seer of those things is neither happy nor sad, neither joyous nor fearful, neither healthy nor sick, but simply Free. As pure and simple Witness I am free of all objects, free of all subjects, free of all time and free of all space; free of birth and free of death, and free of all things in between. I am simply Free.

When I rest as the timeless Witness, the Great Search is undone. The Great Search is the enemy of the ever-present Spirit, a brutal lie in the face of a gentle infinity. The Great Search is the search for an ultimate experience, a fabulous vision, a paradise of pleasure, an unendingly good time, a powerful insight—a search for God, a search for Goddess, a search for Spirit—but Spirit is not an object. Spirit cannot be grasped or reached or sought or seen: it is the ever-present Seer. To search for the Seer is to miss the point. To search forever is to miss the point forever. How could you possibly search for that which is right now aware of this page? YOU ARE THAT! You cannot go out looking for that which is the Looker.

When I am not an object, I am God. When I seek an object, I cease to be God, and that catastrophe can never be corrected by more searching for more objects.

Rather, I can only rest as the Witness, which is already free of objects, free of time, free of suffering, and free of searching. When I am not an object, I am Spirit. When I rest as the free and formless Witness, I am with God right now, in this timeless and endless moment. I taste infinity and am drenched with fullness, precisely because I no longer seek, but simply rest as what I am.

Before Abraham was, I am. Before the Big Bang was, I am. After the universe dissolves, I am. In all things great and small, I am. And yet I can never be heard, felt, known, or seen; I AM is the ever-present Seer.

Precisely because the ultimate reality is not anything seen but rather the Seer, it doesn't matter in the least what is seen in any moment. Whether you see peace or turmoil, whether you see equanimity or agitation, whether you see bliss or terror, whether you see happiness or sadness, matters not at all: it is not those states but the Seer of those states that is *already* Free.

Changing states is thus beside the point; acknowledging the ever-present Seer is the point. Even in the midst of the Great Search and even in the worst of my self-contracting ways, I have immediate and direct access to the ever-present Witness. I do not have to try to bring this simple awareness into existence. I do not have to enter this state. It involves no effort at all. I simply notice that there is already an awareness of the sky. I simply notice that there is already an awareness of the clouds. I simply notice that the ever-present Witness is already fully functioning: it is not hard to reach but impossible to avoid. I am always already in the lap of this ever-present awareness, the radical Emptiness in which all manifestation is presently arising.

When I rest in the pure and simple Witness, I notice that this awareness is not an experience. It is aware of experiences, it is not itself an experience. Experiences come and go. They have a beginning in time, they stay a bit, and they pass. But they all arise in the simple opening or clearing that is the vast expanse of what I am. The clouds float by in this vast expanse, and thoughts float by in this vast expanse, and experiences float by in this vast expanse. They all come, and they all go. But the vast expanse itself, this Free and Empty Seer, this spacious opening or clearing in which all things arise, does not itself come and go, or even move at all.

Thus, when I rest in the pure and simple Witness, I am no longer caught up in the search for experiences, whether of the flesh or of the mind or of the spirit. Experiences—whether high or low, sacred or profane, joyous or nightmarish—simply come and go like endless waves on the ocean of what I am. As I rest in the pure and simple Witness, I am no longer moved to follow the bliss and the torture of experiential displays. Experiences float across my Original Face like clouds floating across the clear autumn sky, and there is room in me for all.

When I rest in the pure and simple Witness, I will even begin to notice that the Witness itself is not a separate thing or entity, set apart from what it witnesses. All things arise within the Witness, so much so that the Witness itself disappears into all things.

And thus, resting in simple, clear, ever-present awareness, I notice that there is no inside and no outside. There is no subject and no object. Things and events are still fully present and clearly arising—the clouds float by, the birds still sing, the cool breeze still blows—but there is no separate self recoiling from them. Events simply arise as they are, without the constant and agitated reference to a contracted self or subject. Events arise as they are, and they arise in the great freedom of not being defined by a little I looking at them. They arise with Spirit, as Spirit, in the opening or clearing that I am; they do not arise to be seen and perceptually tortured by an ego.

In my contracted mode, I am "in here," on this side of my face, looking at the world "out there," on the "objective" side. I exist on this side of my face, and my entire life is an attempt to save face, to save this self-contraction, to save this sensation of grasping and seeking, a sensation that sets me apart from the world out there, a world I will then desire or loathe, move toward or recoil from, grasp or avoid, love or hate. The inside and the outside are in perpetual struggle, all varieties of hope or fear: the drama of saving face.

We say, "To lose face is to die of embarrassment," and that is deeply true: we do not want to lose face! We do not want to die! We do not want to cease the sensation of the separate-self! But that primal fear of losing face is actually the root of our deepest agony, because saving face—saving an identity with the bodymind—is the very mechanism of suffering, the very mechanism of tearing the Kosmos into an inside versus an outside, a brutal fracture that I experience as pain.

But when I rest in simple, clear, ever-present awareness, I lose face. Inside and outside completely disappear. It happens just like this:

As I drop all objects—I am not this, not that—and I rest in the pure and simple Witness, all objects arise easily in my visual field, all objects arise in the space of the Witness. I am simply an opening or clearing in which all things arise. I notice that all things arise in me, arise in this opening or clearing that I am. The clouds are floating by in this vast opening that I am. The sun is shining in this vast opening that I am. The sky exists in this vast opening that I am; the sky is in me. I can taste the sky, it's closer to me than my own skin. The clouds are on the inside of me; I am seeing them from within. When all things arise in me, I am simply all things. The universe is One Taste, and I am That.

And so, when I rest as the Witness, all things arise in me, so much so that I am all things. There is no subject and object because I do not see the clouds, I am the clouds. There is no subject and object because I do not feel the cool breeze, I am the cool breeze. There is no subject and object because I do not hear the thunder clapping, I am the thunder clapping.

I am no longer on this side of my face looking at the world out there; I simply am the world. I am not in here. I have lost face—and discovered my Original Face, the Kosmos itself. The bird sings, and I am that. The sun rises, and I am that. The moon shines, and I am that, in simple, ever-present awareness.

When I rest in simple, clear, ever-present awareness, every object is its own subject. Every event "sees itself," as it were, because I am now that event seeing itself. I am not looking at the rainbow; I am the rainbow, which sees itself. I am not staring at the tree; I am the tree, which sees itself. The entire manifest world continues to arise, just as it is, except that all subjects and all objects have disappeared. The mountain is still the mountain, but it is not an *object* being looked at, and I am not a separate *subject* staring at it. Both I and the mountain arise in simple, ever-present awareness, and we are both set free in that clearing, we are both liberated in that nondual space, we are both enlightened in the opening that is ever-present awareness. That opening is free of the set-apart violence called subject and object, in here versus out there, self against other, me against the world. I have utterly lost face, and discovered God, in simple ever-present awareness.

When you are the Witness of all objects, and all objects arise in you, then you stand in utter Freedom, in the vast expanse of all space. In this simple One Taste, the wind does not blow on you, it blows within you. The sun does not shine on you, it radiates from deep within your very being. When it rains, you are weeping. You can drink the Pacific Ocean in a single gulp, and swallow the universe whole. Supernovas are born and die all within your heart, and galaxies swirl endlessly where you thought your head was, and it is all as simple as the sound of a robin singing on a crystal clear dawn.

Every time I *recognize* or *acknowledge* the ever-present Witness, I have broken the Great Search and undone the separate self. And that is the ultimate, secret, nondual practice, the practice of no-practice, the practice of *simple acknowledgment*, the practice of remembrance and recognition, founded timelessly and eternally on the fact that there is only Spirit, a Spirit that is not hard to find but impossible to avoid.

Spirit is the only thing that has *never* been absent. It is the *only* constant in your changing experience. You have known this for a billion years, literally. And you might as well acknowledge it. "If you understand this, then rest in that which understands, and just that is Spirit. If you do not understand this, then rest in that which does not understand, and just that is Spirit." For eternally and eternally and always eternally, there is only Spirit, the Witness of this and every moment, even unto the ends of the world.

The Eye of Spirit

When I rest in simple, clear, ever-present awareness, I am resting in intrinsic Spirit; I am in fact nothing other than witnessing Spirit itself. I do not become Spirit; I simply recognize the Spirit that I always already am. When I rest in simple, clear, ever-present awareness, I am the Witness of the World. I am the eye of Spirit. I see the world as God sees it. I see the world as the Goddess sees it. I see the world as Spirit sees it: every object an object of Beauty, every thing and event a gesture of the Great Perfection, every process a ripple in the pond of my own eternal Being, so much so that I do not stand apart as a separate witness, but find the witness is one taste with all that arises within it. The entire Kosmos arises in the eye of Spirit, in the I of Spirit, in my own intrinsic awareness, this simple ever-present state, and I am simply that.

From the ground of simple, ever-present awareness, one's entire bodymind will resurrect. When you rest in primordial awareness, that awareness begins to saturate your being, and from the stream of consciousness a new destiny is resurrected. When the Great Search is undone, and the separate-self sense has been crucified; when the continuity of witnessing has stabilized in your own case; when ever-present awareness is your constant ground—then your entire bodymind will regenerate, resurrect, and reorganize itself around intrinsic

Spirit, and you will arise, as from the dead, to a new destiny and a new duty in consciousness.

You will cease to exist as separate self (with all the damage that does to the bodymind), and you will exist instead as vehicle of Spirit (with the bodymind now free to function in its highest potential, undistorted and untortured by the brutalities of the self-contraction). From the ground of ever-present awareness, you will arise embodying any of the enlightened qualities of the Buddhas and Bodhisattvas— "one whose being (sattva) is ever-present awareness (bodhi)."

The Buddhist names are not important; the enlightened qualities they represent are. The point is simply that, once you have stably recognized simple, ever-present awareness—once the Great Search and the self-contraction have been robbed of separative life and returned to God, returned to their ground in ever-present awareness—then you will arise, from the ground of ever-present awareness, and you will embody any of the highest possibilities of that ground. You will be a vehicle of the Spirit that you are. That ever-present ground will live through you, as you, in a variety of superordinary forms.

Perhaps you will arise as Samantabhadra, whose ever-present awareness takes the form of a vast equality consciousness: you will realize that the ever-present awareness that is fully present in you is the *same awareness* that is fully present in all sentient beings without exception—one and the same, single and only—one heart, one mind, one soul that breathes and beats and pulses through all sentient beings as such—and your very countenance will remind all beings of that simple fact, remind them that there is only Spirit, remind them that nothing is closer to God than anything else, for there is only God, there is only Goddess.

Perhaps you will arise as Avalokiteshvara, whose ever-present awareness takes the form of gentle compassion. In the brilliant clarity of ever-present awareness, all sentient beings arise as equal forms of intrinsic Spirit or pure Emptiness, and thus all beings are treated as the sons and daughters of the Spirit that they are. You will have no choice but to live this compassion with a delicate dedication, so that your very smile will warm the hearts of those who suffer, and they will look to you for a promise that they, too, can be liberated into the vast expanse of their own primordial awareness, and you will never turn away.

Perhaps you will arise as Prajnaparamita, the mother of the Buddhas, whose ever-present awareness takes the form of a vast spaciousness, the womb of the great Unborn, in which the entire Kosmos exists. For in deepest truth, it is exactly from the ground of your own simple, clear, ever-present awareness that all beings are born; and it is to the ground of your simple, clear, ever-present awareness that all beings will return. Resting in the brilliant clarity of ever-present awareness, you watch the worlds arise, and all the Buddhas arise, and all sentient beings as such arise. And to you they will all return. And you will smile, and receive, in this vast expanse of everlasting wisdom, and it will all begin again, and yet again, and always yet again, in the womb of your ever-present state.

Perhaps you will arise as Manjushri, whose ever-present awareness takes the form of luminous intelligence. Although all beings are equally intrinsic Spirit, some beings do not easily acknowledge this ever-present Suchness, and thus discriminating wisdom will brilliantly arise from the ground of equality consciousness. You will instinctively see what is true and what is false, and thus you will bring clarity to everything you touch. And if the self-contraction does not listen to your gentler voice, your ever-present awareness will manifest in its wrathful form, which is said to be none other than the dreaded Yamantaka, Subduer of the Lord of Death.

And so perhaps you will arise as Yamantaka, fierce protector of ever-present awareness and samurai warrior of intrinsic Spirit. Precisely those items that pretend to block ever-present awareness must be quickly cut through, which is why ever-present awareness arises in its many wrathful forms. You will simply be moved, from the ground of equality consciousness, to expose the false and the shallow and the less-than-ever-present. It is time for the sword, not the smile, but always the sword of discriminating wisdom, which ruthlessly cuts all obstacles in the ground of the all-encompassing.

Perhaps you will arise as Bhaishajyaguru, whose ever-present awareness takes the form of a healing radiance. From the brilliant clarity of ever-present awareness, you will be moved to remind the sick and the sad and those in pain that although the pain is real, it is not what they are. With a simple touch or smile, contracted souls will relax into the vast expanse of intrinsic awareness, and disease will lose all meaning in the radiance of that release. And you will never tire, for ever-present awareness is effortless in its functioning, and so you will constantly remind all beings of who and what they really are, on the other side of fear, in the radical love and unflinching acceptance that is the mirror-mind of ever-present awareness.

Perhaps you will arise as Maitreya, whose ever-present awareness takes the form of a promise that, even into the endless future, ever-present awareness will still be simply present. From the brilliant clarity of primordial awareness, you will vow to be with all beings, even unto an eternity of futures, because even those futures will arise in simple present awareness, the same present awareness that now sees just exactly this.

Those are simply a few of the potentials of ever-present awareness. The Buddhist names don't matter; any will do. They are simply a few of the forms of your own resurrection. They are a few of the possibilities that might animate you after the death of the Great Search. They are a few of the ways the world looks to the ever-present eye of Spirit, the ever-present I of Spirit. They are what you see, right now, when you see the world as God sees it, from the groundless ground of simple ever-present awareness.

AND IT IS ALL UNDONE

Perhaps you will arise as any or all of those forms of ever-present awareness. But then, it doesn't really matter. When you rest in the brilliant clarity of ever-present awareness, you are not Buddha or Bodhisattva, you are not this or that, you are not here or there. When you rest in simple, ever-present awareness, you are the great Unborn, free of all qualities whatsoever. Aware of color, you are colorless. Aware of time, you are timeless. Aware of form, you are formless. In the vast expanse of primordial Emptiness, you are forever invisible to this world.

It is simply that, as embodied being, you also arise in the world of form that is your own manifestation. And the intrinsic potentials of the enlightened mind (the intrinsic potentials of your ever-present awareness)—such as equanimity, discriminating wisdom, mirrorlike wisdom, ground consciousness, and all-accomplishing awareness—various of these potentials combine with the native dispositions and particular talents of your own individual bodymind. And thus, when the separate self dies into the vast expanse of its own ever-present awareness, you will arise animated by any or all of those various enlightened potentials. You are then motivated, not by the Great Search, but by the Great Compassion of these potentials, some of which are gentle, some of which are truly wrathful, but all of which are simply the possibilities of your own ever-present state.

And thus, resting in simple, clear, ever-present awareness, you will arise with the qualities and virtues of your own highest potentials—perhaps compassion, perhaps discriminating wisdom, perhaps cognitive insight, perhaps healing presence, perhaps wrathful reminder, perhaps artistic accomplishment, perhaps athletic skill, perhaps great educator, or perhaps something utterly simple, maybe being the best flower gardener on the block. (In other words, any of the developmental lines released into their own primordial state, released into their own post-postconventional condition.) When the bodymind is released from the brutalities inflicted by the self-contraction, it naturally gravitates to its own highest estate, manifested in the great potentials of the enlightened mind, the great potentials of simple, ever-present awareness.

Thus, as you rest in simple, ever-present awareness, you are the great Unborn; but as you are born—as you arise from ever-present awareness—you will manifest certain qualities, qualities inherent in intrinsic Spirit, and qualities colored by the dispositions of your own bodymind and its particular talents.

And whatever the form of Your own resurrection, you will arise, driven not by the Great Search, but by your own Great Duty, your limitless Dharma, the manifestation of your own highest potentials, and the world will begin to change, because of you. And you will never flinch, and you will never fail in that great Duty, and you will never turn away, because simple, ever-present awareness will be with you now and forever, even unto the ends of the worlds, because now and forever and endlessly forever, there is only Spirit, only intrinsic awareness, only the simple awareness of just this, and nothing more.

But that entire journey to what is begins at the beginningless beginning: we begin by simply recognizing that which is always already the case. ("If you understand this, then rest in that which understands, and just that is exactly Spirit. If you do not understand this, then rest in that which does not understand, and just that is exactly Spirit.") We allow this recognition of ever-present awareness to arise—gently, randomly, spontaneously, through the day and into the night. This simple, ever-present awareness is not hard to attain but impossible to avoid, and we simply notice that.

We do this gently, randomly, and spontaneously, through the day and into the night. Soon enough, through all three states of waking, dreaming, and sleeping, this recognition will grow of its own accord and by its own intrinsic power, outshining the obstacles that pretend to hide its nature, until this simple, ever-present awareness announces itself in an unbroken continuity through all changes of state, through all changes of space and time, whereupon space and time lose all meaning whatsoever, exposed for what they are, the shining veils of the radiant Emptiness that you alone now are—and you will swoon into that Beauty, and die into that Truth, and dissolve into that Goodness, and there will be no one left to testify to terror, no one left to take tears seriously, no one left to engineer unease, no one left to deny the Divine, which only alone is, and only alone ever was, and only alone will ever be.

And somewhere on a cold crystal night the moon will shine on a silently waiting Earth, just to remind those left behind that it is all a game. The lunar light will set dreams afire in their sleeping hearts, and a yearning to awaken will stir in the depths of that restless night, and you will be pulled, yet again, to respond to those most plaintive prayers, and you will find yourself right here, right now, wondering what it all really means—until that flash of recognition runs across your face and it is all undone. You then will arise as the moon itself, and sing those dreams in your very own heart; and you will arise as the Earth itself, and glorify all of its blessed inhabitants; and you will arise as the Sun itself, radiant to infinity and much too obvious to see; and in that One Taste of primordial purity, with no beginning and no end, with no entrance and no exit, with no birth and no death, it all comes radically to be; and the sound of a singing water-fall, somewhere in the distance, is all that is left to tell this tale, late on that crystal cold night, bathed so beautifully in that lunar light, just so, and again, just so.

When the great Zen master Fa-ch'ang was dying, a squirrel screeched out on the roof. "It's just this," he said, "and nothing more."

CW 7: *The Eye of Spirit*, 672–690

Sources

Books

The Atman Project: A Transpersonal View of Human Development. 2nd ed. © 1996. Excerpts reprinted by permission of Quest Books / The Theosophical Publishing House, Wheaton, IL (www .questbooks.net). Selections reprinted from *The Collected Works of Ken Wilber*, vol. 2. Boston & London: Shambhala Publications, 1999. © 1999 by Ken Wilber.

Boomeritis: A Novel That Will Set You Free. Boston: Shambhala Publications, 2002. © 2002 by Ken Wilber.

A Brief History of Everything. Boston & London: Shambhala Publications, 1996. © 1996 by Ken Wilber. Selections reprinted from *The Collected Works of Ken Wilber*, vol. 7. Boston & London: Shambhala Publications, 2000. © 1999 by Ken Wilber.

The Eye of Spirit: An Integral Vision for a World Gone Slightly Mad. Boston & London: Shambhala Publications, 1997. © 1997 by Ken Wilber. Selections reprinted from *The Collected Works of Ken Wilber*, vol. 7. Boston & London: Shambhala Publications, 2000. © 1999 by Ken Wilber.

Eye to Eye: The Quest for the New Paradigm. Boston & London: Shambhala Publications,1996. © 1983, 1990, 1996 by Ken Wilber. Selections reprinted from *The Collected Works of Ken Wilber*, vol. 3. Boston & London: Shambhala Publications, 1999. © 1999 by Ken Wilber.

Grace and Grit: Spirituality and Healing in the Life and Death of Treya Killam Wilber. Boston & London: Shambhala Publications, 1991. © Selections reprinted from *The Collected Works of Ken Wilber*, vol. 5. Boston & London: Shambhala Publications, 2000. © 2000 by Ken Wilber.

The Marriage of Sense and Soul: Integrating Science and Religion. New York: Random House, 1998. © 1998 by Ken Wilber. Selections used by permission of Random House, Inc. *The Marriage of Sense and Soul: Integrating Science and Religion*. London: Macmillan, 1999. © 1999 by Ken Wilber. Selections used by permission of Macmillan U.K. Text reprinted from *The Collected Works of Ken Wilber*, vol. 8. Boston & London: Shambhala Publications, 2000. © 2000 by Ken Wilber.

No Boundary: Eastern and Western Approaches to Personal Growth. Boston & London: Shambhala Publications, 2001. © 1979, 2001 by Ken Wilber. Selections reprinted from *The Collected Works of Ken Wilber*, vol. 1. Boston & London: Shambhala Publications, 1999. © 1999 by Ken Wilber.

One Taste: The Journals of Ken Wilber. Boston & London: Shambhala Publications, 1999. © 1999 by Ken Wilber. Selections reprinted from *The Collected Works of Ken Wilber*, vol. 8. Boston & London: Shambhala Publications, 2000. © 2000 by Ken Wilber.

Quantum Questions: Mystical Writings of the World's Great Physicists. Boston & London: Shambhala Publications, 1984. © 1984 by Ken Wilber. Selections reprinted from *The Collected Works of Ken Wilber*, vol. 4. Boston & London: Shambhala Publications, 1999. © 1999 by Ken Wilber.

Sex, Ecology, Spirituality: The Spirit of Evolution. 2nd ed. Selections reprinted from *The Collected Works of Ken Wilber*, vol. 6. Boston & London: Shambhala Publications, 2000. © 2000 by Ken Wilber.

A Sociable God: Toward a New Understanding of Religion. Boston & London: Shambhala Publications, 1984. © 1983, 1984 by Ken Wilber. Selections reprinted from *The Collected Works of Ken Wilber*, vol. 3. Boston & London: Shambhala Publications, 1999. © 1999 by Ken Wilber.

The Spectrum of Consciousness. 2nd ed. Wheaton, IL: Quest Books/ Theosophical Publishing House, 1993. © 1993 by Ken Wilber. Excerpts reprinted by permission of Quest Books / The Theosophical Publishing House, Wheaton, IL (www.questbooks.net). Selections reprinted from *The Collected Works of Ken Wilber*, vol. 1. Boston & London: Shambhala Publications, 1999. © 1999 by Ken Wilber.

Spiritual Choices: The Problem of Recognizing Authentic Paths to Inner Transformation. Edited by Dick Anthony, Bruce Ecker, and Ken Wilber. St. Paul, MN: Paragon House, 1987, "The Spectrum Model" by Ken Wilber, p. 248.

A *Theory of Everything: An Integral Vision for Business, Politics, Science and Spirituality*. Boston & London: Shambhala Publications, 2000. © 2000 by Ken Wilber.

Up from Eden: A Transpersonal View of Human Evolution. Wheaton, IL: Quest Books, 1996. © 1981, 1996 by Ken Wilber. Selections reprinted from *The Collected Works of Ken Wilber*, vol. 2. Boston & London: Shambhala Publications, 1999. © 1999 by Ken Wilber.

Other Sources

"Are the Chakras Real?" From *The Collected Works of Ken Wilber*, vol. 1. Boston & London: Shambhala Publications, 1999. © 1999 by Ken Wilber. Originally published in *Kundalini, Evolution and Enlightenment*, edited by John White. Garden City, NY: Anchor Press / Doubleday, 1979, pp. 121–131. © 1979, 1993 by Ken Wilber.

Boomeritis Sidebar E: The Genius Descartes Gets a Postmodern Drubbing(2002).http://wilber.shambhala.com/html/books/boomeritis/sidebar_e/index.cfm. © 2002 by Ken Wilber.

"Death, Rebirth, and Meditation." Selections reprinted from *The Collected Works of Ken Wilber*, vol. 4. Boston & London: Shambhala Publications, 1999. © 1999 by Ken Wilber. Originally published in Gary Doore (ed.), *What Survives?: Contemporary Explorations of Life after Death*. Los Angeles: Jeremy P. Tarcher, 1990. © 1990 by Ken Wilber.

"The Deconstruction of the World Trade Center: A Date That Will Live in a Sliding Chain of Signifiers." © 2001 by Ken Wilber. http://wilber.shambhala.com/html/books/boomeritis/wtc/part3.cfm.

Foreword to Alex Grey, *The Mission of Art*. Boston & London: Shambhala Publications, 1998. © 1998 by Alex Grey. Selection reprinted from *The Collected Works of Ken Wilber*, vol. 4. Boston & London: Shambhala Publications, 1999. © 1999 by Ken Wilber.

Foreword to Andrew Cohen, *Living Enlightenment: A Call for Evolution Beyond Ego*. Lenox, MA: Moksha Press, 2002.

Foreword to David Deida, *Finding God Through Sex: A Spiritual Guide to Ecstatic Loving and Deep Passion for Men and Women*. London: Plexus Publishing, 2002.

Foreword to Frank Visser, *Ken Wilber: Thought as Passion*. Albany: SUNY Press, 2003.

Foreword to Lex Hixon, *Coming Home: The Experience of Enlightenment in Sacred Traditions*. Los Angeles: Jeremy P. Tarcher, 1989. © 1989 by Ken Wilber. Selection reprinted from *The Collected Works of Ken Wilber*, vol. 4. Boston & London: Shambhala Publications, 1999. © 1999 by Ken Wilber.

Foreword to M. J. Ryan (ed.), *The Fabric of the Future: Women Visionaries Illuminate the Path to Tomorrow* (Berkeley: Conari Press, 1998). © 1998 by Conari Press. Selection reprinted from *The Collected Works of Ken Wilber*, vol. 4. Boston & London: Shambhala Publications, 1999. © 1999 by Ken Wilber.

Foreword to Philip Rubinov-Jacobson, *Drinking Lightning: Art, Creativity and Transformation*. Boston & London: Shambhala Publications, 2000. © 1999 by Ken Wilber. Selection reprinted from *The Collected Works of Ken Wilber*, vol. 4. Boston & London: Shambhala Publications, 1999. © 1999 by Ken Wilber.

"The Guru and the Pandit: The Evolution of Enlightenment, Andrew Cohen and Ken Wilber in Dialogue," *What Is Enlightenment?* no. 21 (Spring/Summer 2002), 38–49, 136–143.

"In the Eye of the Artist: Art and the Perennial Philosophy." Foreword to Alex Grey, Ken Wilber, and Carlo McCormick, *Sacred Mirrors: The Visionary Art of Alex Grey*. Rochester, VT: Inner Traditions International, 1990. © 1990 by Ken Wilber. Selection reprinted from *The Collected Works of Ken Wilber*, vol. 4. Boston & London: Shambhala Publications, 1999. © 1999 by Ken Wilber.

"Odyssey: A Personal Inquiry into Humanistic and Transpersonal Psychology." Selections reprinted from *The Collected Works of Ken Wilber*, vol. 2. Boston & London: Shambhala Publications, 1999. © 1999 by Ken Wilber. Originally published in *Journal of Humanistic Psychology* 22, no. 1 (1982): 57–90. © 1982 by Ken Wilber.

"Paradigm Wars: An Interview with Ken Wilber." *The Quest*, Spring 1989, pp. 6–12. © 1989 by Ken Wilber. Selections reprinted from

The Collected Works of Ken Wilber, vol. 4. Boston & London: Shambhala Publications, 1999. © 1999 by Ken Wilber.

"Paths beyond Ego in the Coming Decades." In Roger Walsh and Frances Vaughan, *Paths beyond Ego: The Transpersonal Vision*. Los Angeles: Jeremy P. Tarcher, 1993. © 1992 by Ken Wilber. Selection reprinted from *The Collected Works of Ken Wilber*, vol. 4. Boston & London: Shambhala Publications, 1999. © 1999 by Ken Wilber.

"*Psychologia Perennis*: The Spectrum of Consciousness." Selection reprinted from *The Collected Works of Ken Wilber*, vol. 1. Boston & London: Shambhala Publications, 1999. © 1999 by Ken Wilber. Originally published in *Journal of Transpersonal Psychology* 7, no. 2 (1975): 105–132. © 1975 by Ken Wilber.

"Sociocultural Evolution." Written in 1983. © 1999 by Ken Wilber. Selection(s) reprinted from *The Collected Works of Ken Wilber*, vol. 4. Boston & London: Shambhala Publications, 1999. © 1999 by Ken Wilber.

"Stages of Meditation: An Interview with Ken Wilber." *The Quest*, Spring 1994, pp. 43–46. © 1994 by Ken Wilber. Selections reprinted from *The Collected Works of Ken Wilber*, vol. 4. Boston & London: Shambhala Publications, 1999. © 1999 by Ken Wilber.

"A Ticket to Athens." Interview with *Pathways: A Magazine of Psychological and Spiritual Transformation*, in *One Taste*, reprinted from *The Collected Works of Ken Wilber*, vol. 4. Boston & London: Shambhala Publications, 1999. © 1999 by Ken Wilber.

"Two Humanistic Psychologies?: A Response." *Journal of Humanistic Psychology* 29, no. 2 (1989), pp. 230–243. © 1989 by Sage Publications, Inc. Selection reprinted from *The Collected Works of Ken Wilber*, vol. 4. Boston & London: Shambhala Publications, 1999. © 1999 by Ken Wilber.

"Where It Was, There I Shall Become: Human Potential and the Boundaries of the Soul." From *The Collected Works of Ken Wilber*, vol. 1. Boston & London: Shambhala Publications, 1999. © 1999 by Ken Wilber. Originally published in *Beyond Health and Normality: Explorations of Exceptional Psychological Well-Being*, edited by Roger Walsh and Deane F. Shapiro, Jr. New York: Van Nostrand Reinhold, 1983, pp. 67–121. © 1983 by Ken Wilber.

Index

Absolute, 224–230
Absolute/relative problem, 151, 172–173
Absolute Spirit, 188
Absolute Subjectivity, 171
Action, 52–53
Adam, 154, 157
After Many a Summer Dies the Swan
    (Huxley), 88–89
Agape, 77, 81, 82, 95
Agency, 202
Alienation, 79
All, 96, 154
All-Being. *See* Brahman
Alpha Omega Point, 90–91
Altered states, 17, 41
"And it is all undone," 258
Anger. *See* Hostility.
Apollo complex, 35, 36, 38
Aquinas, Thomas, 144
Archetypes, 36
Art, 189–192, 217–219, 221
Ascending path, 81, 82
Ascent, 93
Atman, 177, 178, 215
Atman project, 177
    nature of, 72, 215
    never occurred, 73, 178
Atman Project, The (Wilber), 41, 64
Attention, 39–40
Augustine, Saint, 157, 164
Aurobindo Ghose, Sri, 109
Authenticity, 132, 213. *See also under*
    Spirituality
Avalokiteshvara, 254
Avoidance, 242
Awakening, 39
Awareness, 136, 137. *See also*
    Enlightenment; Seer; Witness

choiceless, 52
constant, 4
effortless, 17–18
ever-present, 187, 244–253
immediate, 111. *See also* Bodily
    sensations
motionless center of, 43

Basic Moral Intuition (BMI),
    208
Beauty, 47, 190–192. *See also*
    Art
Being, 215
Benoit, Hubert, 26
Bernard, Saint, 236
Bhaishajyaguru, 255
Big Bang, 80, 154
before the, 16, 28, 109, 250
Big Three, the (I, We, It), 208
Blake, William, 124, 243
Bliss, 45, 126
    infinite empty, 127
Blyth, R. H., 107, 236
Bodhi, 235
Bodhisattva, 146, 209
Bodhisattva vow, 165
Bodily sensations, 17, 111
    blocks in, 114–119, 121
Bodily tension, 113–119
Body, 9, 109, 112, 122
reclaiming/connecting with one's,
    112–113, 122
Boethius, 167
Bonaventure, Saint, 228
Bondage, 15
Boundaries, 74, 143, 211. *See also*
    Self/other boundary
    vs. no-boundary awareness, 182–183

Brahman, 158, 226, 236
  as ground and goal of evolution, 75
  is the world, 19–20, 225–227
  meditation and, 75
  nature of, 146, 224, 229–230,
    236–237
Breathing cycle, 112–114
Breathing exercises, 123, 126. *See also*
    Mind-body split: exercise for healing
Buddha, 16, 89, 95, 158, 236
Buddha Mind, 56, 225, 230
Buddha Nature, 232, 235
Buddhism, 52, 147, 158, 171

"Capping exercise," 23
Catherine of Genoa, Saint, 186
Centauric self, 213
Certainty, 163
Chagdud Tulku Rinpoche, 55
Chakras, 37, 142, 143
Chandogya Upanishad, 224
Chenrezi, 60
Chih-huang, 231
Christianity, 157–158, 170
Chuang Tzu, 20, 36, 248
Clearing, 199
Compassion, 127, 128, 131, 254. *See also*
    Agape
  Mahayana path of, 124, 125
  and the One and the Many, 92–93
  path of, 82
Completion stage, ix
Consciousness, 4, 6–7, 39–40. *See also*
    specific topics
  being, 27
  constant, 50, 55–56, 62, 64
  head vs. body, 121. *See also* Bodily
    sensations
  identified with the mind, 145
  integral theory of, 152
  nonordinary states of, 17, 41
Contemplation, eye of, 155, 156, 189, 217
Coomaraswamy, Ananda K., 170, 192
Cosmic consciousness, 52, 106, 165. *See
    also* Kosmic consciousness; One Taste
Cosmic Game, great, 86
Cosmos, 108. *See also* Kosmos
Creation stage, ix
Creativity, 100
Current, 2

Da Free John, 58
Daemon, 198–199
Dante, 36–37
Death, 27–28, 148, 221. *See also under*
    Wilber, Treya Killam
  facing, 71
  imagining the world after one's, 28–29
  as letting go, 52
  and new Birth, 157
  spiritual awareness in relation to, 28–30
Decentering, 185
Derrida, Jacques, 149
Descending path, 81–82
Descent, 93, 94
Desires, 9–10
Devotion, 165
Dialectical analysis, 173
Dichotomies. *See* Dualism(s)
Dionysus, Saint, 237
Divine Ground, 79
Divinity, 166
  ultimate secret of, 1
Dogen Zenji, 107, 147, 177
Dreams/dreaming, 40
  pellucid, 50
  translucent, 40
Dualism(s), 6, 39, 104, 211. *See also* Mind-
    body split; Nonduality; Opposites
  and nondualism, 19, 86
  overcoming, 8–9
  Primary, 144, 145, 180
  Secondary, 180
  Zoroastrian, 77
Dualistic knowledge and Western philoso-
    phy, 141–142
Duhkha, 153
Dzogchen, 135, 136, 167, 219

Earth, 90
Eckhart, Meister, 27, 158, 192, 234, 248
Effort and effortlessness, 22
Ego, 27, 130–131, 194. *See also* Separate-
    self
  body and, 122
  death of, 148, 165, 192
  desire to get rid of, 22, 148
  letting go of, 28, 51
  nature of, 22, 131
Emerson, Ralph Waldo, 103, 170,
    189–190, 198

Emotional release, 118
Emotions, 10
  and the body, 114–119
  resistance to, 118. *See also* Bodily
    sensations: blocks in
Emptiness, 56, 171, 182, 185, 219, 249
  Brahman and, 19
  Buddhism and, 52, 171
  Freedom and, 19, 56
  meanings, 52, 78, 171
  nature of, 3, 171, 173
  omnipresence, 67, 110
  as pure identity, 150
  pure Self/Witness and, 13, 15–17, 171
  resting in, 238
  Zen and, 173
Empty bliss, infinite, 127
Enlightenment. *See also* Transformation
  attaining, 52, 130–132, 135, 137
  defined, 107
  as ego-death, 192
  nature and qualities of, 102, 107, 135,
    136, 147, 158, 254–257
  seeking/desiring, 131, 132, 136
Equality consciousness, 254
Erigena (Johannes Scotus), 226
Eros, 81, 82, 95, 99
Essence, 13
Eternity, 229
Evolution, 74. *See also* Infant self
  other worlds becoming this world, 169
  spiral of consciousness and, 78
  Spirit and, 68, 69, 71–72, 74–75, 98,
    103–104, 109
Existentialists, 213
Experience, 24, 167
  as context, 149
  defined, 37–38
  dichotomy between construction and, 149
  limits of, 37–41, 169
  nature of, 149–150
  sensory, mental, and spiritual, 158–159
  that cannot be put into words, 168–170
Experiential realities, 41
Extrinsic value, 63

Face (of Spirit). *See* Original Face
Falling away. *See* Involution
False self, 213
Feeling-attention, 112–114

Feeling of Being, xi–xii, 195, 196
Female. *See* Great Goddess; Male and
    female
Feminine Face of Spirit, 81
Fénelon, Archbishop of Cambrai, 235
Form(s)
  desire of, 155
  Emptiness and, 21–22, 91, 99, 101–102,
    194
  world of, 101–102, 155
Formless, 91, 155
Four Quadrants, x, 64, 83, 184, 185, 208
Freedom, 14–16, 18–19, 21, 23, 56, 247,
    249. *See also* Liberation
Freud, Sigmund, 37, 108, 210

Game of Life, 85–88
Gateless Gate, 243
Gender differences, 204. *See also* Male
    and female
Genital sensations, 126
Germany, 48–50
God, 3, 7, 238, 240
  denial vs. affirmation of, 159–160,
    163–164
  directions to finding, 2–3
  found within, 1–2
  oneness/union with, 170, 212, 230, 249
  philosophy and, 147
  search for, 249
Goddess, 81, 211
Godhead, 3, 157, 178. *See also* Spirit
Grace, 77, 94, 95
Great Chain of Being, 51, 69
Great Death, 148
Great Goddess, 76–77
Great Nest, 99
Great Samadhi, 167, 231
Great Search, 239–243, 249, 253, 256
Great Spectrum of consciousness, 154
Greek philosophy, 141–142
Ground value, 63
Ground vs. Goal, 97
Guénon, René, 232

Hakuin, 146, 186
Healing radiance, 255
Heart, 2, 47, 216
Heaven, 47
Hegel, Georg Wilhelm Friedrich, 95, 147

Hell, 79, 80
Hildegard of Bingen, 89
Hinduism, 158
History, 97, 198
Holism, 152
Holons, 149, 150, 157, 201–202
Hostility, 114–115
Hsuan-chueh, 234
Hsuan-tse, 231
Huang Po, 144, 229–230, 232, 235
Hui-neng, 89
Humanistic psychology, 199
Humor, 209–210
Huxley, Aldous, 88–89

I, 108, 180
    It becoming, 108–109
    of Spirit, 253–256
I AM state, 7, 127, 248, 250
I-I, 218–219
    nature of, 14, 44, 184, 185
    relaxing into, 174
    resting as, 127
    Witness as, 14, 26–27, 44
    witnessing the world as, 195
I-thought, 25–26
Idealism, 81
Identification, 51
Identity crisis, 11–12. See also "Who am I?"
Illusions, 6, 19
Imagining oneself in the past or future,
    28–30
Immanence, 82, 150
Immediacy, 149, 163
Infant self, development and evolution of,
    79–80
Infinite empty bliss, 127
Infinite space, 33
Infinity/infinite, 95, 228
Integral Approach, ix
Integral studies and practice, 206–208
Intelligence, luminous, 255
Intrinsic value, 63
Involution, 69, 71
Islam, 158
It (one of the Big Three), 179
    becoming I, 107–109

James, William, 144, 159
Jesus Christ, 87, 89, 124, 157

Judaism, 170
Julian of Norwich, Dame, 105, 186
Jung, Carl Gustav, 36
"Just this," 172, 185, 258

Kabir, 104–105
Kalu Rinpoche, 55, 59, 123–124
Kandinsky, Wassilly, 217
Kant, Immanuel, 158–159
Karuna, 82, 93
Katagiri Roshi, Dainin, 55
Kensho, 158
Kierkegaard, Søren, 133
Knowing, 39
    eyes of, 141
Knowledge, 144
Kosmic consciousness, 88, 198, 199. See
    also Cosmic consciousness; One Taste
Kosmos, 13, 81, 129, 153, 154, 198. See
    also Cosmos
    to meet the, 73, 241–244
    nature of, 192, 223
Krishnamurti, J., 153
Kundalini, 142–143

Language, limitations of, 168–170,
    182–183
Lao Tzu, 33, 34
Left-Hand path, 204–206
Level of Mind. See under Mind
Liberation, 3–4, 7, 20, 86, 158, 233. See
    also Freedom
Life, dissatisfaction with, 73
Light, 2
Lila (play), 85
Love, 44, 53, 58, 98–99, 206–207. See also
    Agape
Lowen, Alexander, 112, 121
Lucid dreaming, 50
Luminous intelligence, 255

Maezumi Roshi, Taizan, 55
Maha-ati. See Dzogchen
Mahayana, path of compassion, 124, 125
Maitreya, 256
Male and female, 204, 207. See also Great
    Goddess
Manjushri, 255
Masculine Face of Spirit, 81
Mediation, 149

Meditation, 36, 123, 148, 164–165
  Brahman and, 75
  limitations, 136
Meditative practice(s), 98, 126, 136, 219.
    See also Mind-body split: exercise for
    healing; specific topics
  components of, ix
Memory, 178–179. See also
    Remembering/remembrance
Mencken, H. L., 209–210
Mental experience, 158–159
Metanoia, 157–158
Mind, 180–182
  level and "no-level" of, 145–147
  nature of, 245
Mind-body split, 112, 121
  exercise for healing, 112–119
Mind-body unity, 121–122
Mindfulness, 137
Mirror-mind, 55
Motionless center, 43
Murphy, Michael, 109
Muscle tension. See Bodily tension
Mysticism, 75, 147, 209, 241
  essence, 177

Nagarjuna, 227, 234
Nan-chuan, 38–39
Nature, 34–35, 90, 101, 103
Negation-and-affirmation, 173
Neumann, Erich, 177
New Age, 143–144
Nirvana, 234
Nirvikalpa samadhi, 86
No-self, 171
Nondual awareness/realization, 24, 167,
    182–183, 211
Nondual mysticism, 78
Nondual traditions and schools, 82, 92, 96,
    193, 194, 246. See also One Taste
Nonduality, 127–128, 228
  defined, 96
Norbu, Pema, 55, 59
Notre Dame (Cathedral), 46

Omega, 154–155
Omega Point, 90–91
One Taste, 63, 193
  being/becoming, 8, 22, 23, 51, 194,
    242, 252

Feeling of, 195
Great Embrace of, 9
holons have, 63
inside and outside have become, 9
mistakes on way to, 21
nature of, 23, 51, 52, 252
resting in, 127, 176
tasting, 128
Witness and, 8, 22–23
One vs. Many, 82, 87, 96, 173
  compassion and, 92–93
Oneness, 3, 79
Opposites, 6, 70–71, 120. See also Dualism(s)
Original Face, 28, 30, 91
  nature of, 30–31, 252
  as purist Emptiness, 28, 194
  recognizing one's, 28, 91, 131
Over-human/Over-Soul, 93–94

Pain, 71, 87
P'ang, Layman, 107
Parts and whole, relationship between, 200,
    201
Pascal, Blaise, 236
Passion and passionate philosophy, 133,
    139–140
Patanjali, 15
Perennial philosophy, 69
Perfection, 155
Perfectly Divine, 93
Phenomenal realm, 171
Physics, 96–97
Plato, 92, 93, 142
Pleasure, 126, 127
Plotinus, 36, 93, 228
Pneuma (spirit), 170
"Pointing-out instructions," 136–137
Polarities. See Dualism(s)
Potentials, 105–107
Practices, 23–24
  "perfect," 131
Prajnaparamita (mother of the Buddhas),
    254–255
Prehension, 149
Presence, pure, 150, 184, 220, 242. See also
    Timelessness
Pure Openness, 158

Radiance, 1–2
Radical Truth, 100–101

Ramana Maharshi, Sri, 23, 27–28, 55, 91, 130, 138
  on the awakened one, 106
  on Brahman, 19
  on I-I, 14
  on illusion, 19
  on I-thought, 25–26
  on reality/the real, 30, 54
  on Self, 20, 230
  on Self-Inquiry, 26
  on suffering and death, 221
  and ways of liberation, 25
  on Witness, 14
Real, the, 171
Reality, 35, 151, 201, 226
Reality principle, 35
Realization, direct, 51
Reconstructive science, 161
Rekison Roshi, 232
Relaxation, 186
  "forced," 116
Release, 233
Religion, 100
  functions, 168
  as science of spiritual experience, 155–156
Remembering/remembrance, 73, 74, 87, 108, 177. See also Memory
Resistance, 118, 119, 123
Resurrection, 157–158, 165
Right-Hand path, 204–206
Romantic view, 79
Ruach (Heb., spirit), 170
Ruysbroeck, Blessed John, 38

Sages, 128–129
Samadhi, 167, 231, 242
Samantabhadra, 254
Samsara, 79–80, 234
Satori, 151, 158, 172, 192
Schroedinger, Erwin, 29
Scotus, Johannes (Erigena), 226
Seer, 15, 218–219, 250. See also Witness
  attempting to see, 21, 105, 144, 145, 237–238
  as Emptiness, 17
  nature of, 14, 16
  resting in pure, 16
  and the Seen, 61

Self, 5, 212, 218, 222, 230, 233. See also God: found within; Spirit; "Who am I?"
  alone is real, 19
  creating meaning for vs. transcending, 168–169. See also Transformation
  discovering, 7–10, 20, 144, 166
  finite self vs. authentic, 213
  paths to, 137–138
  there is only One, 174
  True, 171
Self-contraction, 21–23
Self-Inquiry, 26
Self/other boundary, 11–12, 106, 122, 180
Self/other dualism, 124, 184. See also Subject/object dualism
Selfless service, 53
Senses, 111
Separate-self, 21
Sex, Ecology, Spirituality (SES) (Wilber), 63, 64
Sex and sexuality, 45, 148, 203, 207, 211
Sex differences, 204
Sexual union, visualizing, 126
Shadow, 120
Shankara, 19, 226, 229, 233
Shunyata, 158
Silence, object-less, 26
Singh, Kirpal, 37
"Skin hunger," 64
Sleep, dreamless, 54
Soul, 133, 170, 187, 216–217
  "care of the soul," 133
  duty of, 177
  nature of, 25
Soul art, 217
Space, 199. See also Time, space, and awareness
  infinite, 33
Spacelessness, 44
Spaciousness, 254–255
Spectrum, 69
  of consciousness, 180
Spectrum of Consciousness, The (Wilber), 41, 63–64
Spirit, 95, 188, 190, 214, 221–222
  eye of, 253–256
  Great Search for, 239–243, 249, 253, 256
  immanent and transcendental aspects, 67–68

nature of, 13, 20, 55, 66–67, 83, 104, 174
(omni)presence, 4–5, 135, 179
paradox of, 68, 97
reaching, 68, 179
reasons for manifesting, 84–87
return to itself, 72
seeking, 72, 104. *See also* Atman project
self-contraction and, 21
soul and, 25
understanding, 20
within. *See* God: found within
Witness and, 4, 25. *See also* Witness
Spirit-in-action, 66, 98, 99, 188
Spiritual experience, 158–159
Spiritual teachers, 130–131
Spirituality, depth and authenticity of,
    158–160, 163, 172, 222
Splits. *See* Dualism(s)
Subconscious, 37
Subjective space, 207
Subjectivity, 145, 171
Subject/object dualism, 24, 39, 125, 143,
    148, 180. *See also* Self/other dualism
Subtle mind, 51
Subtle realm, 36–38, 217
Suffering, 73–74, 86, 87, 153, 221. *See also*
    Pain
causes of, 87–88, 125, 193
taking on others', 123, 124
Summum bonum, 91–92
Superconscious experiences, 37
Supreme Identity, 68, 157, 170
Suzuki, D. T., 96
Suzuki Roshi, Shunryu, 59

Tantra, 211
Tao, 38–39
Tao-te Ching (Lao Tzu), 33, 34
Tat Tvam Asi (Thou art That), 87, 108,
    170
Tawbah, 158
Teresa of Ávila, Saint, 59
This. *See* Just this
Thou art That, 87, 108, 170
Thoughts, 10, 17–18
Time, space, and awareness, 16, 17, 180
Timeless One, 176
Timelessness, 44, 179, 183–184, 190, 248
Tolerance, 222

Tonglen, 123–125
Touching, 149, 150
Traherne, Thomas, 195
Transcendence, 82, 150, 209
Transcendental aspects of Spirit, 67–68
Transcendentalism, 241
Transcending the self, 168
Transformation, 132–134, 168. *See also*
    Enlightenment
Translation (horizontal), 132, 133, 168
Transpersonal realm, 41
Transpersonal self, 105
Transpersonal witness, 10
Transrational domains, 203–204
Trungpa, Chögyam, 55, 59
Truth
discovering, 133
vs. forms of Truth, 100–101
Tsogyal, Lady, 89
"Turning about," enlightenment as, 158

Ultimate state and human potential, 38, 39,
    106–108
Ultimate State of Consciousness, 230–235
Unborn, 16
Unconscious opposites, 120. *See also*
    Opposites
Union with Divine Ground, 79
Unity consciousness, 70, 122, 242. *See also*
    Bodily sensations
Universe, relation between Self and, 26, 28

Vajrayana path, 125
Value, types of, 62–63
van Gogh, Vincent, 189
Vipassana, 123, 125
Vishnu complex, 38
Visualization practice. *See also* Meditative
    practice(s)
components of, ix
Vital force, 113
Void, 237

Warren, Scott, 63–65
Watts, Alan, 39, 178, 234
Wei Wu Wei, 125
Whitehead, Alfred North, 149
"Who am I?" 7–12, 14, 18, 39
"Who are you?" 26, 62

Wilber, Ken
  on his books, 141
    process of writing them, 63–64
  life history, 33
  living as hermit, 64
  spiritual awakening, 33–37
Wilber, Treya Killam, 192
  beauty, 42
  cancer, 44, 52
  decision to die, 53–54
  terminal condition, 48, 49
  death, 57–61
  description of, 42–43, 47
  Ken contrasted with, 47
  Ken's relationship with, 42–43, 45, 46,
    48, 49, 54, 57–58, 65
Wisdom, 82, 92, 93
Witness (and witnessing), 28, 29, 40, 43,
    62, 78, 125, 216. See also I-I; Seer
  availability, 17
  (being in) pure, 15–17, 24, 28, 165, 166,
    194, 218, 237

  discovering and contacting, 8
  dissolution/disappearance of, 8, 12, 39
  as impartial mirror-mind, 22
  loves and embraces everything, 22
  nature of, 4, 7, 22, 24, 40
  omnipresence, 4, 244–253
  pursuing, 13
  in relation to space and time, 16
  resting in, 7, 15, 18, 19, 21–24, 26–27
  soul and, 23
Witnessing center, 10
Wittgenstein, Ludwig, 148, 226, 227
Women, 204
Wordsworth, William, 2
World as illusory, 19
World Soul, 93–95

Yamantaka (deity), 255
Yasutani Roshi, Haku'un, 172
You-and-I, 174

Zen, 19, 108, 173